THE PREVENT-SYSTEM FOR FOOTBALL INJURIES

DR. JAMES V. CERNEY
President, Professional Research

with illustrations by the author

PRENTICE-HALL, Inc., Englewood Cliffs, New Jersey

Library of Congress Cataloging in Publication Data

CERNEY, J V
The prevent-system for football injuries.

1. Football—Accidents and injuries. 2. Sports—Safety measures. I. Title.
RC1220.F6C47 617'.1027 75-16919
ISBN 0-13-699405-9

Dedicated to my son Jeff who held his All-Ohio high school title for three consecutive years before going overseas to play in war games where winners too often are losers and gold cup awards are not part of G.I. issue.

10 9 8 7 6 5 4 3 2 1

PRENTICE-HALL INTERNATIONAL, INC., *London*
PRENTICE-HALL OF AUSTRALIA, PTY. LTD., *Sydney*
PRENTICE-HALL OF CANADA, LTD., *Toronto*
PRENTICE-HALL OF INDIA PRIVATE LIMITED, *New Delhi*
PRENTICE-HALL OF JAPAN, INC., *Tokyo*
PRENTICE-HALL OF SOUTHEAST ASIA (PTE.) LTD., *Singapore*

CONTENTS

FOREWORD

Chicago Bears physician Theodore Fox has said that a sports injury is most likely to occur: when the player is not physically fit; when he is not well enough developed or coordinated; when he has ill-fitting equipment; or when medical attention is inadequate. Another authority in sports medicine, Robert G. Bashear, M.D., divided the responsibility for injury prevention into three basic areas: the first and foremost area of responsibility is that of the *coach* who controls the greater part of the football environment; the second level of control is in the hands of the *team physician;* and the third distinct area is that of the *athletic trainer.* However, many members of the sports fraternity today realize, that there are additional important areas of control.

The prevention of athletic injuries has many facets: it also begins with sharp-eyed game officials and a fast whistle; it begins with grounds maintenance men who clean practice fields of broken bottles and vacuum water from the Astroturf after a rain; it begins in the administrator's office when a plane is chartered; it begins with an efficient cleanup campaign in the locker room and with properly cleaned equipment; it begins with surveillance of dummies and sleds smeared with impetigo; it begins with careful checking of any eruptions of carbuncles or boils; it begins with the athletic director who books opponents only within the scope of his school's capacity to compete. These are just a few of the working parts of the sports organization that makes a football team possible and plays a vital role in the prevention of athletic injuries. This wonderful group of specialists in the sports fraternity who are concerned with the Prevent-System in football I call *"the Team-Behind-the-Team."*

As I see the Prevent-System for football injuries, it's a combined operation, a coordinated one with the cooperation of everyone concerned. It is made up of the school administrator, the athletic director, the coach, the team physician, the trainer, the team manager and equipment man, maintenance personnel, news media, referees, manufacturers, researchers, stadium and field engineers, and others. The Team-Behind-the-Team is many layers deep, and its combined resources form the prevention program.

According to James Robey, project coordinator for the Laboratory of Applied Physiology at the University of North Carolina at Chapel Hill, the success of a prevention program lies not in knowing who is injured, the type of injury, or when the athlete can be returned to play: *success lies in determining the cause and then developing the prevention procedures that stop the injury.* The answers to the causes of injury lie in all the factors which determined how the injury happened in the first place. These factors could be the condition of physical facilities, the types and uses of field equipment, the condition and habits of the individual player and his protective gear, or even coaching techniques. Robey believes that by analyzing all such factors one can arrive at a well-designed prevention program which can significantly reduce injury in football.

Prior to 1950 there was little or no organized approach to health in athletics. The policy was to wait for an injury to happen and then hope everything would come out right. That was yesterday. Today everyone realizes the necessity for supervision and regulation of health needs in all-year-round conditioning programs for athletes. They recognize the need for the knowledgeable assistance of the team trainer, for more stringent rules, and more adroit officiating. They know there must be a team doctor, a psychiatrist, a dentist, and even a podiatrist. They understand the need for insurance coverage which assures the welfare of cheerleaders, band members, and the folks in the stands. As a result of this thinking it was inevitable that sports and medicine would wed and a system of controls for the prevention of injury would be born.

Today in larger schools the Team-Behind-the-Team has begun to come of age: however, many small colleges do not yet have even a team doctor or trainer. The majority of high schools in the United States have no such assistance, yet paradoxically it is at high school level that an athletic trainer and team doctor, and a prevent-system, are needed most. According to the *Sports Trail* survey six of every ten students who go out for high school athletic teams are injured in competition . . . 450 secondary-school athletic directors queried provided the reasons: (1) lack of certified athletic trainers, and (2) lack of adequate training rooms.

Fewer then half the schools surveyed reported having a team physician to attend home games, while 29 percent said they had no one to call for home games. Since high school athletes in many cases have not completed their physical growth, they have an even greater need for competent trainers and physicians than do older athletes.

A 1968 survey exposed the startling fact that in one football season twenty-six of the thirty-six deaths nationally were at high school level, four on the sandlot, five in college, and one in professional football. All were due to the failure to use one or more aspects of the Prevent-System. This survey, prepared for the American Football Coaches Association and the National Federation of High School Athletic Associations by Carl S. Blyth, Ph.D., reported that since 1941 defensive players sustained more fatal injuries then did offensive players. Blyth's excellent survey revealed that the majority of direct fatalities were caused by trauma to the head and neck. Heart, circulatory problems, and infections also played a role. Fifteen direct fatalities in 1968 occurred from heat stroke. Recommended by the survey were: (1) mandatory preseason medical examinations with complete medical history taken at the beginning of each season, (2) attendance by a physician at all games and practice sessions, (3) strict enforcement of game rules, (4) continued research on safety factors in football, and (5) the outlawing of "spearing" and enforcement of the rules prohibiting it. Blyth also urged conditioning exercises, including those for strengthening the neck.[1]

Football styles such as the "T-formation" changed offensive tactics. One-arm blocking became a weapon. The forearm took on the potency of a battering ram. The elbow was developed as a hammer or spear. The "clothesline" effectively dropped an opponent in his tracks. The "trap" sucked in defensive players who too often were not prepared to be hit at the hip, groin, or knee. "Cross-body blocking" opened up a host of problems, as did the development of the "downfield suicide squad." The passing attack made the quarterback vulnerable to red-dogging and gang tackling, techniques used to soften up the quarterback by injury, intimidation, or exhaustion.

New defensive and offensive techniques have opened a Pandora's box of injuries, so football coaches, athletic directors, field officials, trainers, and team physicians should all play their part in a Prevent-System. They must become more and more conscious of the necessity to lower injury potential. They should know, for example, whether a known diabetic candidate for football has his diabetes under control, whether a youngster has a history of epilepsy, or has only one of his dual organs. They should realize the values of the preseason and postseason "physi-

[1] C.S. Blyth, "Football-Linked Deaths Found to Have Decreased 36% in '69," *Hospital Tribune,* Sept. 21, 1970, p. 21.

cals," know why it is necessary to screen out the handicapped or unfit, and why a year-round conditioning program is necessary. A system like this one demands attention to a thousand and one details because too many athletes are being lost year after year as a direct result of someone who has forgotten about, is unconscious of, or has never gotten around to studying and putting into effect a Prevent-System for football.

Today, sports medicine is coming alive, and bringing with it changes in the rule books. With new know-how in protective equipment, beautifully trained trainers, with controlled coaching techniques, standardization of mandatory national rulings, improved officiating, and improved facilities, it was inevitable that the idea of the Prevent-System open up a new horizon and that traditional injuries, slowly but surely, would be eliminated.

Watching the incidence or injury drop with the help of prevention techniques throughout my own decades of association with sports as a trainer and team doctor and researcher, I began to work out a Prevent-System for many aspects of the fooball program. I fielded it with amateurs and semipros. The system grew. It burgeoned into a total injury prevention consciousness, and out of this came the procedures reported in this text. It's possible, and even probable, that these findings may not agree with all authorities, or with your own views. Anything that leaves the traditional channel is always subject to raised eyebrows. One thing these procedures *do* do, however, is give you a pocket from which to lead your passing attack on injuries in the future. Let this text be your quarterback temporarily calling the signals. Then develop your own plan of action. From then on *you* are the coach! That's when you will not only start sending in your own plays to win games but you will prevent injuries as well!

When your team is not winning games, and a rash of injuries is plaguing your squad, check your Prevent-System! Know how, when, where, and why those injuries occur! Knowing these factors is as important as the care of the injury itself, if you can keep it from recurring in the future. An injury may begin with inadequate gear or with new playing styles; it may begin with the failure to screen out long-necked, fragile youngsters with good intentions but no physique. The Prevent-System must even be used to check out airlines used for away games to prevent such a double tragedy as occurred in 1970 when the football teams of Wichita and Marshall Colleges were wiped out by air disasters. Every loophole has to be plugged, and the responsibility for all this does not belong only to the coach, the team doctor, or trainer; it belongs to everyone in that Team-Behind-the-Team. With this in mind the following text is a positive approach to a very negative problem. All you have to do is field it. Put it to work! See it in action! Add to it or subtract from it according to your local situation. Above all, it's *your* football game, *your* stadium, *your* ball! Play it!

JIM CERNEY

1

THE TEAM-BEHIND-THE-TEAM

Strategy Covered:

Overview of the responsibilities of:

- *The School Administrator*
- *The Athletic Director*
- *The Coaches*
- *The Team Physician*
- *The Trainer*
- *The Game Officials*

THE SCHOOL ADMINISTRATOR

The prevention of athletic injuries, especially in football, begins in the front office. It begins with a school's philosophy of athletics and the rules it lays down. It begins with a school administrator who develops a program of athletic injury prevention based on the recommendations of his athletic staff and keeps it maintained, manned, and financed all the way.

The effectiveness of any Prevent-System for football injuries depends on the school administrator, his understanding, and his feeling for the school's sports program. How he uses the Prevent-System, and develops his Team-Behind-the-Team, determines the destiny of injury prevention in his school.

At the grammar school or high school level, the administrator is usually the school's principal. At the college and university level, he is president. In either case he is the responsible cog. It's his effective control which makes the whole thing click! In an effort to tie down exactly what his responsibilities are I interviewed many administrators. They indicated twenty areas where the administrator's specific efforts are important in the Prevent-System for football injuries.

Twenty Key Points of the School Administrator's Responsibility

1. The administrator sets up a compulsory health conditioning or physical fitness program for all students, not only for athletes. He insists on a "conditioning schedule" for all sports no matter how minor.

2. He sets up "sports safety standards."

3. He selects and gets the best coaches he can afford.

4. He selects an athletic director who is a diplomat and who has administrative capacity and background in sports, then he gives him the latitude and the budget to get his job done.

5. He obtains the services of a doctor versed in sports medicine and a good trainer, dentist, psychiatrist, etc., to play an active role in the prevention and care of athletic injuries. He advises the physician that he is responsible to the school administrator and not to the coach. He provides an examination room, assistants, and all equipment necessary for their work. He does not permit a rotation system of doctors at the school, at games or meets. One person alone has to be responsible. He willingly accepts the offers of service by accredited or licensed men in all professions if such are offered.

6. The administrator goes to city or county boards of education, or to other sources, to solicit the funds necessary for permanent facilities and

operations. (This amount represents monies other than the coach's or athletic director's operational funds.)

7. He sets up training room facilities and provides a trainer, full or part time, and all necessary equipment.

8. He checks all state laws that regulate, define, and control responsibility for the sports program. (All legal aspects should be checked out for the welfare of everyone concerned with the sports program and for the development of a sound basic health program.)

9. He maintains a constant public relations program to stimulate his Team-Behind-the-Team, his faculty, his students, their parents, and alumni. He strives to foster school spirit in the athletic program as well as pocketbook allegiance and support.

10. He insists that his athletic director hires the best officiating personnel for all games.

11. He sees that all intramurals, as well as interscholastic sports are supervised.

12. The administrator arranges insurance coverage for everyone connected with the sports program. This insurance should cover "malpractice" for the trainer, team doctors, and coaches. He insists on travel insurance coverage for the band, cheerleaders, parents, etc., who are traveling with the team. He sets up a separate "athletic fund" for emergencies where there is little or no insurance coverage or help. With the athletic director he makes certain that the insurance covers football. He keeps an eagle eye on all school facilities and concessions for situations that could lead to sickness or injury (for example, contaminated food, worn out bleachers, etc.). He is always aware of all aspects of possible legal entanglements.

13. He insists on a complete record and report system so that there are no legal loopholes in his sports program.

14. He remembers that body-building is as vital as mind-building, and at the same time that sports should remain fun at amateur level. He assures mental and physical conditioning for *all* students, at all levels, a "must" in injury prevention and health maintenance. In his responsibility for triggering and maintaining a physical fitness program, he has to publicize the program to parents and to all involved.

15. He makes rulings on night games and pre- or postseason "all star" games; he does not fit the student program to whims of spectators or officials.

16. He sets up guidelines for sportsmanship and maintains them with disciplinary action, or with incentives as desired.

17. He bans "exhibition" games when athletes are completely un-

ready for competition. He permits no sports competition when athletes have not had at least six to eight weeks of conditioning. He demands, and gets, physical fitness to prevent injury. He does not permit freshman or reserve squads to don broken or hand-me-down, worn equipment.

18. He at no time permits a coach, athletic director, trainer, or team doctor to hide an injury and play a boy, nor does he condone such an action should it occur.

19. He does not permit coaches to treat injuries because injuries and their therapy are not legally within the coach's domain.

20. He does all he can to step up school spirit but at no time permits the demand to win to become the all-consuming desire.

Here I would like to add my own thoughts on a few of these points.

Night Games

Night games have been promoted because of gate receipts and spectator convenience but the administrator must remember that school athletics are for the participants and not for the coaches, the officials, the school, or for the fans. Athletics and physical education must keep pace with mental education of which it is a living part. Night games demand rigid control and supervision. They have to be policed constantly in order not to become occasions for spectator delinquency. This has happened in some large cities to the point where, to prevent audience injury, nighttime football and basketball games have been completely discontinued and only afternoon contests are run. Night games are also a disadvantage because they conflict with the sleep and diet habits of the athlete. As such, night games are an injury risk and the administrator must take a stand to determine how his athletic department will act on this issue.

Choosing a Team Physician

In choosing a team physician for his athletic program the administrator has many considerations. One college president told me that the following were his guidelines for choosing the doctor for his teams.

The doctor chosen as team physician should know, understand, and be trained in sports medicine. Standard medical school training by no means qualifies any general practitioner for handling athletic injuries. Athletic injuries are unique, and diagnosis and treatment for an athlete can't be rendered as for an average person.

A school's team doctor should command respect because of his character, reputation, and accomplishment, and he should ideally have a notable background in sports action himself. He should have an unruffled personality. He should like athletes and be liked by them. He should have a working knowledge of the length of recuperation time, and of surgery, physical therapy, and rehabilitation procedures so that he can properly prescribe to the trainers. He should be able to present a total prevention program to the administrator and his staff, set it into motion and maintain it with the school's support.

The team physician has to have the time, as well as the interest, to do his job and be at all games. Where possible he should be immediately available for practices and scrimmages in the early season when the incidence of injury is highest. He has to be the kind of person who cooperates and works with the rest of the Team-Behind-the-Team. He should provide a standby doctor to fill in if he is away. He has to be one who willingly meets with coaches, trainers and athletic directors to establish policy on athletic injury prevention and care. He should be an individual without professional biases, who welcomes assistance from the trainer or from outside doctors from other professions who offer help.

How the Administrator May Add a Trainer to His Staff

At high school and college level, a lack of funds can kill a lot of desirable programs. However, in the case of adding a trainer to the staff, there is a way to get around the matter. A trainer can be added to the athletic staff at approximately the same pay as that of an assistant coach. How? For the sake of the records the trainer is hired as a teacher first and secondly as a trainer. A teacher's regular salary schedule provides the base pay scale. To the base scale is added additional salary for the trainer and his additional duties.

Publicity Policy

The administrator should insist that his coach, trainer, and team doctor make no public statements concerning players' injuries. Injuries must never be used as a public alibi. All publicity should be cleared through the athletic director, who is completely responsible for the facts and nothing but the facts. There should be a firm policy that athletic injuries play no part in the news. This is good policy for the injured boy, for the team, and for the school. An impulsive public statement, implying, for example, that an athlete "cannot return to sports," could result in needless mental anguish for the athlete.

The Role of the Administrator in Sportsmanship

No athletic program is complete unless it teaches *sportsmanship*. Sportsmanship is the fairness and self-control that athletes learn and that makes them not just better competitors, but also clean competitors. They are taught not to cause injury to others. They are not triggered to hate, to become jealous, or be spiteful, because there is no place for anything but good clean sports in athletics. Therefore, to cut down the possibility of injury that may result from unsportsmanlike behavior the administrator will insist on a *code of sportsmanship*.

THE ATHLETIC DIRECTOR

One hard-hitting athletic director we'll leave unnamed said this to his "Quarterback Club":

> Football has many values. Its greatest value is to the boy. Football provides something that no other sport can give. If a boy wants to play football and is physically fit and capable, and has the best of protective gear and the best of coaching, training, medical supervision, and direction, he participates in the king of sports. . . . To me the boy is everything. In athletics his protection is of first concern. Teaching a boy good clean football and how to cope with hurt and danger teaches him the rudiments of life. Football teaches him courage, cooperation, sacrifice, and perserverance. It deliberately toughens and disciplines him for what he has to face, and no school has the right to ask young men to play football unless the school uses every means possible to prevent injury!

The need for a Prevent-System in football should by now be obvious enough. The athletic director does everything he can to make it complete, often fighting against seemingly insurmountable odds. How he accomplishes this, what his duties are, and how complex his administration has become are broad subjects, just touched on in this book. There are some areas I do want to emphasize, however, where the athletic director is concerned: the legal aspects of injuries in football; the maintenance of permanent records and the athlete's "career file"; how to get authorizations, waivers, approvals, etc.; the importance of choosing referees; using effective field controls and proper hard equipment; and Prevent-System rules for booking air and other travel, to name a few.

The Athletic Director's Annual Report

In a brief, compact presentation, the athletic director should run down the year's injuries in his annual report to the school administrator. This report is not only significant from the standpoint of wins and losses, but it also graphically presents the values of a Prevent-System that has been set in motion. This year's drop in the number of injuries should be compared with the records of previous seasons. This type of evidence is often instrumental in getting bigger football budgets for protective gear for the next fiscal year. When lack of facilities lead to injury, these facts should be dramatically pointed out. They should be emphasized to put across the point that *there has to be a Prevent-System in football!* Credit should go to all personnel involved. No effort should be made at any time to hide injuries. Recommendations should be made that may be of value in cutting down injuries even more in the coming year.

In the overall pattern, the athletic director is a great guy!

An athletic director should be more then a "faculty manager." He should understand athletics and its needs, its problems, and its hurts. Even more than that he should understand everyone who makes the athletic program possible. He has to know his staff, his school's limitations, its needs and its wants, the youngsters, and the community, as well as the wants of the school's administrator, school superintendent, or school board. He must be able to carry on all phases of his job. He has a big business to operate and it has to be run in an efficient, businesslike manner.

The athletic director must continually have an incentive program going to step up local interest in the athletic program of his school. He should go before the P.T.A., "Booster's Club," "Quarterback Club," etc., regularly. He should have a definite understanding of what the duties of the coaching staff are. They in turn should be informed of his duties and needs as well. He should explain to the trainer, the band director, the faculty advisor for cheerleaders, the student managers, the athletes, and everyone concerned the school's policy on all athletic matters. He should tell them exactly what he wants and expects.

As a man with important reins in his hands for the prevention of injuries, the athletic director is responsible for the destiny of the young people in his school who flow through its complex network year after year. He is the watchdog whose objectives and thinking are in accord with those of the school administrator, as well as with the township, county, or state boards of education. In athletics, athletic injury prevention, and management, he is the key to a better program. *From his office and action stem not only a school's athletic success but a lowering of the injury rate as well.* We will go into more detail about his responsibilities throughout this book.

THE COACH

A coach has special duties unique to his job. Said Dayton High School System athletic director William Marquardt:

> In the coach's capable hands can be the overall Master Plan of prevention of athletic injuries. In the prevention of injuries a coach has many con-

> cerns and too often they are more than one man can handle. To stay on top of the prevention program a football coach has to allocate or redistribute some of these responsibilities to the athletic director, trainer, team physician, team and equipment managers, grounds maintenance personnel etc. . . . With the athlete rated as the first consideration and winning the game second, the allocation of duties and responsibilities in injury prevention, and everything else with which he is concerned, has to be brought into focus. Once the coach's awareness of the necessity for a prevent-system is established the drop in injuries becomes readily apparent.[1]

Better coaching techniques are developing a refinement in training and conditioning, the direct result of which has been a general stepping-up of the contestant's competitive capacity. This has meant not only better, more competitive athletes and more broken records, but it has also pointed out that the athletic coach is a vital key in the door of injury prevention. How? Let's take a quick look.

A coach doesn't just *work* with boys and men. He develops them. He controls them. When squad morale drops it is because he has let down somewhere. When fewer and fewer games are won, and there are suddenly more injuries then ever before, it is wise for a coach to look at his injury prevention techniques to discover at what points these injuries begin. This text was designed to touch on these points one by one. In the appendix of this book the coach will find a section of training instructions which he can mimeograph and issue to his boys for his Prevent-System.

Drawing a Bead on the Source of Injury

Big athletic injuries usually begin with multiple small injuries. They may be missed in the preseason screening or in a preseason physical examination if it is inadequately performed. Some injuries may have their inception in poorly kept athletic department records on prior illnesses or injury. Injury may begin when someone overestimates an athlete's abilities or strengths and puts him out of his own league. Injury may begin with a birth anomaly that remains hidden until the explosive dynamics of football reveal it. It may begin with inadequate warm-ups and calisthenics. It may start when a boy is returned to the lineup before he is fully recovered from injury. It may begin with a badly applied adhesive tape strapping, or an inadequate diagnosis of an injury and an even more inadequate treatment. It may have its inception in sticking to traditional exercises like "duck walks" and knee bends when the athlete is known to have had knee injury in the past. This book will attempt to put much of

[1] William Marquardt, personal interview with the author.

this into focus for the coach upon whose capable shoulders rests a heavy trust and an even heavier responsibility.

THE TEAM PHYSICIAN

Physicians are not yet playing a full-blown role in sports. Because there are too few doctors in sports, and too few specializing in sports medicine, many promising athletes are still lost today at grammar, high school, and small college level. Boys going out for football do so at their own risk. Parents in turn are faced with the cost of injury when their boy is hurt. Add to this hazard the problem of the untrained personnel in many athletic departments who are assigned to jobs for which they are not prepared.

In many areas of the United States and Europe, doctors have not yet been utilized in the athletic injury prevention program. In relatively few universities, colleges, and high schools are there sports medicine specialists in that Team-Behind-the-Team. Today, farsighted and progressive school boards, Booster Clubs, and P.T.A. groups are becoming less hampered by the shortsightedness and prejudices of the past. They admit the need for professional personnel who know how to prevent injuries, and especially team doctors.

Seeing and recognizing these necessities, professional people have taken a public stand on prevention in sports medicine. In their new awareness of and alliance with athletics, medical men have brought into focus some exceedingly important ideas. In the state of Michigan, for example, D. L. Hinerman, M.D., conceived an all-important resolution for the Washtenaw County Medical Society. This was presented to the Michigan State Medical Society by Dr. Henry A. Scovill. Let's take a look at this resolution:

> BE IT RESOLVED THAT:
>
> *Whereas* the American Medical Association and the Michigan State Medical Society have demonstrated an active concern in athletics insofar as health problems arise frequently, and this concern is reflected in the recognition of the field of "sports medicine," and
>
> *Whereas* the high rate of injury, the need for prevention of these injuries and the need for rehabilitation of the injured athlete constitute a serious health problem, and
>
> *Whereas* complete records of athletic injuries are nonexistent in many schools, and
>
> *Whereas* the medicolegal aspects of athletic medicine are becoming more and more important, and

Whereas this problem is of national concern and may properly be of interest to the American Medical Association, therefore be it

Resolved: That the Michigan State Board of Education and the Michigan Department of Public Health encourage the establishment of an adequate Athletic Medicine unit in every school where feasible, and

Resolved: That the Athletic Medicine Unit be composed of a duly licensed physician, an athletic health coordinator (trainer), and other necessary personnel, and

Resolved: That the duties of the Athletic Medicine Unit be prevention of injury, provision of medical care with the cooperation of the family physician and others of the health care team of the community, and the rehabilitation of the injured, and

Resolved: That the school be required to submit a complete report of all injuries to the Michigan Department of Public Health, and

Resolved: That medical schools be urged to assume the responsibility of training Athletic Health Coordinators (trainers) as well as specialists in Athletic Medicine, and

Resolved: That copies of this resolution be forwarded to the Governor, the Legislature, the Michigan State Board of Education, the Michigan Association of School Boards and the Michigan Association of School Administrators.[2]

THE ATHLETIC TRAINER

From 1950 to 1960 athletic training changed status! It became an organized career. The National Athletic Trainers Association came into being and answered the basic needs of the sports world with college-trained specialists.

Today, unique in his line, the trainer not only prevents sports injuries and treats them under medical supervision but is also a qualified physical therapist. He may have a dual role as a teacher and author. As an accredited specialist he steps into a long-neglected gap. In direct proportion to his professional growth he has become a responsible member of the Team-Behind-the-Team in the progressive high schools, colleges, and universities of the United States. A few of his many specific responsibilities are: (1) the prevention of injury by all means (exercise, protective equipment, taping, training techniques, etc.), (2) the maintenance of the physical condition of the athlete, (3) emergency care of the injured, (4) nutritional control, (5) physical therapy and rehabilitation, (6) the prevention of undertraining or overtraining, (7) acting as a wailing wall and counselor.

[2] *Journal of the NATA,* Summer, 1970, p. 18.

The Trainer: New Star on the Sports Horizon

Backed up by a wealth of training know-how garnered from university departments of physical education, schools of physical therapy, and postgraduate instruction from the uncommon men in sports medicine, the trainer insures his team against injury when he pounds home the Prevent-System. Prevention is his business and he has unlimited ways for preventing injury. The result is that *the athlete under his care becomes a permanent competitor; he loses little or no practice or game time; his morale is high;* and *he is quicker to reach peak performance.* This is exactly what makes a trainer valuable in any sport.

GAME OFFICIALS

Inasmuch as game officials are a major factor in the prevention of football injuries certain key factors should be considered. These factors are clear-cut and should be used to determine whether a game official should be rehired for the following year. To determine your personal rating of a game official, fill out the following suggested chart. Study your officials. Know them. Keep complete records on all officials you hire.

Referees: Field Control Agents for Injuries

The athletic director hires football officials as field and injury-prevention police. He hires them not just to officiate at a game, but also to guard against misbehavior on the gridiron which may lead to injury. As controllers of rules and regulations of the game, referees are among the best injury-prevention factors in any Prevent-System.

When hiring game officials the athletic director should make sure they are strong enough not to be intimidated by athletes, coaches, parents, or crowds. They must have a fast whistle and quickly penalize infractions of both the rules of good sportsmanship and the game rules. The referee must know all the latest state and national rulings and enforce them.

The athletic director should emphasize to the referees the following points along with any other new rulings.

Referees should prevent gang tackling and promptly penalize for tackling out-of-bounds or direct hits after the whistle blows. They should penalize the face block or nose tackling and be consistent in calls made on illegal defense blocking. They should call and penalize the use of the forearm or elbow on the face or faceguard. Spearing or bull blocking should be called promptly. They should be alert for, and promptly penalize: clipping, kicking, roughing the kicker and violation of the fair catch, piling on, unnecessary roughness after the play is called dead, slugging,

ATHLETIC OFFICIALS
RATING CHART

Date ______________________

Official ______________________ Address ____________

Sport ______________________ Position ____________

	Yes	No
1. Is he on top of the play at all times?	___	___
2. Does he have a sharp eye and a fast whistle?	___	___
3. Are his decisions clear and decisive?	___	___
4. Is he belligerent with the players?	___	___
5. Is he responsive to crowd emotions?	___	___
6. Does he know the rules?	___	___
7. Does he get along with the players?	___	___
8. Are the spectators with him?	___	___
9. Are his violation signals distinct?	___	___
10. Is he consistent in his decisions?	___	___
11. Is he more concerned with the players' injuries then with the game?	___	___
12. Does he establish the rules for and maintain a clean game?	___	___
13. Is he immediately on his toes after the whistle?	___	___
14. Does he stand up to anyone trying to brush aside the rules?	___	___
15. Does he cooperate with other officials and coaches when there is an injury or other problem?	___	___
16. Is he a "take charge type" or does he fade back to let the coach and trainer take over?	___	___
17. Notes:		

Figure 1-1

roughing up the pass-receiver, roughing up the quarterback after the ball has left his hands, the arm lift that snaps the head up and back, and the clothesline (or judo chop) across the throat. Officials should hold up the game and send to the sidelines any player showing signs of injury. Participants guilty of unsportsmanlike behavior leading to injury should be immediately ejected. Referees should show no hesitation in removing spectators, coaches, or unnecessary players from the field. They should halt the action when litter or stray animals interfere with the game or the safety of the players.

All athletic department personnel should have regular health examinations!

The problem of the "unfortunate accident" involving faculty members or athletic department personnel is more common than we want to believe or admit. Therefore, as a method of prevention, *all athletic department personnel should receive complete physical examinations at least twice yearly.* This should include the administrator, the athletic director, the coaches, the trainer, and the team doctor.

For example, there comes a time in every coach's life when he can no longer take the pressure. His nervous system is ready to pop, and his heart, stomach, or small intestine has already popped. He is no longer adapting to emergencies and tension in healthy manner. The examining doctor should advise the athletic director and school administrator of this situation. The athletic director, for his part, can do the following: (1) keep an eye on all department personnel; (2) have the team doctor make a complete scheduled examination of all athletic department personnel; (3) if the grind is getting to the coach, boot the coach upstairs to a job less injurious to his health or have him retire from sports; or (4) take most of the extra duties from his shoulders. To keep a good coach, permit him to coach. Don't saddle him with extra duties not within his domain.

In the big shows put on by the athletic department there are many people who are involved other than athletes. All athletic department personnel share a big responsibility. The whole Team-Behind-the-Team includes the cheerleaders, marching band, team managers, maintenance personnel, and other assisting students. To cover this responsibility the athletic director should make every effort to see that they are protected against injury. He should provide adequate transportation, protected food, insurance, and everything else necessary for their welfare and protection. Most of all he should be concerned about their health. He should make a ruling that cheerleaders and members of the band be given preseason physical examinations and that they go through a training and conditioning process before they are permitted on the field. Such examinations can help prevent a vast number of complications and uncomfortable situations from occurring each year.

2

THE WARM-UP

Strategy Covered:

- *Grammar schools: the cradle of sports injury?*
- *Establishing a physical fitness program*
- *The preseason screening*
- *The preseason medical examination*
- *Guidelines for health disqualifiers*
- *The trainer's athletic examination*
- *Coaching techniques for injury prevention*
- *Football camp*
- *Spring football*

GRAMMAR SCHOOLS: THE CRADLE OF SPORTS INJURY?

University, college, and high school sports injuries too often have their inception at grammar school level. They begin when inadequate physical education programs and inadequate conditioning are allowed by those who feel that only the mind and not the body needs to be developed, and that one is not vital to the other. Yet grammar school and high school years are the very time when regular exercise is necessary and body development is a must to build skill, endurance, and strength. Grammar schools can be the very cradle of sports injuries, and there are certain important areas to watch out for to prevent injuries early.

A more adequate health appraisal has to be made of grammar school children and there should be consistent testing and exercise programs to determine children's progress. The capacity of American children today to maintain physical action is still not completely known. Sometimes the home environment fails to maintain a child's physical fitness or provide proper nutrition. Young children may lack examples of good sportsmanship. Sometimes schools lack health insurance that covers contact sports. Grammar school football or other coaches may not be suited to their jobs.

At puberty a vast number of physical, chemical, and psychological changes take place in a boy or girl and it is at this time that a youth is particularly susceptible to the injuries and illnesses which may affect his or her entire sports career. To prevent injuries at this age level it is necessary for administrators at the high school level and at the grammar school level to initiate a physical fitness program that will not only pave the way for better sports performance in the future but for fewer injuries as well. My friends in school administration insist that mental fitness and physical fitness begin at grammar school level and in preparing that potential athlete there are some vital matters of concern which are listed here.

Fourteen Basic Prevention Necessities for Prepuberty Athletes

1. The grammar school administrator must not permit a youth to participate in sports without a complete physical examination by a qualified doctor. He must not depend on a note from home or vocal clearance from the parents. Children with a history of rheumatic fever, diabetes, or epilepsy should not be allowed to participate in contact sports. When boys or girls show inadequate physical development their participation should be limited.

2. The school should maintain a practical conditioning or physical fitness program. All children not capable of passing given tests should be given special training until they are more capable. A mild weight training program and a program of running (wind-sprints) can be inaugurated.

3. Only qualified coaches should supervise the athletic program.

4. Protective gear should be furnished by the school. When the best of gear cannot be purchased because of lack of funds there should be no *contact* sports!

5. Consistently injury-prone boys should be dropped immediately from contact sports teams and diverted into managerial or other duties attached to thc sport they like best.

6. Quarters for football and other sports should be short.

7. Free substitutions should be made often.

8. Coaches or gym instructors who are assigned must be leaders and motivators. Enthusiasm, faith, and the desire to emulate a leader are important to a child's development.

9. Drop all reluctant players from organized contact sports teams whose parents are pushing them. It could be the best thing that ever happened to them and prevents injuries.

10. Meet with parents and discuss the athletic program and the Prevent-System. Talk over every aspect so that there is a complete understanding of insurance coverage, releases, waivers, car pool responsibilities, etc. Discuss diet and hours of sleep. Hand out mimeographed instructions that specifically point out each and every one of these matters. State the policy of the school and the philosophy of athletics by which the school expects all sports participants to abide.

11. Have an early season auditorium assembly for students and parents that is devoted to sportsmanship.

12. Make sure that special attention is given to the eyes, teeth, feet, and spinal column of these youngsters. Often too little exact attention is given to these areas in the regular medical examination. Since they are at the root of many injuries it is mandatory that they be assessed. Specific examinations covering these areas may be given by volunteer specialists (dentists, optometrists, podiatrists, mechanotherapists, etc.).

13. Use only competent officials who have a sharp eye and a fast whistle for all contests.

14. Make sure these youngsters participate only at their own competitive level.

In maintaining a sports program for the prepuberty participant every possible means should be used to prevent injury. Every angle should be considered. For example: Peewee footballers and Little Leaguers should not be permitted to wear cleated shoes. They should not be permitted to participate until they have had at least a month of preseason conditioning and drills. One of the criminal offenses against grammar school children by adults is the plunging of youngsters into adult-type sports without adequate preparations and protection. Adult delinquents who sponsor injury in this manner give football for children a bad name. There's nothing wrong with children's football except the adults who are trying to relive yesterday.

A desirable Prevent-System for the prepuberty athlete should include: a year-round physical fitness program designed to develop sound minds and bodies. A child's conditioning program should ideally help him or her to develop resistance to injuries and illness, develop stamina, skills, speed, flexibility, and coordination. Body conditioning should include isometrics, weight-training, rope jumping and climbing, gymnastics, tumbling, and running every day if possible. This kind of program not only develops all a child's muscle groups, but also a child's competitive spirit. And remember, a qualified team doctor and trainer should be available for intramural and extracurricular sports teams.

ESTABLISHING A PHYSICAL FITNESS PROGRAM

The administrator should meet at the beginning of each high school year with the children and parents of each new freshman class. This may be on freshman orientation day or on a similar occasion. Along with other printed literature on physical fitness the student and parent should receive a sheet describing health requirements. Parents should be asked for their cooperation in the physical education program after the purposes of such a program are explained.

The mimeographed sheet on physical fitness should not only contain the merits of such a program, but it should also contain a medical excuse form which must be presented to the family doctor if the child is unable to participate in such a program. Included in this literature should also be rules and regulations on deportment in the gymnasium or on other sports facilities. It should detail the necessity and method of taking showers, and the official garb. An example of this form follows.

How to Set Up Criteria for Physical Fitness

The big question most school administrators ask is "Well, what *is* physical fitness?" It's not just a question asked by the athletic department. The same question is asked by research organizations, insurance companies, government agencies, and medical people. The words "physical fitness" are almost meaningless because of the many interpretations that are given to them. Insurance people see it one way; physicians see it another. People in the physical education department give it their inter-

Date______________
Re: Physical Fitness Program

Dear Parents:

It is the purpose of this school to provide an outstanding physical fitness program. We want our classes in physical education to be as effective as possible for your children. We believe that physical education is as vital as mental education, but to provide for our pupils we need your assistance. We need your cooperation in advocating at home the merits of consistent activity. It is the policy of this school to require all boys and girls to have physical education twice a week. In addition there are several other factors to note:

Official Dress: the traditional type of gym shoes will be used. They may be high or low cut. Boys will wear shorts and T-shirts. Girls will wear one piece suits or shorts and blouses. All clothing must be kept laundered. In addition, clothing worn in physical fitness courses may be worn only in gymnasium or on playing fields.

Showering: All students will take a shower after physical education class when time permits and facilities are provided for them.

Excuses for Nonparticipation: Your child, to be excused from classes in physical education, must have his/her Medical Excuse Form filled out and signed by you and your family doctor. If you believe that your child should not participate in our physical fitness program we would like to hear from you. We are happy to cooperate with your doctor to work out a program advantageous to your child.

____
Administrator

Figure 2-1

pretation, and as far as the young folks are concerned, they just don't care.

To define what physical fitness is and to use the definition effectively in the prevention of injury we have to develop a standardized approach and a truly scientific program of action. Knowing the number of times one can run around the gymnasium or track or how many pushups or situps can be done in a given time is meaningless if what the effort is costing the participant remains unknown. This is why it is necessary to set up criteria for physical fitness. The individual's response to action has to be known. For exact answers the AAHPER and Kraus-Weber tests, for example, are inadequate until it is known what change of pulse has taken place during and after a given exercise, or whether that pulse has developed some idiosyncrasy. Further points to determine are: How long does it take the heart to recover after exercise? What is the blood pressure before and after exercise? What variables are there in the blood and blood pressure from day to day? What is the blood sugar count? Is sugar showing in the urine? These and many other questions have to be answered in developing an optimum Prevent-System. When you have the figures on these kinds of measurable matters and can interpret them properly, your physical fitness program, as well as your Prevent-System has begun to function. Through such a program the initial screening of the unfit has begun. We begin to know who should be kept out of contact sports like football. Unfit youngsters are shuttled over to less strenuous endeavors, and this is prevention at its best!

When establishing a procedure to determine a standard of "fitness," consult your team physician. Get his ideas. Check with the trainer. Work out what you feel is the best procedure for making an athletic department estimate of "fitness." Use it consistently year after year. Keep records on your findings. Your yearly summaries will astonish you as your physical education program improves.

THE PRESEASON SCREENING

With tongue in cheek the late Vince Lombardi described a way of telling whether an applicant would play offensive or defensive football. "If the player's hair is combed and he responds to questions with 'yessir' and 'no sir' and says he wants to become a great pro player he's an offensive player. If he checks in wearing a dirty jacket and a few days growth of beard, spits on the floor and asks 'How much you paying me?' he's defensive all the way!" [1]

Of course there's more to preseason screening than that. With injury

[1] Vince Lombardi, interview with the author.

prevention in mind, every candidate should be personally interviewed by the coach, the team physician, the team trainer, the team podiatrist, the team dentist, the team oculist, etc., where circumstances permit. Unfortunately, however, a large percentage of high schools in the United States don't have even a team doctor and trainer.

Whether at high school, college, or pro level, the football coach who screens new candidates should have a completely satisfactory interview before he issues a card qualifying the boy for medical examination. The late Army coach "Red" Blaik once said that he screened them all, and it wasn't just a slender neck that disqualified a candidate. It could be heart problems, congenital defects, hernias, or a missing kidney, eye, testicle, or lung. To coach Blaik's list can be added a host of other health problems brought to light by diligent history-taking and questioning. To forget such an all-important factor as the preseason screening is to lay onesself wide open to the legal consequences of contributory negligence.

It happened in our town. It was the first day of fall practice and the high school youngster suited up and ran out on the field with full equipment. He was a skinny boy with little more than a football hero dream. He'd had no conditioning, no training, and had no know-how. There'd been no earlier screening of candidates. This youngster made his first clumsy tackle on a live target, got clobbered in the neck and died. An "inadequate helmet" was publicly termed the cause, but the helmet was *not* at fault. Fault lay in the lack of a Prevent-System. It lay in the off season that was never utilized to determine whether the kid was physically capable. From the very beginning an astute coach conscious of the Prevent-System and the necessity of preseason screening would have checked him off!

Prevention of football injuries begins before the season starts. It begins with the policies of the state and local athletic departments and the boards of education. It begins with rules and regulations that are enforced. It begins with coaches, with team physicians and trainers, with calisthenics, drills and equipment. It begins with the consciousness of the necessity for an all-year-round training program. As Vince Lombardi put it, "Football is not a seasonal sport. It's an all-year-round program of action for me as well as for the players. Everything is of concern, including the athlete's preseason screening."

THE PRESEASON MEDICAL EXAMINATION

The importance of the preseason medical examination was exemplified when I interviewed football coach Jim Eby who said, "Before any candidate is even permitted to do calisthenics our team physician has compiled a record of the candidate's previous illnesses and injuries. We determine for example whether the boy has such a problem as a short leg, or a rotated pelvis, which could create imbalance and insecurity, whether he is diabetic, epileptic, or asthmatic, or whether he's taking drugs of one kind or another. We feel that the preseason medical examination and medical history are more important than clocking the participant's time running the 100 with full gear."

Your team doctor should be a specialist in sports medicine. In developing your preseason medical examination program utilize a physician who not only knows athletic injuries but who is dedicated to sports. Use a doctor who knows and is trained in athletic requirements and the specific problems of athletic injuries. He must know how these injuries happen and what to do before and after they happen. His findings and prescribed care should be intimately tied to the training and conditioning program of the school or team.

Medical examinations have to be compulsory because all young men are not "physically fit." As you are well aware all grammar and high school candidates who report in to the athletic office or even to football camp are not superstars. Too often they fail to have what it takes for sustained action. They can't stand up to emergency action. This may be because they have a medical problem that precludes a sports career. For this reason all potential candidates *must* go through the medical filter. Findings have to be complete on physical and mental conditions. The coach has to know whether each football candidate is capable of performance under stress and whether he can respond to emergency. For this reason the doctor who makes this compulsory Prevent-System examination should know athletic needs.

Here's a hot item to remember about that athletic physical. Medical information is sometimes misleading no matter what scientific instrumentation is used. As valuable as the preseason medical examination is, there are times when diagnostic equipment and "tests" give a false lead and this is why it is so completely vital that the examining doctor be versed in sports medicine. This was exemplified at the 1968 Olympics in Mexico City. Electrocardiograms of Olympic athletes were found to show remarkable "pathological" traits. Said Tenley E. Albright, M.D., Boston surgeon and former Olympic medalist and women's figure skating champion:

> We now realize a superbly fit Olympic athlete can have a frightening

> abnormal, pathological-looking electrocardiogram and yet be a strong, topnotch competitor with terrific stamina and endurance. Previously such an athlete when found to have such "alarming" heart findings might be barred from the year's athletic competition needlessly. . . . we are getting closer to realizing "normal" is not just average; true normal is really equivalent of the well-trained physically fit athlete—the obvious example of the human body at its maximum efficiency.[2]

I mention this to drive home the tremendous need for a team doctor who *knows* sports medicine, and school administrators, athletic directors, coaches, trainers, and school boards should recognize this.

There's another aspect for consideration: A candidate who appears physically fit for one sport may be totally unfit for another. He may be marked as "approved" but in the Prevent-System this is interpreted only to mean that his degree of fitness determines the sports in which he may participate. For example, a young man turned down for football may become an Olympic medalist in swimming. The school fencing champion may prove totally inadequate for the gridiron and yet be "approved" physically to handle the épée. The screening and preseason medical examination are merely primary steps to assure everyone concerned that the participant is a qualified candidate for his sport.

GUIDELINES FOR HEALTH DISQUALIFIERS

In helping you determine whether an applicant can participate certain guidelines have to be set up. The best I know of to date are those of R. M. Lane, M.D. of Maine. His beautifully developed Prevent-System creates a sharply defined path to follow:

CODE Guidelines for Determining an Athlete's Medical Qualifications[3]

1. *Matching.* Participants should stay in a class of their own weight, physical size, and emotional maturity. There should be minimum and maximum standards for all secondary school athletes.

2. *Acute infections.* Any athlete showing symptoms of an acute infection is to be temporarily restricted from sports participation. This includes chickenpox, measles, mumps, scarlet fever or scarletina, rheumatic fever,

[2] T.E. Albright, *Medicine in Sports Newsletter* 10 (July 1970), p. 1.

[3] R.M. Lane, *Journal of the Maine Medical Association* 60, no. 11, pp. 247–54, 268. I have condensed the original CODE guidelines for this book.

respiratory infections, genitourinary infections, hepatitis, infectious mononucleosis, boils, furunculosis, impetigo, cellulitis, lymphangitis, pediculosis, and herpes simplex.

3. *Blood and related conditions.* An athlete should be disqualified who has a serious problem such as pernicious anemia, hemophilia, etc.

4. *Diabetes mellitus.* Young athletes with diabetes have to be screened for degree of condition and control and approved prior to being medically qualified for interscholastic sports.

5. *Eyes.* Eyes are particularly vulnerable to injury. Thus, candidates who have only one good eye are automatically disqualified by this guideline. Football players in need of visual correction bilaterally should wear contact lenses and never be permitted to wear glasses with frames.

6. *Ears.* External hearing aids are forbidden in contact sports; they are potential weapons. Therefore, bilaterally deaf persons are restricted from contact sports. Unilateral deafness does not preclude participation.

7. *Respiratory system.* Anything causing pulmonary insufficiency disqualifies participation in sports. Good respiration means good performance; interference with breathing spells trouble. Emphysema, bronchiectasis, cystic fibrosis, spontaneous pneumothorax, active T.B., etc., disqualify the participant.

8. *Cardiovascular system.* In sports participation the cardiovascular system (the heart and blood vessels) is most important. Abnormalities which preclude participation are valvular and cyanotic heart disease which has not required surgery, previous heart operations, or operations on vessels to and from the heart, organic hypertension, currently active carditis, significant pulse irregularities, and thromboembolic cardiovascular disease. (Dr. Lane indicates that athletic participation should not be limited because of *situational high blood pressure, transient physiological pulse irregularities, nonpathological heart murmurs,* or *transient physiological pulse irregularities.*)

9. *Liver and spleen.* Enlargement of either organ precludes contact or endurance sports. What appears to be an enlarged liver in a slender athlete, however, may be normal for him. Participation is allowed if the area is padded when the boy is engaged in contact sports. Acute infections of the liver and jaundice disqualify the athlete until he is fully recovered.

10. *Kidneys and genitalia.* Absence of one kidney or testicle (for any cause) disqualifies the participant. Acute or chronic disease of these organs does also. Surgically repaired hernias and scrotal hydroceles *do not* disqualify.

11. *Musculoskeletal system.* The sports participant or candidate is disqualified by: symptomatic structural abnormalities, acute and chronic

inflammatory processes, and functional inadequacies that interfere with skill or performance. Previous injuries that have seriously impaired musculoskeletal function are disqualifiers. The athlete qualifies if healed or repaired parts remain without symptoms during strenuous sports action. Significant injuries that preclude sports action are: history of herniated nucleus pulposus above the fourth and fifth lumbar level, spondylolesthesis (lumbar 5, sacral 1 slippage), previous spinal surgery (above lumbars 4 and 5), and previous cervical bone surgery. Permissable are: spina bifida oculta, lumbar spondylosis, injured discs at lumbar 4 and 5 level, and lumbar 5 and sacral 1 level. Where metal has been used surgically (rods, plates, or screws) for fracture healing, joint prosthesis, etc., the candidate is restricted from active contact or endurance sports.

12. *Neurologic system (brain and intercranial segments only).* Any vascular accident, surgery, infection, congenital abnormalities, malignancy, or trauma to the brain and its covering disqualifies the person from contact sports. CODE, utilizing, the A.M.A.'s *Standard Nomenclature of Athletic Injuries,* spells out the problem of prevention on cerebral concussions in the first, second, and third degrees. This guideline indicates that the athlete who has previously sustained three or more second and third degree cerebral concussions has reached the danger point. Athletes with a "glass jaw" or "punchdrunkenness" are to be excluded from all sports no matter what protective equipment is used. In the case of convulsive disorders, Jacksonian epileptics, active petit mal, and psychomotor epilepsy, aspirants are *not* permitted to participate. Grand mal epileptics under control who have been seizure-free for two years or more may be qualified to participate.

13. *Other unusual medical conditions.* These are left to the examining doctor's decision. Obviously those with a malignancy, cerebral palsy, muscular dystrophy, myesthenia gravis, multiple sclerosis, or Addison's disease would be immediately disqualified.

14. *Special considerations:* (a) Dental mouthpieces are to be worn by all football players. (b) Alcohol and tobacco, if used, lead to direct dismissal at the coach's discretion. The use of pep-up or other *drugs* subjects the participant to prompt dismissal. (c) There must be *insurance coverage* for everyone in the football complex. Medical coverage should be interpreted to mean the availability of a physician, a trainer, a school nurse in her office, a coach with education in health and injuries, an ambulance and/or a first-aid team, or a doctor in a nearby office. CODE guidelines require a responsible and committed medical advisor to be kept informed on *all* sports practices and games. This physician is to be present at all home games. (d) The primacy of medical decisions must be respected, and these decisions must be adhered to

without being contested or resisted. In turn the doctor should render honest and compassionate medical judgment and give explanations willingly when requested, (f) Immunizations are mandatory (tetanus, polio etc.). Hypersensitivity or religious objections are to be individually handled by the physician.

Dr. Lane states finally that CODE is open to review. With advances in medical treatment, technology, changes in athletic rules, equipment, techniques, and social attitudes, the guidelines are subject to change. In the meantime it is the guideline adopted for all Maine secondary schools for their sports program.

Guidelines, as exemplified by CODE, should be used in states other than Maine. This is one of the best medical Prevent-Systems I've seen, and Teams-Behind-the-Teams everywhere should keep it in mind and use it as a point of reference.

Temporary Health Disqualifiers

The University of Wisconsin medical and athletic departments make an effort to discriminate intelligently between athletic candidates with truly disqualifying conditions and those with conditions which are allowable in safe competition. Dr. A.J. Ryan, athletic teams physician at Wisconsin, indicates that there are two temporary disqualifiers: acute infections and obvious disabling injury. He cites *infectious mononucleosis* as a common cause of unnecessary invalidism that should not be given prolonged rest. When x-ray films show a normal spleen the athlete can be gradually returned to activity. Traumatic disabilities should be checked out to determine whether the reason for the disability has ceased to exist. However, he emphasizes this point:

> Acute symptoms may have subsided, but in the absence of sufficient time for solid healing, or in a situation where the part is left vulnerable to further aggravation and new injury, competition should not be allowed. Many disabilities which should have been temporary have become permanent or of long duration due to the failure to realize that either or both of these situations exist.[4]

Permanent Health Disqualifiers

Lasting disabilities in one part of the anatomy shouldn't always keep an athlete from competitive sports. He may very readily fit in another sport or stay in the same sport at a different position. When Babe Ruth's pitching arm went bad he became a good outfielder and an even better batter. The body part is the limitation factor.

[4] A.J. Ryan, *Medicine in Sports Newsletter* 10 (July 1970), pp. 4–5.

When permanent damage has been done there is no question about disqualifying an athlete on the basis of disease or physical impairment. But there must first be a complete physical examination designed to bring all inherent weaknesses to light. No subnormal condition should be minimized or shrugged away. There is no justification for gambling against disaster because the boy shows the kind of talent that wins games. In determining the "health disqualifiers" that cut a participant from the roster, the coach can use a system like the Maine CODE, or abide by a physician's decision on the following athletic restrictions.

There are seventeen major disqualifiers I'd like to mention here. To me they are the most important. Your doctor may add or subtract from the list. Some of them overlap the Maine CODE; all of them are prime problems. They are: (1) permanent damage to one of dual organs; (2) joint instability; (3) locked joints; (4) joints chronically containing fluid; (5) muscle disease or impairment; (6) disease or impairment of the cardiovascular system; (7) diseases of the nervous system; (8) orthopedic problems involving the extremities, pelvis, or spinal column; (9) a history of infective disease that has effected major organs; (10) a history of surgery or wounds creating a physical handicap (for example, a hip operation leaving an anatomically short leg and a metal hip cup); (11) current dislocation or congenital dislocation; (12) chronic "glass arm," "glass jaw," etc.; (13) presence of free fluids (lymph, blood) making the boy a poor physical security risk; (14) history of epilepsy, malignancy, etc.; (15) unalterable anemia; (16) history of multiple concussions; and (17) cervical (neck) fractures. Each of these health disqualifiers prohibit the violence of contact sports. Each is a substantial reason to cut a boy from the squad because each inevitably leads to trouble on the football field.

The physician's diagnosis is the final word. A coach is never freed of obligations by pleading that he did not know about the athlete's physical or mental problem. Lack of knowledge never changes moral obligation. (Nor does it change the element of *contributory negligence* pronounced in a court of law.) Therefore, permit no boy to participate if he demonstrates, or is known to have, or have had, any of the above disqualifiers, or those of the Maine CODE, no matter what pressures are brought to bear on you by the school, the parents, alumni, Quarterback Clubs, etc., if the physician has disqualified the athlete.

When the preseason medical examination and the trainer's athletic examination are utilized to their fullest there is less opportunity to be trapped in difficult legal or moral complications. Place the decision for qualifying the athlete squarely in the hands of the doctors. Also place responsibility directly in the hands of parents. Flatly refuse any boy the right to participate until he has full signed clearance at the beginning of each seasonal sport. Make this clear to everyone concerned by appearing before Booster Clubs, Dads' Clubs, P.T.A. groups, Chambers of Commerce, Quarterback Clubs, and so on. Explain the school's stand in advance. Point out the school administrator's policy and the policy of the board of education or school district. Win the approval of everyone by giving them an understanding of the necessity to protect young people through the preseason physical and medical examination program. Lay it all on the line. Indicate that the life and welfare of each boy is the most valuable commodity an athletic department has.

It's wise to know state or school district laws about physical examinations and athletic department responsibility. Know definitely whether the law in your state requires a yearly examination for all or each sport. Know all possible legal complications and know the rulings before starting your athletic program. Remember that we can no longer live by yesterday's lack of rules. Accidents don't just happen. Something or someone makes them happen. A good football season and a good Prevent-System start with that preseason physical and the trainer's athletic examination!

How to Process Medical Excuses

The school administrator is responsible for the designing and processing of the medical excuse form that goes to the examining physician. When the coach's preseason screening, the preseason medical examination, or the trainer's athletic examination has located a possible health problem, a medical excuse form should be issued to the athlete or prospective athlete. He or she must then take this to the family physician for his decision on the matter. This is especially effective if parents are pushing their youngster. The responsibility and the decision to disqualify the participant for reasons of health become the physician's alone. The school and the Athletic Department are taken off the hook. In turn the school has all this on record. The administrator should furnish an additional type of *Medical Excuse Form* for the student who requests to be excused from courses in physical education. A suggested form follows.

The Invaluable Athletic Career File

It is my feeling that a complete athletic record should follow every participant from grammar school through high school so that a total health transcript—just like a student's scholastic transcript—can be made available to colleges, armed forces, or professional ranks. Every facet of an athlete's career, press clippings and all, should be noted, and his rises and declines recorded. Every injury, every operation, illness, or accident should be noted in the "athletic career file" along with the coach's seasonal summary and the trainer's breakdown on rehabilitation, procedures, and

MEDICAL EXCUSE FORM

To the examining Doctor:

(Name of student)____________(address)_____________
(grade)_____requests that he/she be excused from classes in physical education. We will consider this request only after you have examined the student and filled out this form.

Suggested Activities or Controls

a. The student may take physical education with no restrictions:________________

b. He/she may have the following limited activities:

____

____

c. The student may not participate for the following reasons:

Rheumatic fever_____ Kidney disease_____
Epilepsy _____ Asthma _____
Enlarged spleen_____ Missing one of dual organs_____________

Other conditions:
Nondescent of testes ________________________
Foot defects ________________________
Visual deficiencies ________________________
Spinal defects ________________________
Other heart problems ________________________
Poor nutrition ________________________
Convalescing ________________________
In need of surgery ________________________
Diabetes ________________________
Hernia ________________________

d. If you have checked (c), would you suggest any of the following activities as a substitute?

Scoring _____ Team management_____
Spotting _____ Referee _____
Equipment manager _____

This is to certify that I have examined___________ and recommend the above.

______________________________ __________________
Signature Date

Figure 2-2

treatments used. It should be further fortified by a record of immunizations received and examinations made each year. It should indicate allergies if they exist or develop. Especially valuable is the record of injuries in grammar and high school that have been inadequately handled in the past. Such early injuries lay the groundwork for a disastrous future in college or professional athletics.

THE TRAINER'S ATHLETIC EXAMINATION

A basic preseason testing program to assess the condition of the athlete's muscles, tendons, ligaments, and joints is what I call the "Trainers Athletic Examination." It is an essentially nonmedical function of the trainer/physical therapist, and an integral part of the pre- and/or postseason medical examination each year. Of what value is it? What is actually done? Let's put it in review:

The How and Why of the Trainer's Athletic Examination

By checking muscle, tendon, joint, and ligamentous integrity or abnormality, the trainer's athletic examination cuts down the possibility of injury. He determines the site of and limitations established by previous injuries the notes unhealed or improperly healed injuries, and by this procedure determines the probability of new injury. In other words the participant's injury potential becomes known! The trainer's findings are presented to and verified by the team physician who gives the coach a legitimate and valid reason for cutting a man from the roster even before tryouts begin. Through his athletic examination the trainer determines in advance for the coach the extent to which performance must be limited for a previously injured athlete, and whether or not the injury, even though healed, is going to interfere with a particular sports action. (For example, he might see a collarbone injury and ruptured rotator cuff in the shoulder, which could interfere with a quarterback's throwing arm.) Through his athletic examination the trainer can determine whether a body part is salvageable and whether or not it is going to demand limitation straps, wraps, or other pliable control.

The testing of joint motion through flexion, extension, abduction, and adduction, and against normal resistance is the basic factor in the athletic examination. When a muscle cannot sustain maximum resistance in its range of motion, it should be considered weak, not completely rehabilitated, or a potential site of reinjury. A record of all examination findings should be maintained in the athlete's athletic career file. Each "injury sheet" should record current findings specifically naming all anatomical parts involved and should be accompanied by a small diagram. Where the athlete has been approved to go out for the squad, the trainer should set up and develop a correction program for muscle and joint problems indicated and retest the involved parts at given intervals. Physical therapy for this problem is best on alternate days such as Monday, Wednesday and Friday.

Preseason physicals do more than just determine whether the boy is capable of participation in football. They do more than bring into focus latent weaknesses or improperly healed lesions that someone forgot to report or didn't even see in the past. They demonstrate to parents and young folks the school's protective interest; they prevent harm coming to those unfit for athletics; they provide more exact medical records; they relieve the school and coach of most medical and legal obligations; they prevent unfavorable criticism of the school by making its health policy known; they point up areas that can be rehabilitated or corrected; and they set up higher standards of physical education in the school system. When health disqualifiers are brought to light and the coach has to cut an applicant from the list, the coach doesn't have to explain why. The team physician does it.

Screening Tall Skinny Boys at High School Level

Army trainer Rollie Bevan and I were covering injuries at a national track meet in Dayton, Ohio and I asked that grand old man why Coach Blaik eliminated tall boys with long skinny necks from football. Said Bevan: "Their joints are not yet stable. This makes them immediately susceptible to injury. Dislocations come too easily. In the growing boy—and they're still growing at that age—the growth centers (epiphysis) break away. Muscles are too flabby to act as a splint and all this multiplies the possibility of neck injury. Bones are more susceptible to fracture. When you're screening boys out at high school or early college level cull the tall skinny ones. Shunt them into basketball and gymnastics until they fill out." It was Bevan's opinion that all athletes should be given complete physical checkups in spring and midsummer. Don't wait for the eleventh hour just before the season begins.

How to Handle "Rejects"

Former Dayton Meadowdale High School athletic director Bill Parrish answered my question about what to do about the misty-eyed rejects from sports teams. "We divert tall, willowy aspirants into cross-country running as well as basketball. Boys with bull necks and brawny legs and bodies are promptly channeled into football, wrestling, weight-training, or shotput. The skinny youngsters with enthusiasm, spirit, and inclination are given a chance to associate with their chosen sport as managers, helpers, assistant trainers, and so on. The boy is made to feel that he has found a place in the sports picture. A medical examination and a few hours of preseason screening can save these youngsters, and their parents, many hours, and even years of physical, mental, and even financial anguish."

Athletes and parents may cover up the truth. In taking a complete medical history a number of problems arise. One such problem occurs when the prospective athlete intentionally does not give a true history of weaknesses, previous injury, past disease, birth anomalies, or drug taking. It is possible the boy does not know that a physical problem exists, and does not realize that football has a way of bringing out a physical weakness. Sometimes even the best medical examination may miss a latent problem. In turn, well-meaning parents will often hide a youngster's flaws hoping that they won't surface. These flaws, hidden with or without intent, have a disastrous way of showing up on the football field. The doctor's medical examination and trainer's athletic examination are designed to avoid all this.

The Trainer's Preseason Talk on Prevention Measures

At the beginning of each season all athletes should be given patient, step-by-step, exact instructions on how and what to do about their gear as well as themselves. Full instructions should be given the equipment manager on the matter of regular laundering, drying, airing, and storage of garments and pads. The trainer should insist on the inspection and fitting of all protective gear. It's his problem child, his domain, his responsibility. He may even be given the responsibility for its purchase if he proves himself capable of doing so. He should see that all equipment is maintained, cleaned regularly, and suited to the duties of the player and his football position. The fit of gear is vital to injury prevention and that's where the trainer's job begins!

COACHING TECHNIQUES FOR INJURY PREVENTION

Every coach has his own teaching techniques. Too often these techniques emerge through trial and error, and the football season is littered from beginning to end with injuries. In trying to determine how football injuries could be prevented through teaching football techniques, I asked thousands of questions across the United States. Here are sixteen of the most consistently given answers at high school and small college level.

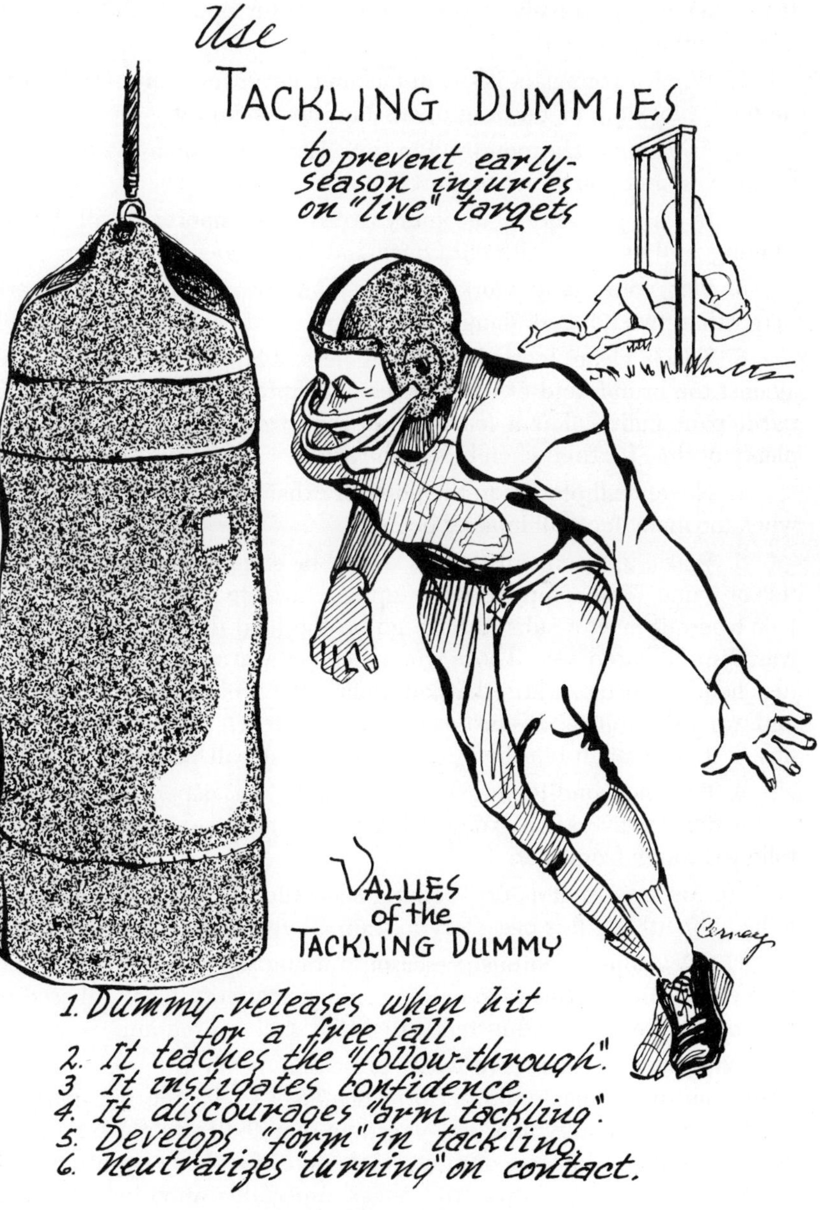
Use
TACKLING DUMMIES
to prevent early-season injuries on "live" targets
VALUES of the TACKLING DUMMY
1. Dummy releases when hit for a free fall.
2. It teaches the "follow-through".
3 It instigates confidence.
4. It discourages "arm tackling".
5. Develops "form" in tackling.
6. Neutralizes "turning" on contact.
Cernay

Figure 2-3

1. Many tackling injuries at grammar and high school level can be prevented by teaching new candidates to tackle dummies rather than live targets. This gives the newcomer a greater feeling of security and control. It psyches him positively. Using live targets for new candidates contributes to nothing but hurt.

2. When a youngster is shy of tackling, never force him. Half-hearted running, blocking, or tackling opens him up for injury.

3. As Tommy Harmon used to say, "Hit harder than the other guy is hitting you and you won't be hurt."

4. In the prevention of injury stress the importance of blocking, running, and tackling with *eyes open* and *head up*.

5. Plot your daily workout. One hour of well-organized work is better than two hours of dangerous unsupervised or disorganized practice.

6. Teach clean football. Nothing else. Play by the book. Caution against the brutal kind of football seen at professional level and give any participant guilty of it a leave of absence from the squad. There'll be plenty of time for that when he's in the pros.

7. Never drill players to the point of exhaustion. Why? That's exactly when too many football injuries begin.

8. Warm-ups and calisthenics should be compulsory before any practice or game. The complete warm-up is a favorite weapon against injury. Don't permit even a substitute to go on the field during a game without warm-up preparedness. Those who renege on warm-ups are automatically benched. Failure to warm that kid up lays the groundwork for a potential and expensive injury. It's just as necessary to teach a player proper warm-ups as it is to teach him how to run or carry a ball without getting hurt.

9. Put the conditioning schedule down on paper. Issue complete instructions. Players will know what you want in advance and you just follow through from there.

10. Set up a mandatory training schedule. Advise your players that to be a top athlete it is necessary to train all-year-round.

11. Develop a vigorous preseason training schedule that doesn't conflict with board of education or state rulings. Parents, when advised as to the benefits for their youngsters, are all for such a program.

12. Don't use any two-week preseason crash program. Bring the participant up to maximum performance level by having him participate in other sports like gymnastics, wrestling, handball, weight-training, and even swimming. When a continuous schedule of training is put into action the rate of injuries drops, and that's especially important in smaller schools.

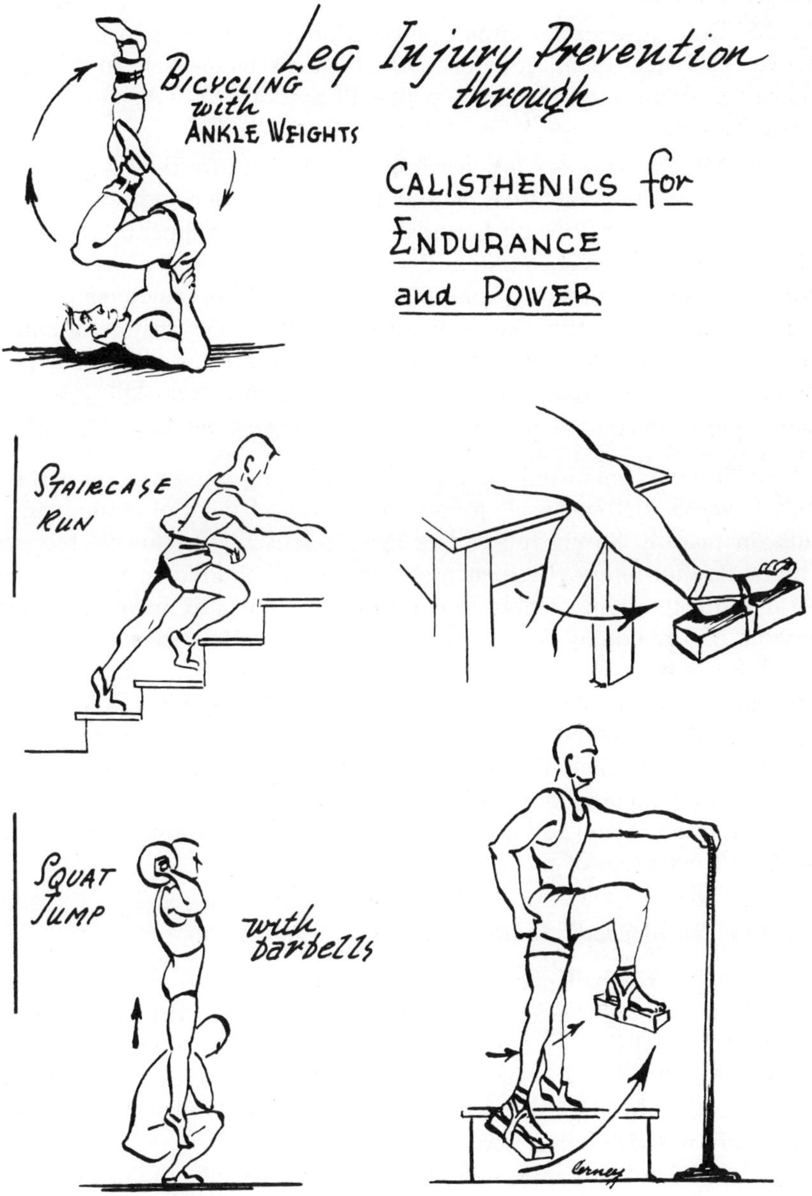
Leg Injury Prevention through
Calisthenics for Endurance and Power
Bicycling with Ankle Weights
Staircase Run
Squat Jump with barbells

Figure 2-4

13. Develop team-action rather than stars.

14. Not wearing *all* protective gear subjects the athlete to immediate disciplinary action.

15. Don't just teach football plays. Motivate the boys to better performance. Teach them how to protect themselves—each in his own football position—and the time spent will pay off. (See Appendix 2 for particulars.)

16. Athletic stars are top performers only because they have developed their abilities and their bodies to meet the demands of football. They do it just that little bit better than the next participant. They have established the physical condition that assures championship performance and championship thinking; and championship performance comes only with physical fitness. Physical fitness remains the major answer to injury, and the majority of my Prevent-System techniques begin with developing speed, agility, endurance, reaction time, strength, and skill, and this comes only with specialized training to meet specific needs.

As fitness is enhanced the possibility of being injured is proportionately lowered. Better muscle tone means fewer chances of strain, sprain, pulls, or tearing. Strong full-bodied flexible musculature lowers the possibility of joint injury. Resilience and strength acquired in working out not only make a more highly tuned athlete, but it also makes one more capable of responding to emergency and stress. He reacts faster. He's tuned for action. He is automatically more resistant to injury. He is schooled to avoid situations that lead to injury. But to protect him against his own enthusiasm and the knocks of practices and game competition, he has to have protection. For this purpose don't try to save a buck on second-rate equipment or gear. Wraps and strappings are also used as part of the program of prevention. Those boys are a coach's responsibility and he doesn't want any of them hurt at any time!

The "Hardnosed" Football Player

Getting a football player with moxie, stamina, and guts, as well as talent, is something that every coach dreams of. This type of boy is the exception. Usually he's a hard-hitting kid who glories in crunching body contact. He likes to clobber an opponent. He's not averse to flattening the opposition by one method or another. In sports jargon this is the player referred to as hardnosed.

When a hardnose appears on the high school scene, the marks of the professional are already on him. He's in a different class than the average player who is out to earn a numeral or letter, or prestige with his peers. The problem with the hardnose is not that he is better than average, but that he is used as an example. Too often the rest of the team bogs down because they are expected to maintain his remarkable pace. And because they can't catch up, or match up, injuries and mental stress begin. So does the mimicking of professional techniques. The end result is the resorting to *spearing* or *nose blocking* and other techniques that ask for retaliation in kind.

How New Football Techniques Contribute to Injury

Injury quite often has its inception in a new brand of football that a coach has just devised. Let's take the example of Red Hickey in the pro ranks when he was coaching the San Francisco *'49ers.* He developed a "shotgun" offensive. Five receivers scattered downfield waiting for a pass. This opened up the defense, and left the quarterback unprotected. Today Hickey admits, "You can destroy a pro defense with the 'shotgun' but you'd better have a healthy quarterback to do it." [5] As a result quarterbacks were decked and broken. Let's quote left tackle Merlin Olson on this matter: " 'You have to bloody-up the quarterback to remind him that you're there. You have to punish him to discourage him. He loses his rhythm and timing. Intimidation is part of the game.' " [6] One of the notorious killers in professional football history was the *Chicago Bears'* "policeman" Ed Sprinkle. This tough 205-pound lineman made his reputation for twelve years on the wreckage he made of quarterbacks. They called him "The Claw." The Cleveland *Browns* had Lenny Ford. The Dallas *Cowboys* had Bob Lilly. Gino Marchetti was hatchet man for the Baltimore *Colts.* Quarterbacks were these players' meat.

In professional ranks every body part becomes a weapon for creating injury. One of these weapons is the forearm. In locker room jargon, the "forearm shivers" was developed to blast quarterbacks and other players. A heavy canvas dummy is shoved forward. On its return excursion an arm is cranked up and as the dummy returns a forearm blast is let loose. The Kansas City *Chief's* 275-pound giant Paul Buchanan uses such a procedure. He admits he likes to use his forearm like a club. "You've got to ring the other guy's bell," he explained, "by larruping him on the helmet." On the field this is called getting "dinged." There's no pain. Nobody knows it has happened until the player who got dinged stops remembering plays. His eyes get an offbeat look. Its brain trauma and another injury.

To get psyched up, some players, at pro level, pray. Some bang each

[5] Red Hickey, press interview.

[6] From W.B. Furlong, "What is a Punter's Hang Time? Why Does a Receiver Seem to Run on Glass? How High is a Cornerback's I.Q.?" *The New York Times,* January 10, 1971.

others' shoulder pads. Linebacker Ernie Clark of the St. Louis *Cardinals* had his own inimitable technique that does not bear copying: he beat his helmeted head against the concrete wall of the training room. Dave Meggyesy tells about his postpractice duels with two rookie linemen by the name of Sam Silas and Bob Reynolds. Each outweighed him by forty-five pounds. Three nights a week, under coaching direction, they'd line up eye to eye and tear into each other. Night after night they'd battle to a standoff. To avoid being annihilated Meggyesy indicates he would work himself up to a fanatical pitch and, "We went at it like animals in a pit." [7] I mention these pro-level techniques because they are no-no's in the minor leagues. I mention them because television has made the art and science of "dinging" an accepted public spectacle that has rattled all the way down to the PeeWee League. Luckily, at high school and college level sports medicine and sports officials and keepers of the code have made some excellent inroads in putting these techniques in their proper place.

Get Rid of That "Cross-Body Block"

Fifty-four percent of 259 knee injuries suffered by football players at Michigan State University, the University of Michigan, the local high schools of Michigan, and the Detroit *Lions* for fifteen years prior to 1967 were said to have been the direct result of cross-body blocking. When a blocker throws himself horizontally at his opponent's knees, his purpose is to upset him. He thrusts 150 to 300 pounds of force at an unprotected knee; the knee gives. However, when the blocker throws a cross-body block he is not only subjecting his opponent to the possibility of injury, he is also subjecting himself to injury. He has voluntarily opened up his spleen, kidneys, ribs, and spinal column to violence, and in our Prevent-System, this is what we are trying to avoid. The cross-body block should be *eliminated.* It is a desperate play used for want of something better to do.

Sports Medicine Breakthroughs

In reporting on the progress of sports medicine from 1965 to 1970, Dr. Alexius Rachun, of Cornell University, had this to say:

> Sports medicine made its biggest contribution in the past five years, when, through group action and lay participation, it clearly delineated a set of rules for the prevention of serious, occasional heat problems in the athlete. Breaking the tradition among coaches of withholding fluids from athletes in hot humid weather, was, in itself, a major achievement. It would be most desirable if the same influences were brought to bear to put an end

[7] D. Meggyesy, *Out of Their League* (New York: Ramparts Press Inc., 1971).

to the practice of "spearing" in football, a major cause of head and neck injuries.[8]

It's my personal feeling that the objective of clean football is to block and tackle to take opposing players out of the play, *not* to take them out of the stadium on a stretcher!

THE FOOTBALL CAMP

As you are already aware, the football camp *away* from school is the ideal arrangement. Such arrangements are sometimes possible but not always economically or legally feasible. Where football camp *is* possible, however, it becomes an integral part of the Prevent-System by giving athletes and coaches unadulterated full-time concentration on conditioning as well as on football drills and chalk-talks. For three to eight days the football candidate lives, eats, and breathes nothing but football. Religion, in some camps, also plays a recommended role.

Football camp not only prepares the boy for the fall season but prepares him for life as well. There's no need for preaching and philosophizing here. This is prevention at its best. When a coach sends out his spring letter about football camp he should describe glowingly what the camp can do for boys. He should explain the general camp schedule, the role it plays in injury prevention, how valuable it is in preparing in advance for the season. He should advise what clothing the boys should take. This diplomacy and preparation is all part of a Prevent-System that puts more than victories in the win column.

Suggestions About Minor Football Camp Hazards

Poison Ivy. One week in advance of camp have your team trainer or team manager scout the edges of the practice field and environs for poison ivy, poison oak, or poison sumac. Spray all such patches. If spraying is not permitted, mark the areas with red warning flags or tags.

Sunburn. To prevent sunburn during opening days of camp have all candidates apply ointment or cream on the nose, neck, cheeks, forehead, back of the knees, and calves of the legs. (Note: never permit a sunburned area to be bandaged.)

Mosquitos. Have your student manager fill all local water holes with dirt weeks in advance. Where this is not possible or practical, spread a film of used crankcase oil or kerosene over the water. This kills the larvae.

[8] A. Rachun, *Medicine in Sports Newsletter* 10 (July 1970), p. 2.

Workouts and Warm-ups. Permit no athlete to play or go through calisthenics without his sweat clothes on. This not only prevents chilling and preseason stiffness, but acts as insulation for the avoirdupois boys who have to lose weight.

Humidity. Keep track of heat and moisture in the air. Do not practice in the heat of day. Permit no colored clothing. Allow only whites to be worn. (More on this later.)

Gear. Permit no wearing of heavy gear at football camp. The helmet should be worn but only gym shoes should be on the feet.

The Coach's Letter Home on Year-Round Conditioning

Vital to improved sports performance and injury prevention is the year-round conditioning program. To the sports fraternity its values are already obvious. To the new candidate and the folks back home it's a whole new ballpark. Therefore, the coach should send a preseason letter to each candidate and his family *after* the preseason screening has been completed. The following letter is a suggested form you may use, mimeograph, and mail.

SPRING FOOTBALL PRACTICE

Spring practice is always justified from the standpoint of injury prevention because (1) it cuts down injury in the fall season and (2) it becomes a functioning part of the year-round training program. In spring a greater number of sports participants are available. It is the time for developing preseason organization and cutting away the problems that confront a coach when he enters the fall season stone cold. Spring practice has other advantages. It weeds out the disinterested. It eliminates participants who are not gung-ho about blocking and tackling or otherwise working out; in fact these participants automatically weed themselves out. A high schooler who thinks enough about football to want to spend additional time with it in spring, and who is emotionally as well as physically right for fooball, and has his parents or guardian's consent to do so, deserves the right to try out for a place on the squad.

Set Up Your Lines of Communication Early

In February or March another letter should go to the parents or guardian of the prospective high school or college athlete. The same letter should appear simultaneously in the school paper. As an open letter to candidates it should explain the goals for the football season and the program of preseason conditioning. It can also make suggestions for

Date:

Re: Year-round conditioning
and the summer program

Dear :

Your physical fitness and your mental conditioning for sports depends on a year-round conditioning program. Our objective is to have strong and tough squads. We want you to be ready to go when the season opens, not just beginning to get into shape when the season ends. For this reason the following program is excellent for you to follow if you are sincere in maintaining a tiptop condition.

DAILY ROUTINE

FOOD

Proper diet is a necessity. Cut to a minimum all carbohydrates (pastries, candy, soft drinks, etc.)

Make breakfast the biggest meal of your day. Eat a substantial protein breakfast to give you the day's "hold-energy." Remember that sweet rolls and sugar covered "breakfast foods" are not the diet of champions. The energy they deliver is quickly lost. The exhaustion level is reached faster. So avoid vapid breakfast foods. Eat foods with substance. Don't overload at noon. Eat a light meal in the evening.

SLEEP

Get at least 8 to 10 hours of sleep each night. At the risk of being a bore to others hit the sack at a regular hour. You are only as good an athlete as your body is capable of producing. So store up the necessary energy. Don't store fat.

CONDITIONING

RUNNING

Endurance comes with distance running; speed is developed by sprinting. Running is one of the best conditioners, but you must learn to run relaxed. If you like to run distances maintain a

Figure 2-5

fairly flat-footed stride. The moment you sprint come up on the ball of your foot. Dig in. Move with a forward thrust. Keep your toes pointed straight ahead. Develop a stride about the length of your body and learn when to "float" to regain your wind. Relax and don't tighten up.

Here's a tip on relaxation: Place the tip of your fourth finger into the palm of your hand. Maintain your consciousness of this and you will never make an arm-tightening fist.
Maintain a forward lean and pump your arms in rhythm to your leg action. Always be completely warmed up (by calisthenics) before taking off on a run. Stretch all muscles. Work only in sweat clothes and don't uncover. Follow your workouts with a warm shower climaxed by a cold shower. Rub yourself down with a towel until you glow and then go about your regular business feeling like a million!

SCHEDULE

Springtime:

1. Run daily for distance and endurance. (No sprinting.)
2. Develop a weight-training program suited to your needs (see the school trainer).
3. On days alternate to the weight-lifting get in some golf, tennis, handball,or rope-jumping.
4. Maintain a daily weight chart. Weigh in and out.

Midsummer:

1. Step up the distance run each day.
2. Continue daily calisthenics and rope jumping.
3. Begin to sprint as well as run distances.

August:

1. Double your workout schedule.
2. Add a heavier sprinting schedule. Develop speed.
3. Start all special drills that will be of advantage to your position in your sport.

EXERCISE PROGRAM (The Daily Dozen)

1. Shoulder girdle stretcher: Grip a horizontal bar or limb and just hang suspended for the

count of 30. Release. Relax in standing position and then repeat the shoulder girdle stretch for a sixty count.

2. Side stretcher: Clasp hands overhead with the arms straight up. Keep feet eighteen inches apart. Now bend to the right. Bend your knee. Go as far as you can and then return. Now repeat to the left.

3. Knee stretcher (only if you have never had a knee injury).

Note: your trainer should outline the balance of this sheet according to your needs.

Coach____________________
School____________________

summer training, types of jobs, what not to do, etc. The letter should establish a date and time for a preseason physical examination by the doctor and trainer. Be sure to restate in it all eligibility requirements. With the letter enclose a return card for the prospective player to fill out indicating his interest in spring practice, and indicate the time and place for the first football session and what to do upon checking in.

In Appendix 2 of this book you will find a manual describing how each player, in each position, can prevent injuries. Copy or mimeograph it. Issue it at the beginning of spring practice. Add or subtract from it as you desire. You will find that issuing such a how-to-do-it on paper will save you a lot of talking time!

Setting Age Limits to Protect Young Athletes

To keep young athletes from competing out of their class it is necessary for the school administrator to see that his Athletic Department fixes, establishes, and maintains, rulings on such matters as age limitations, weight, and size. At high school level these age limits may extend from fifteen to nineteen. Since the age factor is not always the best criterion, weight and size have to be considered. Some youngsters have the build of adults at an early age. As a result the administrator must be conscious of his school's manpower and its limitations, working out his own limiting factors accordingly. Small schools, hampered by a paucity of football "talent," often have to use secondary athletes to complete a team roster.

Such teams should not be played against the teams of larger and better-equipped schools.

Reserve squads demand as much attention as the varsity!

Tomorrow's varsity often springs out of today's crop of reserves and every effort should be made to preserve them. Failure to maintain their physical health as well as their competitive spirit invites disaster. This means that the same rigid attention has to go into their training, conditioning, officiating, and protective gear. To fail in this is to contribute to negligence and this negligence is unfair to the boys, to the school, to the parents, to the coaches, and to the team doctor and trainer, and athletic director. There is no logical reason for getting caught in such a position.

To alleviate the possibility of injury to the reserves the athletic director should see that the following guidelines are carried through.

An Injury Prevention Program for Reserve Squads

1. Reserves should have a strenuous conditioning and training program.

2. Their injury care and prevention should be comparable to that of the varsity squad.

3. The reserves should be issued comparable gear and not be subjected to hand-me-downs.

4. The coach must make sure not to permit anything broken or unrepaired to be used.

5. The coach must assure complete sanitation measures.

6. If the squad is too large for available supplies, it should be cut until the facilities are available.

7. The athletic director should see that all facilities are free of hazard.

8. The athletic director should see that reserves play by rigid game rules and exhibit good sportsmanship.

9. The athletic director should provide the best possible coach at reserve level because it is at this point that many injuries begin.

10. The athletic director should maintain eligibility standards and check the eligibility lists daily.

11. Games must be scheduled with team capacity in mind and not for the convenience of officials or viewing audience.

12. Game time should be cut to prevent exhaustion or injury. This is especially true in grammar school or high school.

Information to Parents

An athletic director or coach may convey the necessity for injury prevention to parents in many ways. One way is to have a preseason meeting with all parents to give them complete information about the football program and school policy, its philosophy of athletics and the rules and regulations by which everyone has to live. Before such a meeting takes place the coach or athletic director should send the parents a letter on rules concerning sleep habits, eating, smoking, and drinking alcoholic beverages, practice schedules, working out with weights, off-season workouts, penalties and losses of privilege to play in interscholastic games for breaking rules, etc. In addition to the written list these rules may be reemphasized during a sports award banquet or preseason sports smorgasboard which provides a get-together to solicit the cooperation of parents. An example of such a letter follows.

Date ______________________

School ______________________

Dear Parents:

We want your child to have every possible advantage in this school. Our school is here to not just give our students a scholastic education but to educate them physically as well. What concerns them concerns us, and in our effort to develop a good student and a good athlete we need your cooperation. We cannot be expected to do the entire job alone and so we depend on you. We know that "going out for sports" takes a lot of time. We know that it often interferes with regular evening meals and other family activities while the sport is in season. But to produce a good team and in excellent physical condition there is more to the job than our activities at school. There are certain matters with which you have to be concerned at home:

Sleep: Your boy should have at least eight hours sleep a night. On nights before a game he should sleep even more. To go without sleep could lead to exhaustion and injury.

Figure 2-6

Smoking: If your boy is found smoking, or it is proven that he has been smoking, he will be suspended from the squad. There is no excuse for anything that deteriorates health and this is our stand on the matter.

Drinking: If a player is caught drinking, or is proven to have been drinking, he will automatically be suspended from the squad. There is no place for the drinking of alcoholic beverages by any young person, and certainly no place for it in sports.

Food: Athletes require good food and lots of it as you are already well aware. Most mothers know what their children like and they do a good job of feeding them, but I would suggest you make certain they get plenty of vegetables and fruits as well as meats. Use rye and whole wheat bread instead of white. Avoid fried foods of all kinds. Cut down on the desserts. Remember that the energy your boy needs to perform at his best is derived from good food. Remember too, that the energy he needs in the afternoon comes from food he has eaten at breakfast, so give him a substantial meal. Avoid commercial breakfast foods. They have little substance as do the people who eat them.

Studying: To help him maintain better grades that keep him on the team, see that your child cultivates regular study habits. Give him a study area. Then prod him to study when it's necessary.

When Injury Occurs: It is the policy of this school (fill in the school's policy on injuries, insurance coverage, etc.)

____

____

And if you have any question on this matter, or if we can cooperate with you, please advise. We are as close as your telephone.

Travel: Some of our games are at other schools. To get there we have to use various kinds of transportation. But no matter what kind of transportation is used it is necessary for the school to obtain a signed travel release, or waiver of responsibility, from you. Your son will bring this home.

Physical Examination: At the beginning of each season your boy will receive a complete physical examination. This is to assure us of his continued welfare and to assure you of a healthy youngster.

Insurance: Please remember that no athlete is permitted on the practice or playing field, nor will he be issued gear, until he has complete insurance coverage. Your family health and accident policy must cover football!

With your cooperation at home, and the work of our excellent coaches here, we can develop the kind of championship teams and bring out the championship ability in your son and all of us can proud.

Yours truly,

____

Athletic Director

3

THE EQUIPMENT

Strategy Covered:

- *Football gear—why you can't cheat the budget*
- *How to choose football gear, clothing, and padding*
- *Headgear and head injuries*
- *Neck and shoulder protection*
- *Footgear*
- *Field equipment and injury control*
- *Sanitation in the athletic department*

FOOTBALL GEAR

The incidence of football injury in the past decade has dropped in four significant areas: (1) head, neck and spinal column injuries, (2) knee injuries, (3) foot and ankle injuries, and (4) injuries due to heat. New understanding of injury, new coaching techniques, better facilities, improved equipment, sounder engineering, and scientific construction of football protective gear has brought about a dramatic change from that injury and death-laden era prior to 1935. In the early part of the twentieth century, football had its "flying wedge," and a host of crippling and fatal injuries. The problem was so flagrant that president Theodore Roosevelt threatened to outlaw the game if something wasn't done to clean it up. So the flying wedge was outlawed. Football gradually became a game emphasizing skill rather then brute force. A new day dawned for rules, regulations, and equipment. Protective football gear was coming into its own.

By the 1970's the injury rate in football had dropped significantly at all levels although some grey areas still persisted. Today, at the professional level, football has never had it so good. Television carries games throughout the world via satellite. Current TV spectaculars recall the former glory of Rome with football gladiators in the modern manner. It's organized mayhem under floodlights; entertainment with color, drama, spectacle, and pageantry. It's a fascinating melange of sensations that audiences enjoy, and a goal toward which the amateurs spend years working. It's the amateurs, in most part, with whom we're concerned in building a Prevent-System. New understanding of the how and why of injuries is eliminating the grey problem areas that remain. Improved football gear is helping in all this.

This section on gear, field equipment, and sanitation is not as extensive as it could be. It covers only a few pertinent aspects. Its purpose is to stimulate your own thinking on the matter of protection through the Prevent-System so that you will do something about it and make the advantages of the twentieth century even more significant. With this in mind, this chapter is short but to the point.

There are many kinds of football injuries and various ways of classifying them. Allan J. Ryan, M.D., feels that sports injuries can be classified in three rough groups: (1) those which are self-induced (tennis elbow, for example), (2) those which result from interaction with others (for example, throwing a body block which results in an injury to the knee of the player stopped), and (3) those resulting from impact with the environment (for example, hurdling the line from the one yard marker and knocking oneself out against a goal post).[1] There are ways

[1] A.J. Ryan, "What Injuries in Sports Can Be Prevented by the Use of Protective Equipment." Lecture, University of Wisconsin, June 1968.

to prevent all of these types of injuries in a good Prevent-System. The answer lies in keeping the injury from happening and in this gear plays a significant role!

There are no hard and fast rules in the prevention of football injuries. There are no exact scientific regulations that predict the dynamics of football action. In fact there are times when prevention has to be "played by ear." Despite this there is one thing that's certain: *the football player is an athletic department responsibility.* His protection is mandatory at all costs, and the cost shouldn't be to him or to his parents! Football injuries do seem to follow general, recurring patterns. As a result, rules and regulations have been devised by coaches and committees to cut down on situations that lead to injury. The development of improved equipment and gear has followed from such regulations, along with better coaching methods and better facilities.

On-the-Scene Supervision

Early detection of the how and why of injuries is part of the prevention program. This often means being on the scene to see injuries happen. Isato Hirata, Jr., M.D., Surgeon-in-Chief at the Yale University Department of University Health, believes in this implicitly. He states that major football injuries at Yale such as broken legs, fractured clavicles, dislocated shoulders, etc., have constituted only 10 percent of the total disability time for the football squad throughout the season since the Yale form of prevention by being on the scene was instituted. In the Yale Prevent-System (my terminology) Dr. Hirata, and his trainer, O.W. Dayton, hold clinic hours every morning, including Sunday, during football season. They are present at all afternoon practice sessions and games, and are available to other varsity participants. Being on the scene is the significant aspect in their prevention program because seeing is understanding!

What Factors Should Be Known to Prevent Injury?

In the determination of the how, when, where, and why of injury to various body parts, attention has to be paid to *all* factors associated with these injuries. Being on the scene, Dr. Hirata and trainer Dayton see the kind of equipment being used, the circumstance of the injury, the habit patterns of the athlete, his physical condition, his mental attitude, the coaching techniques that are being used on him, and all the other factors that are brought into focus to create that injury. Analyzing this information lays the groundwork for the Prevent-System and a lower incidence of football injury.

James Robey, Project Coordinator at the University of North Carolina, in his epidemiological study of football injuries said, "The significance of this project centers on its uniqueness. It is unique in that it attempts to apply a standard health research approach to a not too well-recognized or understood health problem. It is significant because it is a project interested in the cause of injury and not the treatment of injury. Such a study could dramatically reduce the injuries sustained by young men participating in one of the country's most popular recreational activities." [2] In other words, Dr. Robey is telling the story of the Prevent-System.

At Northwestern University, Doctors Stephen Reid and Verner Swan, in their two-year study of varsity football injuries, reported that the number of football injuries is relatively small, and that the bulk of injuries occur prior to a player's reaching peak condition. They found that the platoon system reduces the number of tired players and, consequently, the number of injuries associated with this condition; [3] They studied how equipment improvements and improved rules have reduced and helped prevent injuries. They also found that with the advent of ankle taping, the knee has become the area most commonly injured and once a knee is injured, it is likely that the injury will recur. Proper conditioning of the leg of the injured knee can reduce the possibilities of recurrence. Finally, they noted that the de-emphasis of football, expecially in terms of abolishing spring football, will not necessarily make the game more safe.

Football Gear Is One Place You Can't Cheat the Budget

When purchasing football gear, there are four significant areas in which there can be no economic cheating. When working out your equipment requirements you can't cut corners on: helmets, shoulder pads, shoes or neck guards and pads as safety devices.

A rough rule of thumb for an athletic department on how to judge the school's capability for having a football program or a good season with the minimum amount of injuries is this: If your school can't afford the best of equipment for injury prevention it cannot afford football!

Obviously helmets, shoulder pads, shoes, and neck gear should be the best available. The best is none too good for the boys who are your

[2] J. Robey, "An Epidemiological Study of Football Injuries," *American College of Sports Medicine News* 4, no. 3 (July 1969).

[3] Liberal substitutions help solve the problem of game-tiredness. For example "Bear" Bryant used sixty-five men in the first half of the 1973 national championship fray between Alabama and Ara Parsegian's Notre Dame.

responsibility. To bring this all into focus I established the following set of reminders. Check them out. Each factor is a key to injury prevention, so put these reminders to work.

HOW TO CHOOSE FOOTBALL GEAR, CLOTHING, AND PADDING

Football gear has certain inadequacies. Most of it is cumbersome, overly heavy, awkward, and in turn can serve as an offensive weapon. At college or semipro level its aggregate weight checks out at twelve to fourteen pounds for each man. Much of this gear has nonadaptive edges that become weapons for and against the wearer. Edges of such gear should be "feathered out" and made of flexible material with quick recovery characteristics. Hard gear only partially buffers a blow. It is meant to spread trauma rather than to absorb it. As a result, hard gear aggravates a blow and merely transfers the impact to available pressure points. Most of today's gear does not adapt to contour changes or flow with the action of the underlying musculature. Neither does it expand. Because of all this, our safety gear sometimes causes self-inflicted injury. For example, shoulder pads and their restraining straps can cause chest pain when poorly fitted. Because a great deal of our football gear is nonadaptive and nonmobile, it is not designed for the spasmodic and explosive efforts of football. Too often protective pads create pressure, bisect muscle action, and restrict the freedom necessary to unhampered athletic action and maximum performance.

A thigh pad, for example, is a relatively nonflexible flattened mass laid over the quadriceps. Everyone accepts pockets in the pants into which these pads are slid. They believe these pockets are positioned *normally*. There's one problem: there is no norm in the development of thigh muscles. Look down the rows of thinly clad players at spring and summer practice: some have big thighs, some small, some medium. All of their legs show different levels of development, length, and circumference. Since there is no uniformity of development, no standardization in thigh formations, there's no one particular position for a thigh pad pocket in football pants cut to standard patterns. The pad thus becomes a pressure point over the larger muscle or muscles. The athlete doesn't feel this for the most part, but the skin and the underlying soft tissues do. So do lymph vessels, blood vessels, and nerves. It's like putting a rubber band around your finger: local circulation slows down. Needed blood supply can't get in. Waste in veins and lymph vessels can't get through and there you have the beginning of a "charley horse," cramps, or muscle pulls. You should take a close look at the gear worn by the athlete who comes off the field limping because of a thigh problem. It's cause and

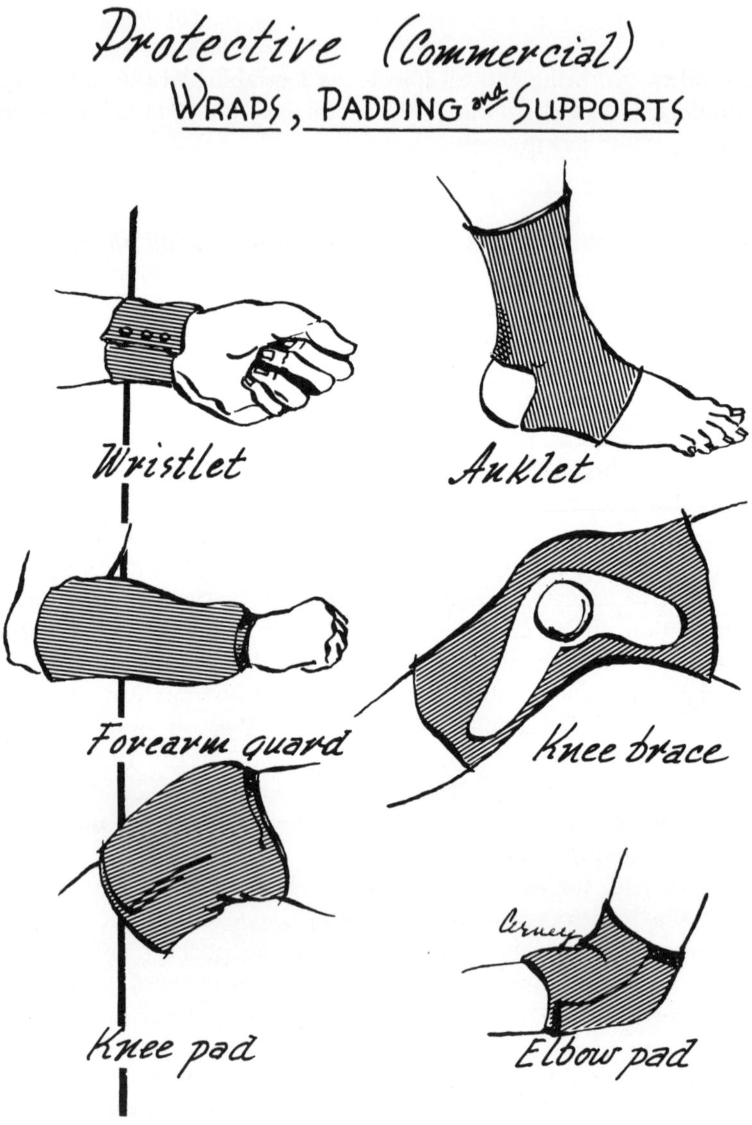

Figure 3-1

effect: the inadequacy of gear and the end result.

Equipment, uniforms, and improperly applied adhesive tape strappings, like thigh pads, have long failed to provide for the fundamental requirements of underlying functioning structures. They too often restrict mobility when needed most and contribute to injury. Many an inadequately applied ankle bandage has done just this to the knee. Many a well-meant "protective device" has become a cause of injury.

Examples are the use of helmets for spearing, or of face masks for nose blocking.

When a leg goes into action it must do so unhampered. So must a shoulder, ankle, or knee. It must have cooperation from its environment. Clothing and gear provide this environment. A uniform, for example, should stretch when the athlete stretches. A shoulder protective device should follow contour and provide no harsh edges. It should be capable of mobile adaptability as it protects. Here are some key points to watch for in gear.

Warm-Up Jackets

Warm-up jackets should have raglan or bi-swing shoulders to prevent shoulder restriction and limited arm action. They should be zippered in front and of windproof lightweight waterproof material. This material should be free of rubber or plastic, and be inexpensive to launder. The wrist bands should be elastic but of a cotton or wool knit rather than rubber or plastic.

Figure 3-2

Sideline Parkas

Sideline parkas should be of lined waterproof material (nonrubber). They should have bi-swing shoulders, a full "skirt" to ankle length (to keep the athlete sheltered from rain, hail, sleet and snow), and have big slash pockets in which he can bury his hands without restriction.

Figure 3-3

Jerseys

In your Prevent-System there are a number of factors to be aware of in considering jerseys, which you will learn with experience. For example: *don't* use dark colored jerseys in hot weather practice or games. *Don't* use jerseys made of rayon, nylon, or other acetates, because they are cold, clammy, and chilling when damp with sweat or rain in cold weather. *Don't* launder jerseys in powerful solutions that destroy the material. *Don't* use cleaning solutions that will cause allergic skin reactions when it comes in contact with a warm sweaty skin. *Do* use jerseys made of mesh material in hot weather. *Do* use "V" necks that allow for any size neck and put no pressure on the carotid artery, thyroid gland, or any musculature at the base of the throat. For regular workouts use mixed wool and cotton jerseys. Controversial as they are, "tear-away" jerseys have been known not only to get you more yardage but save injuries by preventing those clawing fingertip tackles. Game jerseys should be of medium-weight wool for cool weather.

T-Shirts

T-shirts should be of white cotton. They should be replaced at half-time with dry ones. For longer lasting service from these shirts, get them with nylon reinforced V-necks. Washing and rinsing procedures should avoid any cleaning material or fluid which can lead to possible skin allergies.

Football Pants

Football pants should have a form or contact fit. They should be of lightweight tough material with triple-stitched seams. The material should not sag or bag. The pants should have multiple-panel construction combined with elastic cloth to adapt to contour changes during action. The leg section should be flare cut at the knee for adaptation comfort and have goring around the legs, through the crotch, and over the sacrum to be functionally pliant and feel good.

Football pants should not restrict motion at any time or in any position. They should not be of cheap material. Hip pads should not be suspended from a belt nor should thigh pads be sewn in. The trainer does a better protection and prevent job with custom fitting. Pants should not tear. On this score I remember Michigan State's *Spartans* playing the *Golden Gophers* of Minnesota. The year was 1953. All-American Leroy Bolden had the ball. He was off and away in his usual manner when one of the *Gophers* got close enough to get a handful of pants. The pants ripped but Bolden kept going. He ran fifty-seven yards for a touchdown with one hand cuddling the ball and the other clutching his cup. The crowd roared. Inside the goal line his teammates clustered around him while he donned spare pants. From the sideline Duffy Dougherty was yelling: "Boldie, that's the best showing you've made all season!"

Padding

Iliac contusion padding ("hip pointer") should be streamlined to adapt to its position so that at no time can it become a "foreign body"

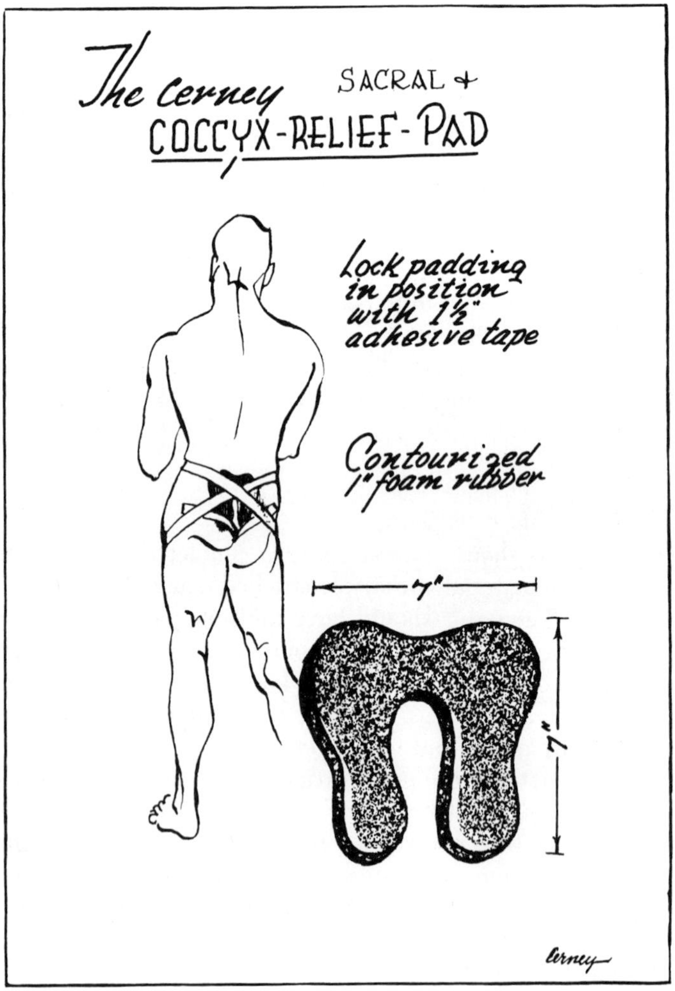

Figure 3-4

and contribute to injury. It should be held and harnessed (by the trainer) to protect the crest of the ilium and still adapt to the mobility of the player.

Sacral padding should bridge the gap between the "hip pointer" pads with blow-absorbing material. This material should have fast recovery characteristics.

The testical cup and *athletic strap* should get special attention to prevent contusion to the contents of the scrotum. As a requirement beneath football pants both cup and strap act as a form of padding that

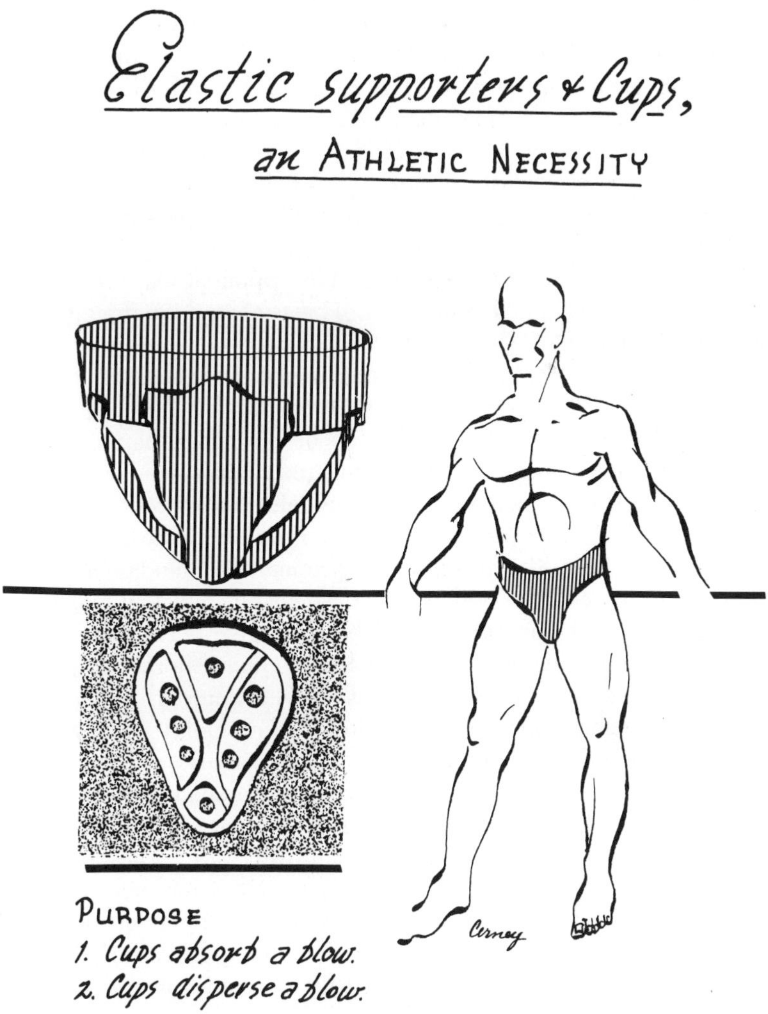

Figure 3-5

has to be custom fitted for shape and size. In the fitting make certain that the edges of the cup are well padded, and that a web-type jock strap locks the cup in position.

HEADGEAR AND HEAD INJURIES

Head injuries in football find their beginnings in such things as inadequate helmets, fractured helmets, or even good helmets that have been improperly fitted. How do head injuries happen? Head injuries may begin in the "pileup" in which feet fly. A head injury may begin when a player makes a flying tackle and gets a foot or knee in the face or jaw. It may come when a player makes a front-on tackle with the head lowered and eyes closed. It may come when a coach puts a boy back into play too soon after a previous head injury. It may come when facemasks are used and a false sense of security is developed behind them. When a player opens up he can get "nose blocked." When he retaliates in kind he may get subjected to the battering ram of his opponent's headgear or a forearm brought up fast into the heart area. His opponent may even grasp his facegear and twist it to take him down. This is always laughingly referred to as "part of the game."

Neurosurgeon Donald F. Dohn, staff member of the Cleveland Clinic Sports Medicine Department, feels that to prevent head injuries, you have to utilize your specific knowledge of how they happen. This information, he feels, not only promotes preventive medicine but also a keener diagnostic acumen on the playing field. To prevent head injuries, he stresses the need for: preseason conditioning and inseason exercises to strengthen the neck, the teaching of proper play fundamentals, good protective equipment, the outlawing of "spearing" and low tackling, and use of only the best and safest available headgear. "The helmet should be well-fitted, since herein lies one of the frequent sources of protective error. Unless the suspension apparatus is well adjusted to fit properly, the impact-absorbing properties are lost." [4] Dr. Dohn feels that every head injury should be checked for associated injuries to the neck and that every neck injury should be checked for accompanying head injuries. He feels that any injured player with an injured head or neck should be watched for his level of consciousness. Answers to questions to the athlete should be noted (if he is conscious). Does he know who he is? Where he is? Does he know his teammates or the last play he made? Is he totally awake? Does he seem normal? Can he speak clearly? Does he react normally when spoken to? If not fully conscious how does he react

[4] D.F. Dohn, *Medicine in Sports Newsletter* 10 (July 1970), p. 3.

to questions? When pinched, what is his reaction? For the player rendered unconscious due to head injury on the field he recommends that any player who does not "come around" must be taken to the hospital immediately; "log roll" the player on a stretcher to prevent aggravation of a possible spinal injury. Lock the athlete's head in position and support it on a level with his spinal column.

The best headgear today is still not right. It is still not the total answer to head and neck protection, but the major manufacturers have demonstrated responsibility in developing a better product. The football helmet, for example, is a shell that envelops the skull. It contains a suspension system of webbing which distributes the force of blows to the head. The purpose of the suspension webbing, and the inner padding, is to keep the helmet from making direct contact with the skull.

Stringent rulings and even more stringent follow-up by referees at games is vital, but the best way to prevent head injuries is to play only a boy who is well-conditioned, healthy, has a strong neck, and has a happy desire for competitive contact sports out on the field. The best equipment is valueless when it encases a scrawny youngster who dies of head and neck injuries sustained while trying to make his first tackle on a live target!

How to Handle Loose Helmets

To get better fitting, keep the suspension webbing in balanced tension. The trainer or equipment manager should check this out daily as a matter of routine. Apply blow-absorbent material with quick recovery characteristics to areas where direct blow transference or dispersal is likely. When a helmet gets loose issue a new one. Remember that a helmet, like a pair of shoes, is never "broken in"! If it doesn't fit in the beginning it never will! It will continue to cause stress points and contribute to injury through constriction, restriction, friction, and pressure.

Where helmets come low on the neck, cut away a half-moon segment at the posterior inferior border and cement a chamois-covered section of absorbent material back in for an added neck guard. Use exactly the same method that armor makers used for hundreds of years with helmets of the middle ages. Cut up, in, and over the nape of the neck. Add a pliable protective flap. It not only feels good but it helps close the vital gap on the neck where a karate chop can be so adeptly placed.

No helmet minimizes trauma to the brain!

Years ago George Barclay was credited with having devised the first football helmet. It was for the Lafayette game against Penn State. The year? 1896. Basically it was a leather skull cap. Today, manufacturers demonstrating their ingenuity have come up with an *air suspension helmet*. This helmet is contoured inside with pneumatic pads which are filled through five openings in the plastic shell. The helmet comes in two basic sizes. Pneumatic pads absorb the blows. According to experiments at the University of Colorado the force of blows to the head in regular suspension helmets can be cut 15 to 40 percent by placing foam padding between the football helmet and the headband straps at the bottom of the helmet's equator. But despite the kind of helmet, no matter how sophisticated, the point remains that no helmet can stop trauma to the brain! The brain rests within the skull. Between the brain and the bony shell, is a small amount of fluid and a thin membrane. Hit the head and the brain inside gets two blows. *First,* on the impact side; *secondly,* as the brain continues in the forward motion of the blow and slaps the opposing side of the skull. It's a one-two punch.

Here's another factor to think about: *the head does not turn with the helmet on impact!* When a blow is delivered the head continues to turn *after* the helmet has come to an abrupt stop. This means that the head and neck sustain two blows, and the brain, riding inside the skull, sustains another blow as it knocks against the inside of its bony boundary.

The helmet is blamed much too often for head injuries in football. Too little concern is given to a player's history of having been "knocked out." Too little concern is given to the lack of conditioning of the athlete, or to that fragile neck. If you are concerned with the helmet as a protective agent, and if the player has had a previous concussion, use a helmet that is ovoid, or oblong in shape and contains no hard or solid padding that can become a direct referral point for trauma. Neither felt nor hard rubber should ever be used for padding inside the helmet. Check that helmet thoroughly for fit. Check the suspensions. Check the chin strap. Maintain this inspection on a day-to-day basis as indicated earlier because that helmet that feels OK today may cause an injury tomorrow.

Plastic Helmet as an Offensive Weapon

As good as it is, the plastic helmet of today is not yet the answer to head injury prevention. Because it is hard, it has become a battering ram and a sledge hammer. It is used to hurt rather than to protect. To obviate this, various football authorities have suggested using the same shell covered with a blow-absorbent material. It should further be engineered and padded to fit the neck and forehead. Certainly it would tend to change the use of the helmet as a battering ram. It would eliminate the multiple small injuries to the brain that tend to collect and finally cause trouble. Most of the time these blows go unnoticed. The athlete is not conscious of them.

Just how a blow to the head can go unnoticed at the time of conflict or impact was exemplified in the Super Bowl of 1969 when the Minnesota *Vikings* went down to defeat against Kansas City. Viking quarterback Joe Kapp had been completely contained and was getting nowhere. In the fourth quarter Aaron Brown decked him. The previously unhurtable Kapp was hurt. Prior to that Brown's counterpart, Jerry May, had also gotten to Kapp but Kapp belted him on the helmet with his follow-through from a forward pass. Wham! On the head. Mays pointed at his helmet when he came to the sideline. There was a jagged crack over the ear hole. "You know," he said puzzled, "that guy Kapp is so tough he didn't even feel it when he dinged me." But neither had Mays.

Helmets May Contribute to Postural Imbalance

Postural balance in football is vital, and the weight of the helmet, strange as this may seem, is a part of it! A helmet not only protects the head and face, but also adds a certain amount of weight at the top end. To accommodate this weight and establish a compensating balance, a player should wear all headgear during spring and summer practices so that he gets the feel of it. It is interesting to note in our Prevent-System research that *athletes who are "off balance" for any reason are the ones who are accident-prone.* Whether it's an insecure balance center, bad feet, postural defects, or even the additional weight of headgear, the imbalance results in poor timing, slowed reflexes, and inadequate coordination. These conditions lead to future injury. Helmets *do* contribute to postural imbalance and accentuate it if a player has fallen arches, an anatomically short leg, a rotated pelvis, or inner-ear balance-center deficiency.

Headaches and Headgear

Football players who wear glasses off the field but not on the field often complain that their helmets cause headaches. More often than not the "headache" is from tension or eyestrain. A factor which may seem unusual if you are unacquainted with oriental acupuncture is that pain occurs when the helmet is riding on acupuncture points in the scalp and forehead.[5] The headache may also come from photophobia (fighting light) due to lack of Vitamin A. To prevent further eye problems get reports from the eye doctor before blaming the helmet. Then check with

[5] J.V. Cerney, *Acupuncture Without Needles* (West Nyack, N.Y.: Parker Publishing Company, 1974), pp. 8–98.

the internist. He may want to administer vitamins for nutritional deficiency. When the athlete continues to fight the light, prevent sun and stadium glare with a few smudges of blacking under the eyes.

Figure 3-6

FACE INJURY

Mouthpieces and Oral Injury

Fast disappearing from the gridiron scene is the "football smile." With the advent of the mouthguard or mouthpiece, having all one's front teeth knocked out is no longer the price of playing the game. In the Prevent-System a mouthpiece has become the answer not just to fractured teeth but to various injuries to the head and jaw.

Teeth come in two decks: sixteen upstairs, sixteen down, normally. The way they come together is called *occlusion.* The teeth of high school boys are not yet totally tough and hard. Permanent teeth have replaced the deciduous teeth of childhood, but their central pulp has not yet been strengthened by dentine. Minor blows may break them. Because young permanent teeth in high schoolers are not yet firmly set, the molars may become *impacted* as the result of a direct blow to the jaw. Where there are misaligned teeth (usually molars), the possibility of jaw fracture is multiplied when a blow occurs. The answer to such blows has proven to be the mouthpiece, and it's the prevention procedure to use. There are three types: *the mouth-formed, the custom-fitted,* and *the boxer,* or stock-style.

The trainer should assist the team dentist when fitting these guards. When a dentist is not available for the squad, the trainer should have this responsibility. Mouthpieces, in rules laid down at the beginning of the preseason workouts by the coach, trainer and team doctor, are to be worn in all practice sessions as well as during games. Since the mandatory mouthpiece regulation was passed January 5, 1962 by the National Football Alliance, the incidence of dental injury has dropped dramatically to less than 1 percent! It's proof positive that the Prevent-System *can* work! The fittted mouthpiece prevents concussions, prevents misaligned teeth, and prevents loss of or injury to teeth, which can affect health and appearance, inhibit normal jaw growth, bring on tooth decay, or cause cosmetic deformities that can be emotionally upsetting to the athlete.

The 1962 official rulebook of the National Federation of High Schools, in Rule 1, Section 5, Article 1, provided that a coach, trainer, team doctor, or school administrator was obligated to protect the student athlete by every means. The National Alliance of Football Rules Committee developed the same ruling. This applies especially to mouthguards.

Lawyers check for use of mouthpieces immediately. The negligence factor erects its ugly head if coaches, trainers, team doctors, etc., have not provided the athlete with a mouthguard. They are subject to lawsuit when this protective device is not used. Although not 100 percent effective, the mouthpiece, along with the face mask, has proven highly effective in the Prevent-System.

Tips on Choosing and Fitting a Mouthguard

Heated "bite-down" or other plastic molded plates take a quick impression. If the athlete already wears dentures he should keep them in while being fitted and when playing football. If any of his teeth are missing above or below, he should be sent to the dentist for a bridge.

This prevents the possibility of mouth laceration where gum spaces (if two or more teeth are missing) are open. Where there are just lower teeth and no uppers, or vice versa, any blow to the lower jaw may result in a torn mouth. The flexible mouthpiece has cut the frequency of this injury to almost nothing. But it's not just the number of fractured teeth that has been reduced in court. That mouthguard also decreases the incidence of brain concussion, and this makes the mouthpiece a necessary protective device.

The right mouthpiece should be based on certain qualifications and advantages. For this purpose here's the guideline: The best mouthpiece is nontoxic, odorless, tasteless, easy to install, comfortable, absorbs and disperses high impact blows, reduces tooth and jaw fracturing, and permits speech. It guards against the dislocation of the temporomandibular joint and protects the inner cheeks and gums from laceration. It is *sterilizable,* refittable, and still meets the requirements of all official rulings. It is easy to clean and should have at least a two-season life. Standard forms should be available to fit all ages and sizes.

Statements of Satisfaction for Dental Injury

Athletes with new dental injuries should be referred immediately to licensed and qualified dentists who may or may not be members of the Team-Behind-the-Team. When the dentist has satisfactorily completed his job the boy is to be returned to action *only after he has presented the proper form* to the athletic director. (See Figure 3-7.)

Facemasks and the Role They Play

Facemasks range in variety from plastic to steel covered with plastic. They are protective, but can also be a source of trouble. They not only protect the face but also provide convenient handles upon which to exert leverage in snapping a neck. I've seen face masks whip loose and lacerate a throat. Leather covered double bar guards protecting the nose and mouth are preferred, but are still inefficient because they tend to limit vision. Despite their excellence, there still continues to be facial contusions, lacerations, and fractures of facial bones.

"To aid in the prevention of mandibular injuries, the NCAA has declared spear tackling illegal," say Doctors E. and M. Rontal. "Heavier padded chinstraps are also needed. The final prevention is to urge the education of players, coaches, trainers, and team physicians on the mechanism and sequelae of facial injuries." [6]

[6] E. Rontal and M. Rontal, *Journal of Sports Medicine* 11 (1971), pp. 241–45.

STATEMENT OF SATISFACTION

Date______________________________________

Name______________________________________

Street____________________________________

City and State____________________________

Telephone_________________________________

To whom it may concern:

I have satisfactorily completed all necessary dental work on____________________who sustained dental injuries (nature)_______________

____

on__________(date). He is now ready to return to athletic action.

____
Dentist

Figure 3-7

In reducing the number of facial injuries the facemask has made some excellent forward strides. Three general types of masks have been developed and are available today: the *full cage,* the *single bar,* and the *double bar.* These are rigid guards attached to a plastic helmet. They are designed to guard the face on a horizontal level against large masses but not against fingers or the opponent's own face guard. Despite the "guard," the nose, zygomatic process, and the mandible continue to be hurt the most often. Getting "dinged" on the helmet may drive the front of the helmet down on the nose if the helmet has been fitted improperly or if the suspension straps are not properly fitted and adjusted. A forearm blow or fist to the mask may cause facial injuries. The full mask prevents most of this by warding off blows from most angles. Forces from all directions are absorbed as long as the suspensions in the helmet are under control, balanced, and/or the helmet is padded to the size and shape of the athlete's head. The full mask does cut off a small bit of peripheral vision, but from the standpoint of general protection, even the backfield men and ends admit it's great.

The Eyes Have It

Vision specialist Dr. A.I. Garner of Harrisburg, Pennsylvania, indicates that of the 1360 football players he tested, some had vision so poor "they couldn't see the side of a barn," much less an opposing player. Dr. Garner reported that one out of every four had visual problems worse than 20/40 in the better eye and that many would be considered legally blind, yet they were out on the football field. He stated that players with visual problems risk serious and permanent damage to themselves. "Many of today's finest American athletes are in reality visual cripples! They are playing with eyesight that would prohibit them from driving an automobile on today's highways." [7]

Contact Lens

From the standpoint of injury prevention, Dr. Garner suggests contact lenses since they have advantages over regular glasses: (1) they protect the eyeball; (2) they improve peripheral vision; (3) they follow the movement of the eyes; (4) there are no "blind spots" as with framed glasses; and (5) they are impact-resistant and nonbreakable.

Framed Glasses

Where framed glasses have to be used, no matter what the reason is, the glass should be shock-proof or unbreakable. Football goggles should have the following requirements: (1) they should feel comfortable, (2) there should be no templates (use adjustable headbands instead), (3) the lenses should be of case-hardened glass or plastic, ground to prescription, (4) they should provide wide-angle vision, (5) they should have nonfogging ventilation, (6) they should have a cushioned nose piece, and (7) the lens should be contoured to prevent "smash-back" on the eyeball. Cornerback Joe Lavender of the Philadelphia *Eagles* (1974–5) is the only professional football player I know who uses framed glasses. Those who are playing it smart have gone to "contacts."

NECK AND SHOULDER PROTECTION

Neck Collars

Neck collars have as much psychological as physical value for the football player. This solid tube of plastic-covered foam rubber encircles

[7] A.I. Garner, Lecture to the Eastern Athletic Trainers Association, spring 1973.

the base of the throat and anchors to the shoulder pads with laces. The amount of pull on the laces determines the amount of restriction imposed on the neck. The diameter of the tube ranges from one to two inches and controls excursion of the head on the neck and shoulders.

Does the Collar Restrict Vision?

The neck collar *does* tend to restrict the visual area by limiting certain movements, but this can be compensated for simply by teaching the athlete to roll his shoulders. There is no loss of the visual field, or any restriction, when the neck is flexed. The visual field *is* limited when the neck is hyperextended.

To prevent neck injury, a thick collar is suggested for the *lineman*. A less thick collar for *defensive ends* and *linebackers*. The middle thickness, or intermediate size, may be used for *offensive ends, quarterbacks, backs,* and *safety men*. The trainer should supervise the fittings of all collars and check their relationship and anchorage with the shoulder pads daily to prevent complications. For more protection you should apply talcum powder with a large proportion zinc oxide liberally to the neck. This prevents irritation and rubbing. In cold weather encase the tube with gauze because the collar gets hard and contuses the flesh beneath. Here's another trick to use: simply encase the collar in orthopedic stocking or tubular gauze. In warm weather see that all players wear V-line T-shirts because of the heat accumulation in the collar (plastic tube) itself. When properly adjusted and used the neck collar is an excellent prevention method indeed.

Shoulder Gear

Be highly selective in choosing commercial shoulder gear. Choose padding in accordance with football position being played. The following is not a hard and fast ruling but a general guideline for style and type:

Maintain regular checkups on all shoulder gear. This should be done daily by the trainer or equipment manager. Do not leave this to the athlete. Check all laces, straps, hinges, etc. Check for security and pliability.

Cover shoulder padding with foam rubber to keep it from being used as a battering ram.

Check for fit. Remember that chest pains may begin with poorly fitted shoulder gear gouging the musculature and nerve supply of the chest.

Avoid the overly-large pad. Outsized paddings, ostensibly to protect old injuries, may also contribute to knobs of angry tissue on the shoulder that can feel like a boil. Further, to the perceptive opponent this is a signal. It points up where a weakpoint lies.

CHOOSING THE RIGHT SHOULDER PAD

Football Position:	Commercial Pad Style:
Guards	Inside/outside cantilever pad
Centers	Inside/outside cantilever
Backs	Inside cantilever
Ends	Linebackers pads
Quarterbacks	Flat padding

Figure 3-8

Instruct the athlete to block with the shoulder and not the arm. Issue instructions such as: "Never throw an arm at a helmet." By sticking to these simple rules the athlete can avoid "blocker's disease" (calcification of the arm muscles) by proper use of his shoulder.

Shoulder Pad Problems

Shifting of the shoulder gear during action can cause a nonadaptive shoulder "cushion" to become a fulcrum on which the power impact of a direct blow takes its toll. *Notice how often the athlete works his shoulders or hitches his padding with his hands to check for shifting of shoulder gear!* When fitting shoulder pads in the Prevent-System don't depend on jerseys to hold shoulder gear in position. Gravity does not hold padding either. This means that all possible security measures have to be used but the shoulder gear should remain fluid with the flow of the athlete's motion. It has to prevent injury rather than cause it. Protection has to be built right in.

FOOTGEAR

One of the most important pieces of equipment an athlete has is his shoes. The football player is no exception. When improperly fitted, or of inferior construction, shoes are his worst enemy and he doesn't even know it! The ideal football shoe, like the ideal football helmet, has yet to be devised from the standpoint of foot environment and postural balance.

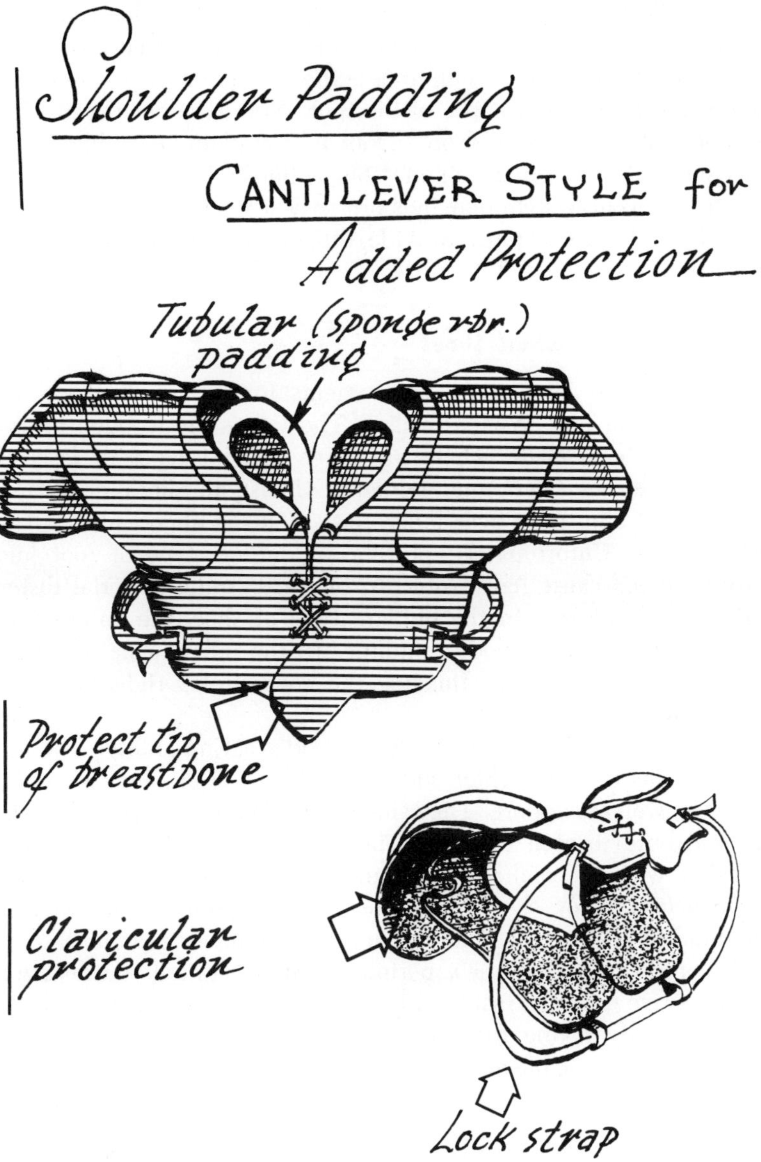
Shoulder Padding
Cantilever Style for
Added Protection
Tubular (sponge rbr.) padding
Protect tip of breastbone
Clavicular protection
Lock strap

Figure 3-9

For this reason, examine the internal structure of shoes that are available before ordering them. If the shoe is of Goodyear welt construction, for example, check for a steel bar running between the soles from heel to toes under the arch. Check the medial inner aspect of that shoe and note whether it is supportive enough to take the pressure off leg muscles which support and control the bones of the foot. Note whether the athlete has any foot problem or "arch drop." Does he complain of "sliding forward" in his shoe, of "loose heel," or of "shin splints"? If such complaints are made the Prevent-System demands properly fitted shoes and the addition of padding. The shoe must provide the football player with a feeling of security.

How to Fit Football Shoes

Shoes should fill certain requirements for proper fit. They should be of the proper last. What is a last? The last is the wooden form over which the shoe is made. There are three general types of lasts. They are: *inflare, straight last,* and *outflare.* Almost all shoes manufactured in the United States are over inflare lasts. This is almost always true of football shoes. Unfortunately, putting an outflare type of foot into an inflare shoe can cause foot problems, physical strain, or serial distortion up the spinal column. In the outflare type of shoe, the anterior of the shoe goes lateral of the body's midline. In the inflare shoe, the forepart of the shoe goes medially. Imagine the conflict! It's right here that so many injuries begin!

The shoes should, of course, have good wearing ability. The uppers should be made of a lighter softly pliable material. They should give comfort as well as support. They should give "ground grip." They should not contribute to arch collapse. They should provide an environment adaptable without conflict or pressure to the dynamics of the football foot in action. They should grip the heel to guide the forefoot. They should aid at all times the biomechanics of the lower extremity.

When fitting shoes *do not* permit the athlete to tell you his size. *Do not* take a size from the inside of his street shoes. Most civilian shoes are badly fitted. By taking the same shoe size, you merely compound the damage by repeating the error.

Measure the foot only on weight bearing!

Measure the athlete's foot only on weight bearing. The player's weight should be evenly distributed on both feet as he stands on the measuring stick. Width as well as length should be taken. Note the difference in the widths of the two feet and fit the larger foot. The most efficient procedure to get an exact measurement of the foot is to have the boy hold a bucket of sand in both hands equal in weight to the amount of gear he wears. Remember that the function of the foot in football is dependent upon all metatarsal heads and toes coming down for that prehensile grip that assures the next forward thrust of the foot. Limiting the environment of the foot by placing it in a shoe too small only leads to injury.

After width and length are taken keep the numbers on file but remember they won't be much good next year. An athlete's shoe size is not static. It changes from year to year, and I've proven this after long arduous research. Here's another fitting tip: Make a rough allowance of a thumb's width from the tip of the longest toe to the tip of the shoe. Allow space for the foreward "ride" of the foot in the shoe. Don't try to inhibit the "ride" completely by fitting on narrow shoes. Forget the old shoe fitting philosophy that says: "You've got to grip the ball of the foot and hold up the arch." Nonsense! Do that and your boy is in trouble. You not only ruin his feet but you successfully contribute to leg misery and possibly to the end of his sports career.

Allowing this controlled "ride" in the shoe helps to eliminate blisters and calluses. The athlete will also stop having "ingrown nails," "corns," contracted toes, metatarsalgia and metatarsal neuritis, tarsal strain and sprain, ankle sprain and strain, heel spurs, and "charley horses." It all begins with how you fit that shoe, using the Prevent-System.

The point here is, "Know feet, footgear, and how to fit them!" Don't take the word of the athletic goods salesman whose major interest is in sales, not in feet. Many know nothing about the anatomy of the foot, or how it functions in the dynamics of football.

The decision between high and low football shoes is one you have to make. If all the coaches, players, trainers, and team doctors in the world were queried on the relative merits of the high versus the low shoe, their decisions would all boil down to personal preferences and the position played by each athlete. In developing your own Prevent-System guidelines for footgear keep the following points in mind:

High Shoes: High shoes give mild ankle support and minor ankle support by pulling the uppers together with the laces. The high upper also acts as a guard against blows to the ankle. On the other hand, high cuts are heavier. The amount of arch support and ankle protection they render is almost negligible.

Low Shoes: Low cuts are light in weight and give go-power when the legs get weary. To a degree this is true if you use high cuts on your boys in the first half, and then give them wings the second half with lighter weight shoes. Low shoes, however, do not protect the ankle. They offer less binding support to the arch, provide less "heel lock" control for management of the forefoot, and can bring to a head all the biomechanical faults of the lower extremities.

Football Shoes Maintenance

In your Prevent-System, be concerned with more than the fit of football shoes. Be aware that shoes are carriers of bacteria, spores, fungus, and other microorganisms. Cleanse the outside of all shoes with soap and water. Rub them with sorbitol to keep them soft. Cleanse the inside with a germicide. Never use a drying machine on shoes when they get wet. A size 9D suddenly shrinks to an 8B. Hang wet shoes up to dry. Keep them on lasts or stretchers in the drying process or during storage time.

Preventing Foot Problems

An aching foot is a warning: pay heed to it. It is a sign indicating that all the Prevent-System rules are not yet in action. Don't expect shoes or appliances (arch supports, prosthetics, etc.) to prevent all foot problems. Yes, good shoes are necessary. So is a good fit. But many other matters are also vital to injury prevention. Here are some things to remember.

Place heel cups in the low cut shoes of backfield men. They not only stabilize the heels but also prevent blisters and help establish more security in the arch and ankle joints. They also eliminate pressure on the Achilles tendon.

Punters should wear highcut shoes to protect the tarsal bones, their joints, and the soft tissues and tendons anterior to and below the ankle. Further protection may be achieved for the dorsum by placing soft foam rubber padding along the length of the shoe tongue. This dispels the blow when contact is made with the ball. The wise coach or trainer does not permit punting with gym shoes or bare feet. The barefoot kicker is quite a spectacle it's true but barefoot kicking can cause arthritis, tendonitis, bursitis, cellulitis, and a dozen other problems.

Do not use football shoes in preseason workouts. Use basketball or gym shoes. Football shoes in early season workouts cause latent foot problems to show up. Badly fitted football shoes hasten this process. Do not use shoes with spikes, cleats, or rippled soles.

If cleats are used check them systematically. Bad positioning of a cleat leads to foot and leg problems. Make certain cleats are under weight bearing points. Keep cleats greased to prevent them from stacking up mud and debris. Replace broken cleats immediately because broken cleats become an offensive weapon.

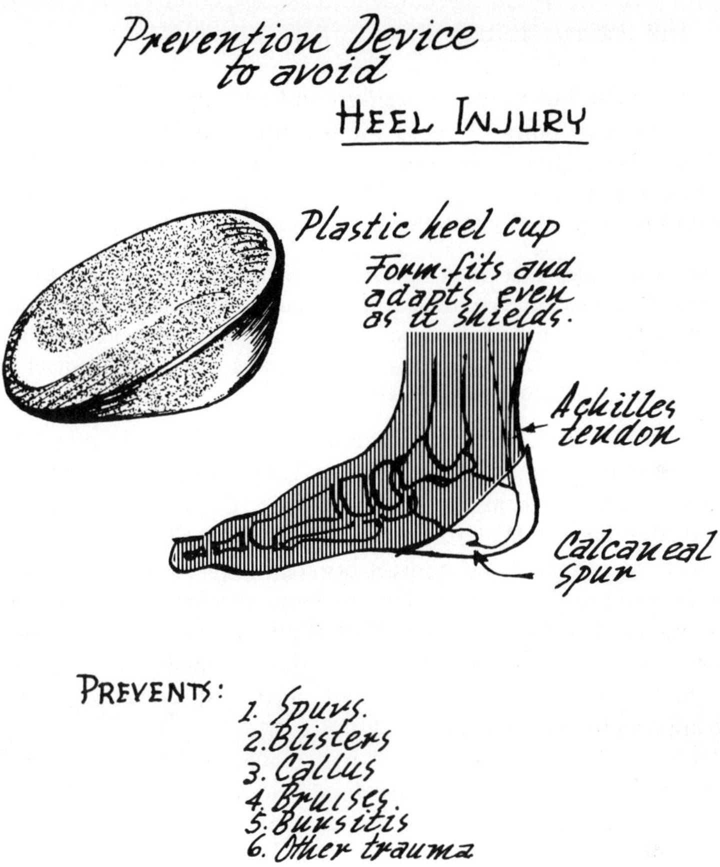

Figure 3-10

Remove heel cleats when knee injuries occur. The heel cleat has long been known to have a significant relationship to knee injuries. The traditional approach to guarding the integrity of the ankle and knee has been to apply adhesive tape or other wraps to these two joints, develop the hamstrings and quadriceps, remove the standard heel cleats and replace them with a bar or swivel heel, and teach the athlete better techniques for "cutting" and running. The weight of the body should be in postural balance over a slightly turned-in forefoot. Dr. D.F. Hanley, of Harvard University, back in the 1950's reported an appreciable drop in knee injuries after using the heel bar. The New York State Public High School Athletic Association screened forty-four high schools in 1968. It found that low cut shoes with disc heels were most injury-free yet with no loss in playing efficiency.

Linemen should wear hard-toed shoes.

Players should use basketball or gym shoes on frozen turf. Cleated or rippled soles can fail to grip frozen ground and injuries can result. Have players wear two pairs of socks for warmth and remember that while basketball shoes give more security on frozen turf they do not protect against frostbite!

Said Professor Karl K. Klein, at the University of Texas:

> Tradition holds that the heel cleat is absolutely necessary for better function. But what players run on their heels? Any coach who understands the mechanics of the human body should realize how useless the heel cleat is and how it locks the heel in cutting, turning and player contact, intensifying major strains thrown on the knee.[8]

Eight Iowa high schools abandoned the traditional spiked football shoes to prevent ankle and knee injuries. They replaced old-style footgear with soccer shoes with molded rubber cleats. Dr. Ed Martinet, Chief of Physical Medicine at Wake Forest's Bowman Hospital, advocates swivel heel cleats to reduce knee injuries because they prevent the foot from becoming fixed to the ground. This cushions the force of a block thrown into a runner. Dr. Martinet, Dr. Carl Blyth of the University of North Carolina, and Dr. James Whitehurst of the University of Houston went so far as to advocate the use of short cleated shoes on synthetic turf, which apparently works well.

Athlete's should wear shoes that are a bit wide to prevent "blood blisters" and pinching. When this doesn't work check the player's style of pivoting

Socks and Blisters

As the old lady said, "When my feet hurt I hurt all over." Shoes and socks can emphasize and create problems. Here are the Prevent-System techniques I have used effectively for years.

Early season blisters can be eliminated with the following procedure: Lubricate the bare foot with petroleum jelly or lanoline before applying lightweight socks. Sprinkle the socks liberally with talcum powder, and put sweat socks on over them. The petroleum jelly, the two pair of socks, and the powder provide a frictionless "ride" for the foot inside the shoe, eliminates procedure of toughening the foot with formaldehyde, salt solutions, or tincture of benzoin.

Thermal socks may be used as the first pair of socks in cold weather. Always fit them two sizes larger than the athlete's actual foot size. This allows for shrinkage in laundry. Socks don't "break in." At no time should athletes wear "stretch socks"! They are one of the worst offenders in

[8] K.K. Klein, "The Heel Cleat: Its Contribution to Football," *Journal of the NATA* 5, no. 2 (Summer 1970), p. 20.

5 Steps
for
PREPPING THE FEET
JELLY
1
Apply petroleum jelly liberally.
2
Put on light-weight socks
3
Sprinkle socks with powder.
4
Don heavy-weight socks.
5
Shoes
to
PREVENT
BLISTERS
23

Figure 3-11

athletics. There is constant pressure from the stretch material, in direct opposition to the normal anterior ride of the foot inside the shoe. To prevent shrinkage, wash socks with lukewarm water. Rinse with cold water. *Never* use hot water. Before socks are placed on the drying line or in the drier, pull on the toe and heel to restretch the material.

Avoid darned socks: they start blisters. Don't use harsh detergents or bleaches on socks. They not only shorten the life of the sock but may also contribute to contact dermatitis (inflamation of the skin) if a player is allergic to the substance used. All socks should be absorbent, soft, have a springy cushioned heel, be made of nonbunching material, maintain flexibility, and have a cotton elastic (not rubber) woven top.

FIELD EQUIPMENT AND INJURY CONTROL

The term "field equipment" as used here pertains to all hard gear in the practice and playing fields, in the stands, locker rooms, showers, training room, weight-training room, and gymnasium. To prevent infection and injury you have to foresee every possible cause of injury: debris on the field, uneven turf and holes, rusting equipment, equipment lying around to be fallen over, spectators, photographers, newsmen, TV cameras, marching bands, or drill teams too close to the football action, etc. Following are procedures to be followed in preventing injury in all such areas.

Do have your maintenance men keep the practice field and stadium turf in good condition. Keep it patched and at its best at all times. When planning or redoing a football field study the engineering of tiling, sloping, drainage, etc. If you are in the financial position to put in artificial turf, I find that some brands can give good footing when wet and thus insure against ankle and knee injuries.

Do assign a squad of students to keep all areas free from sticks, stones, glass, and equipment of all kinds. When line markers are applied, *do not use lime.* Use material that will not burn the eyes. Do have your field maintenance man use fertilizer on grassy turf rather than manure. Manure is a conveyor of tetanus. When fields are dusty have them watered down so that there will be no problem for players subject to asthma or sinus problems. Do be careful of all sprays used on or around the gridiron. Weed poisons and chemical fertilizers can aggravate allergies and lead to dangerous physical complications.

Do enforce (through your student equipment manager) the ruling that loose gear must not be on the field at any time. Players' benches should be kept as least five to ten yards back from the sidelines. Yard markers and stakes should be collapsible to prevent injury should the athlete fall on them. Linemen should drop chains and markers immediately in the face of an advancing play. Goal line flag pedestals should also be flexible.

Do demand that tackling dummies (not live targets) be used for first-year participants. Goal posts on practice and stadium fields should be generously padded. Insist that all sleds and other equipment are painted and the padding clean and secure. When obstacle courses are used for dodging and drills be certain that ground-locked posts are padded.

Do make a schedule of agreements with the music department about the use of the field by the marching band, the majorettes, etc., for practice sessions during the week and for halftime during a game. Bands and drill teams can be a real hazard on the playing field and their on and off the field times should be run by the clock. Practice sessions for the band and drill team should ideally take place away from the playing fields.

Do be concerned about your bleacher seats. Have them checked and rechecked regularly, even to the bolts underneath. Tragic accidents in the stands can be prevented by regular inspection and observation.

Do be judicious about the equipment you purchase. A few points on this matter follow.

Soliciting Extra Money for Equipment

When costs have risen and income has dropped, when city or county school system support has been stripped, providing there are no local rulings about accepting donations, it's a good idea to take advantage of outside groups who are willing to solicit the money you need for a better prevention program. A well of funds can flow from the projects of "Booster Clubs," "Quarterback Clubs," "Dads' Clubs," Parent Teacher Associations, etc. They can often find ingenious ways of getting it.

At the high school level funds are easier to raise. Parents play an interested and prideful role in athletics and become not just ardent fans but a living part of your campaign against injuries. Their projects can get you the prevention gear your department needs but can't afford. Don't be ashamed to ask for help. Tell them the circumstances. Show facts and figures and explain how protective gear will save their youngsters a lot of harm. When they ask, "How much do you need?" lay it on the line. Then sit back and wait. They'll come up with it sure enough!

SANITATION IN THE ATHLETIC DEPARTMENT

Infections seldom occur in the athletic department when the necessary standards of sanitation are maintained. Sanitation methods have to be practical, effective, and relatively economical. A state of total asepsis is not necessary but it is vital to take all necessary precautions. Lockers, showers, equipment, floors, toilets, etc., are all possible centers for contamination. Laundry bags and trash containers are prime places for bacterial growth; unsterilized protective pads, restriction binders, and braces can be menaces; bacteria are constantly carried by the parade of athletes. Therefore, an effective germicide should be used. Constant attention to infection prevention is needed.

The Qualifications of an Athletic Germicide

To determine whether a germicide is right for your athletic department's Prevent-System it should fill the following requirements: It must kill bacteria, viruses, spores, and fungi. It must be effective against antibiotic-resistant bacteria such as staphlococcus aureaus and against fungi and their spores, as well as the trychophytons (athlete's foot) that can infect a whole squad overnight. The athletic germicide must kill on contact and be lasting. It must continue killing air-borne bacteria several days after application without hurting the person, the gear, or equipment on which it is used. Its odor must not be obnoxious. The athletic germicide should work synergistically with detergents, be nonirritating to the skin or mucous membranes, and leave no film. It should not harm the surfaces upon which it is applied, yet it must still be capable of cutting through surface tension.

What to Police With Germicides

Wood, metal work, walls, and floors must all be treated by mop, brush, or machine. The locker room, the shower, gymnasium, training room, and athletic offices should be disinfected regularly. Floors of the shower and locker room should be treated daily. Apply germicide full strength to heavy smudges.

Training room floors, walls, windows, and equipment (scales, tables, cabinets, etc.) should be scrubbed with germicidal solutions at least once weekly. *Note: if one infected boy comes in scrub everything!* Clean and hose down areas of vomit, blood, etc., immediately. Rinse and swab with germicide. If there are colds and influenza in the department, clean everything, because any surface can be contaminated by coughs and sneezes. Maintain clean covers on the training tables. Soak them with germicide before laundering.

In the gymnasium, gymnastic and weight-training equipment are constant carriers of infective organisms. One boy with a broken boil can contaminate an amazingly big area in a short while. To prevent others from being infected, apply germicidal cleansing agents liberally to this

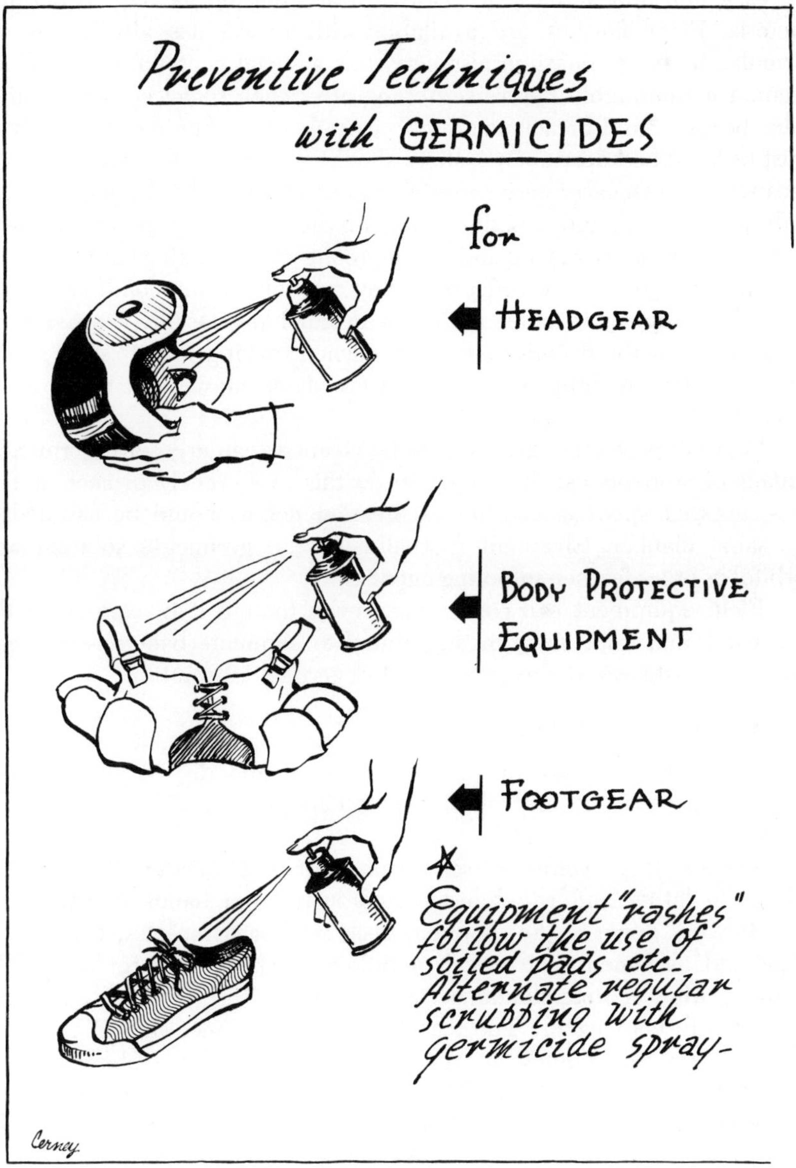
Preventive Techniques
with GERMICIDES
for
HEADGEAR
BODY PROTECTIVE EQUIPMENT
FOOTGEAR
Equipment "rashes" follow the use of soiled pads etc. Alternate regular scrubbing with germicide spray.
Cerney

Figure 3-12

equipment. Mechanical floor scrubbers are best for this. To the germicidal solution add deodorants and detergents. *Do not use soap!* Soap leaves a greasy film and actually increases surface tension locking in harmful bacteria. Floor finishes are available with germicides already in the formula. If the gymnasium also serves as a social center for the school, vacuum it thoroughly before scrubbing after each social occasion. Since mats, benches, and bleachers are also carriers of contamination they, too, must be scrubbed down. Gym shoes should go through the washing cycle because they can carry germs inside and out. No one should be permitted to drop toweling, bandages, or clothing on the floor or equipment. Shower rooms, locker rooms, drying and storing rooms etc., as well as gymnasiums, have notoriously poor ventilation. They are seldom air conditioned. To solve this problem in older buildings install blowers and vents. Permit no smoking on the premises. Provide efficient drying facilities for stored material. Store nothing in rooms that are damp or without windows or vents.

Football protective gear should be cleaned regularly with germicide. Squads of students can be taught to do this as a weekly project. A few moments thus spent saves athletes. Leather goods should be handled in the same manner. Clean all footballs. To the germicide solution add sorbitol or other leather-softening agents.

Field equipment can contaminate even though it is exposed to the sun, wind, and rain. Keep metal painted to eliminate bacteria-collecting rust areas and swab down canvas with a germicidal solution.

Showering Procedures

Showering does not just get rid of sweat and dirt, it also removes offensive bacteria. Proper showering techniques should be taught to everyone.

Showering Procedure: Use warm (not hot) water. Instruct the athlete to lather and rub himself vigorously from hands to shoulders, then to work down to the shoulder, neck, and back muscles, then to the chest and abdomen. The crotch and lower extremities are last in the washing. Shower time should be no longer than three minutes. End the shower with cold water. The team manager or trainer should check an athlete's skin for coolness as the athlete exits from the shower room. It is just as necessary to cool out an athlete after practice sessions or games as it is to cool out a racehorse. The athlete's physiology should be back to normal before he leaves the shower room. He should be wearing adequate clothing and have a covering on his head and neck if it is cold outside. This ounce of prevention once again is worth a pound of cure. Too often that post-workout soreness began in the shower room because someone forgot that an athlete, like a racehorse, must be "cooled out."

Injury Prevention Rules for the Shower Room

Sanitize and clean shower rooms regularly with a mechanical scrubber (mopping is nearly valueless).

Inspect showerheads to prevent scalding.

Maintain orderly conduct; the rules of shower room decorum must be laid down at the beginning of the season. Discipline all horseplay.

Do not permit hoses in the shower room. They become weapons for injurious horseplay.

Do not permit gear, clothing, shoes, toweling, bottles, etc. in the shower room.

Do not allow wet trails to the locker room. The trainer should mark off a drying-out area in which the towel-drying should take place.

Make sure shower room floors are rough in texture to prevent slippage but not so rough that they are hard to keep clean or will house bacteria.

Do not use duckboards. Wooden platforms are dangerous, unsanitary, and an insecure base for feet when wet.

Maintain shower room temperature at 68°F to 72°F.

Keep the shower room well lighted.

Use psychologically soothing colors (like light green) on the walls.

Believe it or not, one part of my Prevent-System is watching for whistling and singing or its absence in the shower room. The shower should be a healthy experience after a good workout or game. When showers are taken in glum silence, something in your Prevent-System has broken down. This is a signpost that directs you to look for areas of trouble with the athletes, the coaching staff, the facilities, or for unsuspected problems.

Guidelines for Prevention in the Locker Room

The locker room is only one of the responsibilities in the sanitation program but it is an important one. Rules and regulations should be laid down by the athletic director at the beginning of each season so that there is no question as to what is expected of each person who uses it. Injuries can be prevented in the locker room if you stick to the following program.

Your team or equipment manager should be placed in charge of policing the locker room for sanitation, decorum, and personal cleanliness of the participants. All athletes should be advised that proper action will be taken against those who break the rules. Set up a "drying area" for after showering as well as a drying room where all gear is hung as soon as it comes in from the field and provide convenient hampers for dirty jerseys, underwear, etc. Instruct all athletes to be completely dried off before they enter the locker room. Rubber floor runners should be provided in the drying area to prevent athletes from slipping.

Keep locker room floors dry. Establish proper ventilation to eliminate odors and airborne bacteria. Clean floors with germicidal detergent at least twice weekly (daily is even better). Instruct the trainer and coaches not to allow glassware (shampoo bottles, etc.) to be taken into the shower or locker room. Horseplay in the locker room (which causes most of the locker room "accidents") should be totally outlawed. No one should be permitted to wear cleated shoes in the locker room or any other part of the athletic plant. They should be carried to the outside door and only then put on.

The person in charge of departmental sanitation should order off the premises such contaminating devices as the "foot powder box," which is a carrier of many dangerous organisms. He should assure that toilet rooms have complete sanitary care. At the beginning of the season the athletic director should issue written instructions on laundry handling. Printed rules and regulations must be issued to everyone using the facilities to establish athletic department requirements.

At the beginning of the season, individual lockers are usually assigned to each player. To prevent the spread of contact infections, no locker should be shared. Lockers should be of sufficient size, well ventilated, convenient, strong, and easily cleaned with germicides. The doctrine that no dirty or sweaty clothing is to be kept in the locker should be established early. When dampness prevails in the lockers, have a dehumidifier set in the locker room. Spray lockers with germicide, or swab them, at least twice each season. *Use no strong insecticides.* Strong insecticides are irritants to the nose, throat, sinuses, and lungs causing symptoms that appear to be due to a disease but are actually manifestations of an allergy. Insecticides can take an athlete out of action as readily as a broken bone.

The Athletic Director Sets Up a Laundry Room

Clothing and toweling are carriers of disease organisms and parasites, and proper laundering is necessary to any Prevent-System. More and more schools are putting in their own laundry room and economy of operation is not the only reason. This home service not only produces cleaner laundry but also has it ready when needed. The athletic director who is considering a laundry room should consider five major factors: hygiene; the operator's health; the prevention of the spread of infection; and the economy of operation and sanitation.

The majority of schools give little or no thought to hygiene and prevention. They have a laundry room and they are happy, but as a result of their indifference many things can happen. The laundry operator's respiratory system can be affected, for example, by harsh vapor. Therefore, in planning the athletic department laundry room the following specifications should be written into the student operator's *Laundry Bill of Rights*.

LAUNDRY BILL OF RIGHTS
FOR STUDENT OPERATORS

1. There shall be mechanical ventilation to remove steam and heat.

2. A slotted wood or insulated platform shall be provided for the worker to stand on to prevent the possibility of electrocution, cut down on slipping, and provide foot comfort.

3. Floors shall slope to the drain.

4. Rubber aprons and boots shall be provided if there is excessively wet work.

5. A unit that sterilizes clothing and gear shall be provided. If it is possible to purchase autoclave units, and the drier doesn't provide the heat to sterilize a garment, then a gas or electric unit shall be installed for boiling clothing.

6. Nonbreakable dispensers shall be provided for bleaches, soap powders, detergents, etc., to eliminate the possibility of cuts from broken glass. Containers that pour shall be used to prevent the laundry operator from coming in contact with possibly harmful chemicals.

Figure 3-13

It is quite true that most laundry is done by machinery. Manufacturers of such equipment claim that they are easily operated and that all one has to do is throw the soiled articles in and then haul them out when they are finished. This also is true. But what is equally true is that the operator still has to touch the garments that may or may not be contaminated. He still has to breathe bacteria-laden dust from these garments when he gathers them up to throw them into the machine. It is necessary to keep the laundry operator from being infested with parasites or bacteria. The laundry operator breathes steam and noxious irritants from the cleaning agents used. These irritants can adversely affect the eyes, ears, nose, and throat, as well as the upper respiratory tract. Preventing these damages from harming the laundry operator is the athletic director's responsibility, so the athletic director should set in a stock of surgeon's masks as a partial means for coping with this situation.

The purpose of boiling contaminated clothing is to destroy spores and spore bearing bacteria which are so virulent that they will resist boiling up to twenty minutes. The clothing of boys who have carbuncles, boils, impetigo etc. should get rigorous sterilization.

In smaller schools the athletes usually have their own personal clothing and toweling. The "Booster Clubs," "Dads' Clubs," or "Quarterback Clubs" of such schools will sometimes pay for commercial laundering. In large schools the boys are usually issued clean items as they are needed and the school laundry does the job. In all cases the athletes should be instructed never to exchange garments, toweling, soap, or gear among themselves, and that a daily change of underclothing is necessary.

To provide a working program for the care and prevention of laundry problems, I have set up the following chart (see Figure 3-14). It explains to your laundry assistants what should be done.

Training Room Germ Carriers

A trainer, as an important member in sports medicine, can't help but be conscious of the role of sanitation in the athletic program. For example, a player whose resistance is down is susceptible to disease and injury. Vigilance against bacteria is as important as football drills. The whirlpool bath, a dirty "warbag," the floor, the walls, the gear: all of them are possible carriers of germs.

The Immunization Program

Most youngsters carry their tetanus-diphtheria-whooping cough triad of toxoids as part of their earlier pediatric protection. In contact sports, however, lacerations and penetrating wounds are not unheard of and may pick up spores and germs against which there will be a need for additional shots. As a preseason "must" these shots should be administered by the

LAUNDRY METHODS CHART

DRY CLEANING	WITHOUT CLEANING FLUIDS	DETERGENTS/SOAP 110-120°F	MILD SOAP 110-120°F	MILD SOAP 130-140°F
clothing or gear	clothing or gear	clothing or gear	clothing or gear	clothing or gear
Award jackets.	Sideline caps.	T-shirts (baseball)	Baseball uniforms.	Practice football jerseys and pants.
Wool baseball jackets.	Sideline coats.	Baseball dickies	T-shirts.	Socks
Wool warm-up jackets.	Directions: Sponge the outer surfaces with germicide-detergent and rinse very well.	Sweaters.	Football pants and jerseys	T-shirts
Basketball jerseys.		Directions: Do rinse well and dry flat on towels	Track pants	Athletic supporters.
Softball jerseys.		Note: Do not tumble dry or wring dry.	Socks	
			Scrimmage vests, Game jerseys Warm-up clothes. Nylon jackets	
			Special Note: Do rinse and hang on rustproof hangers.	
			Don't bleach, or tumble dry.	

Figure 3-14

team physician weeks before the practice season begins. This avoids the complications of postshot reactions that may arise. The trainer should keep complete records as to time, date, dosage, etc. He should see that it gets done if the school nurse, team doctor, or family physician has not yet gotten to it.

Equipment as a Germ Carrier

Coaches, trainers, and team doctors often forget that equipment can be a carrier of infection. Following is a list of specific equipment which may be invaded by foreign organisms, and what to do about them.

The Hydrotherapy Tank. Pulling the plug in the hydrotherapy tank does not remove all foreign organisms. Harmful organisms collect on the inside of the tank and motor shaft mechanism as well as the outlet. Test after test of scrapings from the inner tanks of many high school and college "hydros" revealed spores, molds, yeasts, bacteria, and fungae. Many spores take twenty minutes of boiling time to kill, but the following procedure handles the majority of microorganisms. Check hydro tanks daily. Remove deposits with janitor's bowl cleaner or bathroom-type cleaners that foam the dirt up and out of crevices. Use no cleansers that scratch or "eat" the metal. Apply germicide and dry the tank after hosing and draining. Clean the tank after each player uses it. Swab the tank with undiluted germicide, rinse it and cover the tank top. For further insurance, place a small portion of nonallergenic detergent in the water to loosen the dirt and decrease the surface tension that clasps bacteria to the hair and skin. Add germicide.

The Foot Powder Box. This is one of the most flagrant purveyors of disease. I have done a great deal of research on foot powder boxes and suggest that they be run out of the county. Here's the story: Everyone's feet go into a common place, and so do microorganisms. Another flagrant offender in the powdering process is the tincture of benzoin bottle and its attached brush. Tincture of benzoin in itself is not even mildly antiseptic and has no self-defense. As a result it becomes a carrier for disease. In turn, the bench attached to the powder box is a carrier of germs. It distributes infective organisms impartially to everyone sitting on it. The rectum and scrotum become affected and too often this is misdiagnosed as "jock strap itch." The powder box should be eliminated! It is a public trough for transplanting organism from one athlete to another despite advertising claims to the contrary. Powders in themselves provide an excellent environment for breeding bacteria.

Medication containers. Like the tincture of benzoin bottle, containers are subject to everyone's hands. For this reason analgesics, "gunks," etc., must be kept sealed and used by the trainer only! This rule must be laid down at the beginning of the season.

Trainer's hands. The trainer's hands and clothing may be carriers of infective organisms. The trainer has to be as strict about himself and his personal antibacterial techniques as the team doctor is. He should keep his fingernails trimmed and clean and skin soft. His uniform should not be just distinctive and smart but clean. He should maintain his own health and keep his equipment clean so that he himself is not a carrier of germs.

Protective pads and gear. There's nothing wrong with reusing pads, hip protectors, etc., for protection. Just keep them sterilized. Since the more easily available oven heat method of sterilization is hard on rubber and plastic it is wiser to simply soak all pads and similar gear in germicidal solution and rinse them well before drying. Store them when dry in a plastic bag.

Trainer's Warbag. This bag should be cleaned regularly. Everything should be dumped out, the inside and outside cleaned meticulously and sprayed with germicide. Air the bag in the sun. Place all gauze, tape rolls, etc., in closed sterile containers. Don't permit anything to "kick around loose" in the bag or kit. This includes oral screws, splints, scissors, etc. Maintain a strictly "handsoff" policy on this bag and set the rules early. It's the trainer's ensignia which he carries with dignity, and *doesn't* carry full of bacteria and microorganisms.

Physical therapy apparatus. Such apparatus is seldom used on areas of active infection. However, when used on healthy boys who are carriers the bacteria may be transferred to someone else through indiscriminate usage. To prevent electrodes from becoming carriers, sterilize them in germicidal solution or in the sterilizer, or boil them. Shortwave arms and pads should be swabbed regularly with germicide. Sand bags used to hold electrodes in position should be kept in throwaway plastic bags. Latex rubber straps used for locking an electrode to an extremity should be rinsed with germicidal solution and thoroughly dried.

Blanket sterilization. Simply washing a blanket is inadequate. However, if a 2 percent solution of o-phenylophenol and p-tertiary amylphenol (trade name Amphyl or Lysol) is added to the rinse water of the laundry washing cycle, the problem of blankets holding bacteria is averted.

Dry brooms, dry mops, wet mops, and dusters. Mops, dust rags, and straw brooms are nothing but breeding places for bacteria. Worse than this they simply spread infective organisms around in clouds of dust. The wet mop slops them around as well. Eliminate this method of cleaning. Vacuum everything first and be certain that your vacuum has a cleanable filter system. Then use a mechanical scrubber on everything with a strong germicidal-detergent solution.

Wastebaskets. Line all containers with throwaway plastic bags. If the budget won't permit that, simply use large grocery bags. Scrub and rinse the inside of all waste containers regularly with germicide. *Do not rely on spray cans to do the job*! Their nebulous spray is inadequate.

Laundry hampers. All laundry hampers in the athletic plant are continuously full of dirt and germs. Line them with plastic throwaway bags before permitting laundry to be thrown in them.

Visitors. Since visitors cannot be decontaminated, to keep the training room free from external contamination as much as possible, keep a large sign posted: *"Visitors Not Allowed!"*

Training table pads and sheets. Don't rely on an ultraviolet machine or airing to do a "sterilizing" job. Neither will do so. Scrub all pads and mats with germicide and permit them to dry in the sun.

Vacuum cleaners. Most vacuum cleaners are spreaders of contamination. Make sure they have a filtration system, or they will fill the air continually with waste.

Gauze mask ruling. To prevent the spread of colds and influenza by coughing and sneezing, put "surgical" masks on all players with colds or flu who are indoors.

Fans and air conditioners. Mechnical devices that keep air moving may also be spreading bacteria and spores, as they do in hospitals. Where such equipment is used it should have an air filter attached. The filter should be cleaned regularly.

Shoes, pants cuffs. The moment anyone with shoes on walks into a trainer's room from the outside, he is shipping in contamination that will be spread to the barefoot athletes making the same excursion. To prevent this problem, the athlete should wear clogs. They're better then nothing. Clogs, and their thongs, must be kept fairly free of bacteria by frequently soaking them in germicide solution. The trainer should not have cuffs on his trousers; they are constant holders and dispensers of microorganisms.

The washing-down process. The necessity to wash walls and floors regularly is obvious. What is not so obvious to the uninitiated is that mechanical washers are the more effective in coping with a sanitation process.

Germicides alone are not always effective. The use of chlorinated compounds, phenolated detergents, or even benzalkonium chloride, are only partially effective used alone. They do not get through the accumulated debris or into the cracks. Quite often they even fail to penetrate the surface tension and this makes scrubbing an act of necessity.

4

THE GAME

Strategy Covered:

- *Pregame procedures for injury prevention*
- *Halftime prevention procedures*
- *Food control for athletes*
- *Conditioning, drills, and warm-ups*
- *Injuries and heat*
- *Weight loss and other warning signs*
- *Field controls*
- *The transportation problem*
- *The gridiron and the bleachers*

PREGAME PROCEDURES FOR INJURY PREVENTION

The following suggestions are not hard and fast rules. They are simply common sense procedures based on experience that have been found to be practical and workable. They are as follows:

1. *Prohibit pregame sightseeing tours.* Make sure the athlete gets a rest period before the game and has had at least eight hours sleep the night before.

2. *Eating on Game Day* should go like this:

   Morning: Up early, *big* wholesome breakfast, tape athletes if taping is necessary.

   Luncheon: Light. No meals for at least four hours before a game. A boy plays better on an empty stomach. The cliché that an athlete should have a thick steak before a game is ridiculous. This is false, misleading, and makes him less capable of performance. (Stop and remember how lazy you felt after that last big meal you had.)

   Dinner: After the game, moderate.

3. *Suit up at least forty-five minutes before game time.* Have your trainer check out all tape jobs for security and comfort. Apply wraps where necessary. The trainer and/or the equipment manager should also check out helmets and other gear, replacing damaged equipment.

4. *All emergency equipment and personnel should be immediately available.* The team physician should be called earlier to assure his attendance on the bench.

5. *Have a complete squad warm-up before game time.* Stretch those muscles! Get adrenalin flowing. Get the boys sweating and charged up. *Then keep them under wraps* until time to go.

6. *A salt-down and vitamin C should be administered at least an hour before game time.* Avoid letting the boys drink large amounts of water. Body salts don't need dilution at this time, and the sodium chloride balance has to be maintained.

7. *Permit no visitors in the locker room or clubhouse.* Screen out everyone! Permit only necessary personnel. Too often disaster-merchants destroy the players' peace of mind.

8. *Mild pregame rubdowns may be administered via the "buddy system."* (At no time is a massage or rubdown to be construed as taking the place of the warm-up!) This not only keeps the boys mutually occupied but is also invigorating.

9. *Additional pregame fortification may be given with vitamin B complex and honey.* Lemon juice or vitamin C liquid with the bioflavonoids may be added.

10. *Recheck all emotional problems.* The trainer is the in-man in the locker and training room. Let him be your conning tower into the emotional status of your squad.

11. *For "psych value" a coach should not see his squad until just moments before the game.* He should make his entrance, deliver his message and rejoice in how beautifully this method works. It's the Prevent-System in action!

HALFTIME PREVENTION PROCEDURES

Indoctrinate players on the psychological necessity of moving off the field looking as fresh as when they came on to it. This not only deceives the opposing team, but is also a great preventive against deflation of team spirit. On entering the locker room, the injured should report immediately to the trainer or team doctor. Cold wet towels should be issued to be wrapped around the neck or applied to the base of the skull. Neck and shoulder muscles may be massaged by the buddy system before the athlete lies down on blankets which have been laid on the floor. Permit no players to sit on benches with their legs drawn up under them or to sit down on wet ground, wet straw, or on bare cement flooring. After the buddy system neck massage, the assistant trainer should issue honey and B-complex liquid in tea or lemonade. Dispense oranges to those who want them. Give personalized attention; it shows that you care. As for liquids, I suggest that carbonated beverages or cola drinks be *eliminated.* They are *not refreshing* as advertised; they are palatable, but that's all. They do not provide quick energy! Instead they promote a thick mucous slime in the mouth and throat leading to "dry mouth" or "cotton mouth" which is a mucous membrane injury in itself.

FOOD CONTROL FOR ATHLETES

Depending on your school of thought and personal biases, you may or may not advocate a controlled food schedule for athletes. You may be one of those hiding behind the statement: "The American diet provides everything a person needs." Many people are becoming more and more aware that this is far from the truth. All federal agencies today admit that our foods do not provide what we need and this is especially true of athletes. In designing food control procedures for the football player there are many facts to be considered.

Top research men such as Thomas K. Cureton have found, for example, that wheat germ, which contains a large amount of vitamin E, is an asset to swimmers for endurance. Vitamin B complex is a necessity in all sports activities, as are amino acids, those protein-building-blocks of the body. Vitamin C and the bioflavonoids may be used as a preventive against contusions and aid healing. Vitamin C is also necessary for building resistance against infections and colds. Vitamins A and D are also part of the Prevent-System and should be studied for their values to sports and sports injuries.

Meal Suggestions

It is abnormal to load the body with "three square meals a day." However, school hours, jobs, etc., set the pattern so that food is consumed at given hours, whereas for best assimilation meals should actually be eaten in smaller quantities more often. Foods eaten at breakfast usually do not make their energy available until afternoon. A big breakfast is therefore a necessity. Early morning workouts may find an athlete at his lowest ebb despite the coolness of the morning. In the afternoon a player always demonstrates a slump if his breakfast has been sparse. It might be noted that a more steady flow of energy is maintained when five or six lesser meals are eaten in a day. The digestive system is better able to cope with smaller amounts. No lethargy follows. Most of all, the multiple smaller meals are more apt to efficiently serve athletic requirement.

Getting Parent Cooperation on Food Control

The training table in college, or even in pro ranks, may be used effectively to control "bad" eating habits. At high school level, however, parents must be advised about nutrition for athletes. Despite protests to the contrary, most homes provide an almost completely inadequate diet for a child engaging in strenuous sports. Thus, it is advisable for the trainer to give a preseason talk to parent groups. Parents should be advised not only on what kinds of foods to serve but *when* the athlete should eat his or her bigger meals. If a family is known to be without funds arrange for the athlete to get a job in the lunchroom or school cafeteria so that he or she can get better meals. Remember that *a stomach should be empty before* and during games. This also holds true of practices. Eating should not take place for at least four hours before a game for the sake of the game and the player.

Controlling Early-Season Weight Gain

1. Weigh all athletes in at the beginning of each season as part of the preseason physical examination.

2. Sound out the players' attitudes on food and conditioning. Are they ready and willing to cooperate in the food control program?

3. Black and white printed instructions should be issued by the trainer on food during his preseason trainers talk.

4. Send a letter home to all parents (of high school students) indicating the need for quality nutrition. Indicate that good food doesn't have to be expensive, just wholesome. All families do not have big allowances for food, so be diplomatic.

5. Indoctrinate the athlete to the habit of eating several small meals instead of three big ones a day.

Clint Thompson of the Department of Athletics, Colorado State University advocates that the stomach be comparatively empty at event times and that the pre-event meal should consist of nutritious foods that leave the stomach rapidly. Such foods are *soup, fruit juices, cereals, bread, candy* (carbohydrates), *lean meats,* and *puddings.* He recommends that the meal should include nothing which leads to the formation of intestinal gas or distress and that drinking large amounts of liquid at meal time be stopped because liquids tend to delay digestion. In the wake of traditional approaches to diets for athletes many fallacies and fads continue. Thompson suggests that the athlete should eat what he knows will best agree with him. However, Thompson adds, there are very few athletes who know what is best to take care of their needs.[1] Because of this I devised the following menu: (see Figure 4-1)

The pregame meal should not only satisfy appetite but should digest easily, go through the stomach without complication, provide nutrition, and be palatable. Such a meal lowers the probability of pregame vomiting and the accompanying feeling of nausea. Because of pregame tension and its concomitant vomiting and diarrhea, the athlete not only loses any food that has been eaten but also becomes dehydrated and experiences all the symptoms that indicate salt deficiency. In one vomiting session a player may lose up to a pound or more of water. With this may come a feeling of weakness, abdominal cramps, or leg cramps; any one of these problems may take him out of the game. So why gamble on losing a boy because of traditional thinking, or because of a pregame meal that doesn't adapt to the physiology of the boy or the psychology of the game? To feed him immediately before a game may not only take him out of the competition, but make him more susceptible to injury. This is not prevention!

As a rich source of immediately available carbohydrates there are various pregame liquid meals that are easily available and are easy to transport. These liquid meals should be given to athletes two to four hours before a game in place of conventional food. One warning: Read

[1] C. Thompson, "A Brief Evaluation of Certain Athletic Dietary Practices," *Journal of the NATA,* Winter 1969.

RECOMMENDED GAME-DAY MEALS FOR ATHLETES

BREAKFAST

* Fruit - grapefruit, oranges, apples, prunes, etc.

* Fresh juices - from all fruits and vegetables. Do not serve canned or frozen juices that contain preservatives or other additives. They may be easy to transport and serve, but they are not good for athletes.

* Meats - ham or bacon in small portions, lean steak, well done in 4 to 6 ounce portions.

LUNCH

* Soup

* Beef or steak - Roasted or broiled, but no fried meats or gravies.

* Vegetables - all kinds.

* Toast and jelly

* Light dessert

* Cheese - if desired.

* Milk and/or tea

PREGAME MEAL
(two to four hours before game)

* Poached egg on a thin slice of toast

* Dry toast

* Fruit salad

* Tea or milk - one serving.

* Cool water - no iced!

* Chocolate bar - if desired.

Figure 4-1

the label on the container! If that pregame liquid is rampant with artificial additives, forget it. Beware, too, of synthetic vitamins. They are the same in formula as a natural vitamin, true, but the body doesn't know this. Foisting synthetics in concentrated doses on the liver and kidneys is a contribution to future physiological disaster.

Travel Hazards and Food Control

Food poisoning raises its ugly head when least desirable on road trips and away games. The cramps, nausea, vomiting, chills, and diarrhea that knock a squad out may come unsuspected and unchallenged in contaminated meat, canned juices, or beverages. It may come as a result of bacteria causing botulism or in a chemical spray that has been used on foods to prevent spoilage and make them more stable in shipment. Plant parasites may also contribute to food poisoning.

To prevent food poisoning on roadtrips it is vital for the trainer to assure in advance that the water and milk supplies are state tested and approved, that restaurants are dependable, and that there are no foods on the menu of these restaurants such as ham salad, chicken salad, or tuna salad. These all contain mayonnaise which can too easily become contaminated and are on my hate list. Orange drinks, root beer, and cream sodas have also consistently given my boys problems.

Chemical Food Additives That Can Cause Poisoning

At the risk of being called a food-faddist and crackpot I want to mention man-made "preservatives" in food that should be known to and avoided by everyone. Everyone, that is, who is interested in prevention. The criminal chemicals with which many foods are endowed are as follows: acidifiers, antioxidants, alkalyzers, bleaches, buffers, deodorants, disinfectants, drying agents, dyes, emulsifiers, artificial flavors, fortifiers, fungicides, gases (agene, phosgene, etc.), maturers, sweeteners (other than sugar), thickeners, and artificial vitamins in so-called "health drinks."

The United States Food and Drug Administration commissioner George Larrick warns that *there is always residual risk in permitting the use of even small quantities of poisons in foods* and no one can possibly know what new and dangerous compounds may result from chemical combinations that are mixed in the human stomach as the result of taking in so many additives. So-called "harmless chemicals" may combine into complex and disastrous compounds that can become poisons and may cause vomiting, diarrhea, and nausea. Today the FDA reports that 1500 known chemicals are dumped into foods such as bread, milk, cheese, vegetables, candy, desserts, and fruits. Each amount of foreign chemicals in one package may seem small enough, and in itself may be "nontoxic," but when these preservatives are united with other additives, they become destructive. They are filtered out and stored in the liver and kidneys and can trigger the beginning of chronic disease.

Nature will do its best to eliminate poisons from the body by vomiting and diarrhea. When this begins the trainer should pinpoint the source of the problem as quickly as possible. He should get this information to the team physician immediately. When poisons are absorbed, however, and get to the kidneys and liver, they are "in." Thus the trainer must not only be concerned with short-term toxicity, but also with the long-term and more to be feared end-products of food additives. He *has* to be concerned despite those who will charge him with being a food-faddist and call him other inappropriate names. The enterprising trainer should be interested in male and female athletes and in prevention of injury and illness all the way. His duties and responsibilities lie in more than adhesive tape and arnica. These responsibilities extend to what the athlete eats, what he drinks, and every other Prevent-System procedure vital to his welfare. All of this is just as important as conditioning, drills, warm-ups, and chalk talks.

CONDITIONING, DRILLS, AND WARM-UPS

After the preseason physical and athletic examination have been passed, and the welcome mat to the practice sessions has been laid out, the training and conditioning program begins. The second line of defense against injury begins right here. The conditioning program that is set into motion is another facet of the Prevent-System that guarantees a better season and should be the beginning of a continuous program that goes 365 days a year. A team is no better than its collective conditioning and no stronger then the men on the squad who are its weakest links. The story is told about Bobby Layne who took a rookie out for an all-night bash. They were back in time for morning workouts. Bleary-eyed they went into the washroom. Bobby sprinkled water on his face, put on his gear, and headed for the field. He gave his usual whirlwind performance. His young friend went out on the field and collapsed. Layne stood over him, and shook his head. "The trouble with you," he said, "is that you are out of shape!"

The Bobby Laynes and the Babe Ruths are the exceptions to the rule. Physical conditioning cannot be violated by the average person. The average individual needs a perpetual training program to develop endurance, speed, agility, specialized function, and muscle and joint suppleness. All-year-round conditioning is necessary. This was pointed out specifically in a lecture by Dr. H. Royer Collins, head of the Sports Medicine Clinic at Cleveland Clinic in Ohio.

> As with most injuries and illnesses the best treatment in sports is prevention. This can best be accomplished by proper, gradual conditioning with emphasis not only on building muscle mass but also increasing endurance, increasing the range of motion by stretching exercises, and agility drills. The musculotendonous unit should be loosened up with warm-up drills and proper techniques of running.[2]

Conditioning means training, and training should be undertaken by desire as well as by design. High morale and spirit are a consequence of good training habits, and winning becomes a natural consequence as well. When athletes are filled with the desire to win, the physical conditioning program is less difficult. For the best sports performance, conditioning has to be an all-year-round procedure and to this there is no alternative when you're thinking about cutting down injuries or preventing them. The secret of prevention lies in the conditioning program which makes the athlete less prone to injury. He is less accident-prone. He accommodates to emergency. He adapts to stress without loss of continuity of muscle, tendon, ligament, or motion.

No athlete must under any circumstances, be permitted in active competition if he is physically unfit. To subject an unconditioned athlete to the explosive stress of football may set up a chain of disasters. Each link may be small but all links lead finally to physical breakdown. It may mean destruction. It may mean the loss of the boy to all sports in the future or have medical and/or legal repercussions. It may defeat everything for which football stands.

Capacity to Condition

There is a variation in the ability and capacity of athletes to become conditioned for performance. Often it is this variable in the rate of training that makes a difference in the player's readiness for athletic action. The degree of "readiness" may also predict the number of injuries, and readiness for action can be charted. I divide athletes into two classifications for this purpose as far as *readiness* is concerned. Athletes may be classified in terms of *slow tempo* and *fast tempo* conditioners. Here's what I'm talking about.

Slow Tempo Athletes:

1. Slow tempo athletes take longer to case-harden.
2. They demand more personal attention.
3. When they hit peak they remain there with few deviations.
4. They remain faithful to sleep schedules, diet, and stick to schedules.

[2] H.R. Collins, author's lecture notes

5. Slow tempo athletes need a longer preseason workout. They should have at least eight to ten weeks of preseason conditioning before being permitted to play.

6. Their training work load should begin small and build gradually toward a maximum.

FAST TEMPO ATHLETES:

1. The fast tempo athletes take a shorter time to get into top condition.

2. They have less endurance than slow tempo athletes.

3. They have a greater tendency to become prima donnas.

4. Their improvement at a given position is faster.

5. They tend to get injured because they tire quickly of routine and rigid training. When they break training they get injured.

6. Their best performance is never constant.

7. As the season wears on the fast tempo athlete's interest and go-power tend to peter out. It is during this let down that he becomes accident-prone.

Injuries incident to Phase One adjustment to all stress can be cut down appreciably through the all-year-round training or conditioning program. They can be substantially lowered by maintaining physical fitness through (1) participation in other sports, (2) a daily weight-training program, (3) a daily running schedule such as the Fartlek or other system, (4) remaining on a high protein (amino acid building blocks) food control program.

Injuries incident to the Phase Three "letdown" may be avoided by giving the boy a surprise rest, cutting down heavy workouts, stepping up psychological techniques for morale building, anticipating the letdown by warning the athlete against it early in the season, loosening up on rigid rules which offend the prima donna looking for an excuse to "goof off" or kick over the traces of routine, and, using the athlete in key situations only if his endocrine cycle is at its peak.

Endocrine Glands: Controllers of Athletic Action

Both slow and fast tempo athletes have their ups and down in conditioning and I believe that some of this rise and fall in performance is partially controlled by endocrine action. The athlete, of course, is completely unaware of this monthly cycle. Too often the word "overtraining"

THREE PHASES IN THE ATHLETIC
CONDITIONING AND PERFORMANCE CYCLE

PHASE ONE: Pretraining Adjustment	This period should be elongated to adjust the player to the sport. This is especially true for "slow tempo" athletes (see above). How well a player adjusts mentally and physically in preseason training determines his capacity to perform and the number of injuries he will sustain during the season.
PHASE TWO: Conditioning, Maintenance, and Top Performance	In this phase the athlete is adjusted to routine. He adapts to new functions without tiring. His training and conditioning schedule can be less rigorous. He is strictly on a maintenance schedule that keeps him ready for top performance.
PHASE THREE: Performance Decline	Once the conditioning peak has been reached the athlete tends to level off, affecting the perfect polish of Phase Two. "Seasonal letdown" sets in. The problem is more mental than physical. Lethargy prevails. It is at this time that the incidence of injury is high!

Figure 4-2

is applied to an athlete who has actually reached a turn in his endocrine cycle, which moves in a twenty-eight day rhythm, and these cycles in the male make a swing just as in a female menstrual cycle. During the "lows" he is not at his emotional or physical best. During his highs he can whip the world. He can meet any stress.

The stress factor, says the renowned physiologist Hans Selye, is dependent on the ability of the pituitary and adrenal gland to adapt to stress. The action of the pituitary and adrenal glands is further enhanced by thyroxin, the hormone from the thyroid gland. The thyroid, once called the racehorse of the body, plays an active role in the performance cycle and the alert trainer can plot out the athlete's peak periods each day, week, and month because these peaks and lows are prominent and methodically regular. As a result, the "high periods" can be anticipated. You will know exactly when a boy is going to be at his peak. He will be riding the crest of euphoria and will be in the best of condition. He will be less susceptible to injury and less negligent about training habits. His digestive system will be capable of consuming boiler-plating and he will run three miles "just for fun." He will be capable of taking on heavier training assignments, learn plays faster, and he can be depended upon to be mentally alert. By setting up such a biorhythm chart and studying it, you will suddenly become aware of why the boy acts the way he does. Suddenly a lot of unanswered questions will have answers. Suddenly you will find yourself capable of predicting his ups and downs and you'll say "For Pete's sake, it works!"

Calisthenics in Athletic Training

Calisthenics exercises are individual activities designed to train and develop the body when performed repeatedly with purpose. There are specific objectives in such a physical training program. Elementary as these objectives appear to be, let's catalog them just to refresh memory.

Calisthenics develop agility and flexibility. They develop strength, power, endurance, and resistance. Calisthenics are instrumental in improving posture and body symmetry, as well as body metabolism and the function of body organs. Calisthenics step up and adjust the cardiac system to the action of the respiratory system. The purpose of calisthenics is to prepare the body for any specialized action in sports and make the athlete less prone to injury.

Warming Up

No pitcher goes to the mound without warming up. Yet time after time athletes in many other sports are thrown into a crucial action "cold," and their failure to be ready for best performance not only makes them less adequate to cover their assignment and meet emergency but also makes them more susceptible to injury. Many a benchwarmer thrown in at the last minute has been blamed for the loss of a game when the fault lay not with the boy but with his body's lack of readiness. Many a sub sent into the game has been promptly injured for the same reason.

The degree of warming up needed as a prerequisite to athletic action is determined by the strenuousness of the event, the condition of the athlete, and his capacity to handle exercise. It must be noted that there are two kinds of exercise: the nonfatiguing warm-up exercises which stretch muscles, and the exercises which build muscles and are capable of straining or fatiguing them. Both forms of exercise are meant to reduce injury by promoting healthy physiologic action, raising the physical capacity for performance, and maintaining maximum efficiency. With this improvement comes better circulation in the blood and lymph vessels and better adrenalin flow, and a new sense of innate rhythm and coordination, and along with the stretching of the joint capsules and the loosening of the muscles come endurance and stamina. This is injury prevention at work! (See Figure 4-3 for suggested warm-up exercises.)

FOUR PHASES OF WARM-UPS

PHASE ONE	Running until perspiring
PHASE TWO	1. Foot rotation 2. Hip and waist rotation 3. Back bending and arching 4. Head and neck rotation 5. Tumbling: rolls and somersaults 6. Hurdlers stretch Note: No knee bends!
PHASE THREE	Heavier exercises: 1. High kicks 2. Push-ups 3. Sit-ups 4. Four-point crouch starts, only if knee and thigh permit and never in early season 5. Chinning and arm suspension from horizontal bar Repeat entire routine as endurance develops.
PHASE FOUR	The resting stage should include walking and/or sitting with the legs extended.

Figure 4-3

Warm-ups can be injurious! Admittedly not all exercising is good. Exercising can be injurious (1) when neither the coach nor the athlete knows the participant's physical capacity, (2) when too strenuous warm-ups cause overfatigue, (3) when fast movements are overemphasized, (4) when muscles are stretched beyond their elasticity, (5) and when muscles are strained beyond the strength and/or body weight of the athlete. *The warm-up should be progressive!* The athlete should begin exercises slowly but vigorously and continue until the muscles are supple, flexible, and loose. The warm-up should include slow stretching movements for all tight and little-used muscles.

14 DON'TS to Keep in Mind When Warming Up Your Squad

Don't use fast movements that strain muscles, tendons, ligaments, or other soft tissue joint structures.

Don't stretch muscles to the point where an antagonistic muscle is pulled. Muscles pulled past their elasticity will tear.

Don't permit warm-ups unless the athlete is under wraps.

Don't let the athlete rest in the sun or on benches with his legs drawn under and back.

Don't make the athlete snap the body forward when touching toes. It should all be one free-flowing motion.

Don't allow the athlete to do deep knee bends!

Don't require any early season crouches or fast starts.

Don't ask for speed running at the beginning of practice sessions.

Don't use slow exercises on speed-runners. Backfield men get a different kind of warm-up.

Don't allow any prolonged rest period after a warm-up. Send the boys directly into football drills.

Don't rush your warm-up program! Use moderation and your boys will get there soon enough, without injuries!

Don't permit an athlete to wear any kind of warm-up clothing that makes him feel cold and clammy when he begins to perspire. (Rayon and nylon, etc., are offenders.)

Don't allow any more than four minutes between warm-up and performance at a game.

Don't permit massage or medication to take the place of the warm-up at any time!

11-Point Prevention Program for Early Season Stiffness

Early season stiffness is an athletic injury that can be prevented. The following eleven-point program is recommended to circumvent this problem.

Point 1: Maintain an all-year-round conditioning program.

Point 2: Maintain a year-round running schedule and run, run, run!

Point 3: Complete warm-ups prevent stiffness. Many early season injuries are caused by inadequate warm-ups. Muscle "pull" and muscle fatigue, tearing, and inability to stretch stem from the player's inadequate preparation for action. Once again, the first answer to this is an all-year-round conditioning program. The second answer is "plenty of stretching exercises" until the player is warm and ready to go.

Point 4: Prevent chilling. When the athlete is not in action keep him moving under wraps. Enforce this rule. If a boy shows fatigue or some functional limitation, send him to the showers. Don't risk early season injuries by permitting him to chill while hanging around the field. Allowing him to do so also results in stiffness.

Point 5: Make sure a player gets a mild massage after each workout. This alleviates stiffness. Lactic acid and other waste is expelled from the musculature. Massage may be done by the trainer but should preferably be done via a buddy system in which the boys work on each other *after* the trainer shows them what to do and how to do it. Massage should start at the feet and fingertips and work in toward the heart.

Point 6: Stress showering habits to avoid stiffness. Warm showers should begin with a soap massage from the feet up. Follow this rub with a warm rinse followed by a *cold* rinse. As a prevention procedure I've found it wise to check the boys out for cool skin as they exit from the shower room. This cooling-out process is just as vital for football players as it is for racehorses. It's a must in preventing stiffness.

Point 7: Prevent wet-heads from going out on cold days. Departure from the locker room and clubhouse with a wet head and skimpy clothing too often lays the groundwork for muscle stiffness. It's also an open door policy to flu and colds. Unnecessary exposure after a strenuous workout and shower accents muscle fatigue and early season stiffness.

Point 8: Regulate early season workouts to the condition and size of the participant. Place candidates in their own weight and class. Never expect grade-A performance from a regular grade-C performer. Overworking that grade-C performer exposes him automatically to hazard and injury. One of those hazards is early season stiffness.

Point 9: Make regular pre-, post-, and mid-season physical examinations pay off. That "stiffness" may be something other than what it appears to be.

Point 10: Dietary supplements such as vitamins and minerals should be administered as a preventive against stiffness. No conditioning program should be without supplements. The average American diet does not give the athlete what he needs! It's a no-man's land of vitamin and mineral destitution, and nutritional experts are beginning to admit it with grave concern. Nutritionist June Gibbs at the University of Arizona warns about tampering with the diets of athletes. She indicates that this is especially true at the high school level. Ms. Gibbs claims that football players are gorged on calorie-loaded, unbalanced diets to keep them within weight ranges designated by the coach. Sometimes the boys are placed on unusual diets to lose weight. These practices seriously impair the physical fitness and future health of the young persons involved. With vitamin C always give salt as replacement therapy for loss of sodium chloride on hot days. When nutrition is out of balance so are the athlete's muscles. They simply get stiff when used.

Point 11: Indoctrinate your squad on "graduated exercising" all year round. Staying in good shape all year is one of the preventives for early season stiffness. When the athlete is at "go," the incidence of injury drops dramatically. There are fewer men on the sick list or riding the bench. To maintain this level of readiness have all football participants do gymnastics, wrestling, swimming, weight-training, isometrics, and handball. Keep them busy at all times. Avoid those few high-stress weeks of crash conditioning and drills.

Luckily changes are being made in this area. Two- and three-week crash programs are being prohibited. For example, the Alabama State Medical Association has gone to bat on this matter. On recommendation of the Committee on the Medical Aspects of Sports, the Alabama High School Athletic Association adopted a ruling that any school practice or assembly may be held during summer months, provided that the equipment used for football is not used. A New York club, with former Fordham University trainer Johnny Dziegel as its head trainer, has set up a physical fitness department. The all-year-round program includes rehabilitation therapy, weight-training, and isometric drills. As a result there is little or no preseason stiffness.

How to Recognize and Prevent Staleness

An athlete should build up to maximum performance gradually. When he overextends himself and his capabilities, he not only sets the stage for injury but he becomes subject to a lot of bad habits and a problem called "staleness." Athletes who run all-out in practice sessions early in the week may never recover for the weekend game. Athletes who go stale have a slump mentally as well as in performance. To diagnose staleness in an athlete look for: listless action, exhaustion, easy tiring, drawn face, disinterest in the sport, loss of appetite, "worrying about nothing," insomnia, and weight loss. Recognize the problem for what it is and not for what it appears to be. That appearance of "staleness" may be the beginning of an illness.

Too often, when an athlete's weight goes down, the tendency is to say that the boy has "gone stale." This may be partially true, but it may also not be true at all. A number of other problems may be occurring concurrently. One of these problems may be that of the thyroid "low." The thyroid, an endocrine gland at the base of the throat, operates on a twenty-eight day cycle, as indicated earlier. As the "racehorse of the body" it creates highs and lows in emotional and physical levels. A thyroid "low" does not necessarily mean a deficiency. It merely means that the athlete is at the bottom of a traceable cycle. His metabolism is low. Everything is low including his morale. However, the moment he starts on the upswing of the next cycle he readjusts and feels great again. Metabolism is reestablished. The emotional factor readjusts. The boy is no longer stale. His edge is back. By making a graph on these ups and downs you can actually predict when the boy will be at his best and when he is going to go "stale."

Getting an athlete up for a contest is often a necessity, but one that has to be kept under control. Remember that when edge is prolonged it also becomes devitalizing. More then one team has maintained its edge all season and then lost it just before the state championship finals to go down to ignominious defeat with everyone wondering why. An emotional high can wear a boy out even before the game begins. Because of this, an athlete should be kept busy with activities rather than lectures and chalk-talks before a game to avoid pregame tension. He should have no work-outs but he should do something that keeps his mind occupied. For want of something better, bed him down three hours before the game. If he's the nervous type permit him to read or watch a calm television show. He should not eat. Before the game he should be given a ration of orange juice and a peppermint tablet, a little praise, and some psychological buildup. This should be followed by a rigorous warm-up to get the adrenalin flowing. A stimulating massage may be added to the routine. Do this and the boy will be ready. He'll have his edge.

Road Trips and Edge

To some boys, road trips are exhausting. To others a road trip stimulates. All this is part of individual personality. To find a means of making sure that no one loses his edge during a road trip it is unwise to unload from the bus, train, or plane right into the stadium for a game. Plan your trips away so that the squad is there well in advance. A light meal two to four hours *before* the game is advisable, followed by walking back to the hotel, motel, bus, or stadium. Sightseeing is temporarily avoided and everything that can contribute to friction or disagreement is studiously avoided. Trips away are hazard courses that kill edge. Remember that no boy is mentally or physically ready for a game after riding for a long distance on any kind of conveyance. With this in mind, the game should be booked or arranged to give the athletes time to recuperate from the ride as well as from the pregame practice sessions. This holds true especially when athletes are taken from moderate to warm climates or from low altitudes to higher altitudes. Conveyances used for the trip should be big and roomy. No cramped quarters!

Fast Way to Stimulate Athlete With Lost Edge

1. Cold fast shower, with a sharp impact of hard spray on the back, or an ice rub.
2. A brisk rubdown with toweling.
3. A hot pack on the back of the neck.
4. A liniment rub on the calves of the legs.
5. An overall massage immediately *before* the game.

INJURIES AND HEAT

According to Thomas E. Shaffer, M.D., Director of the Division of Adolescent Medicine at Ohio State University,

> The development of ways to prevent illness and death from the effects of heat is, in my opinion, the outstanding advance in sports medicine during the past five years. Deaths from heat stroke occur among sports participants every year. In 1969 there were six such fatalities in football in the United States. We now have definite measures to prevent these fatalities and less serious disorders due to heat, but unfortunately they are not known or they are not carried out. . . . Illness due to heat can be prevented by gradually acclimatizing athletes to hot weather through limited workouts in the hot part of the day; by insisting on frequent replacement, on the field, of fluid lost by sweating; by increased salt intake, and by paying careful attention several times a day to the temperature and humidity on the playing field. Humidity is measured by a wet-bulb thermometer, and when this is above 70°F strenuous prolonged workouts must be scheduled in the cooler times of the day, with light weight clothing.[3]

[3] T.E. Shaffer, *Medicine in Sports Newsletter* 10 (July 1970), p. 1.

David G. Moyer, M.D., Medical Director of Germantown Academy and team physician at Lafayette College, had this to say: "Though it would appear that knowledge of water balance and prevention of heat prostration have finally gotten past the horse and buggy stage, the state of one's team in hot weather is still a great cause of concern."[4]

Dr. Moyer feels that constant methods of prevention are in order. He advocates a ceaseless vigilance because of the longer seasons, preseason scrimmages under game conditions, and warm climates. In hot weather the big boys have to be watched constantly. Heavy interior linemen have less evaporative surface for cooling off. The bulk-boys should be watched both on and off the field and given additional education on hydrating themselves and "salting down." Strongly advocated by Dr. Moyer are mesh jerseys, proper fluid and salt intake (salt taken twelve hours before game time), replacing the salt and fluid losses, and cooling-out at rest time.

Hot days are hard on the bulky boys in any league. It's even harder on the player who is unconditioned and getting older. At the pro camps during early season training it's not uncommon to see veterans in that first week of training camp doubled up along the edge of the field. Dry heaves shake their bodies. Even worse than the dry heaves is the scorn hurled by those who go unaffected by the heat or are in good physical condition. Too often this problem is looked upon by an athlete's peers as a sign of personal weakness.

Symptoms and Results of Salt Loss

Sweating and fitness go hand in glove. Chief of the Institute of Sports Medicine at Charles University in Prague, Dr. Jiri Kral, indicates that his studies show a definite relationship between physical fitness and perspiration. He discloses that the well-trained and fit athlete with a low pulse rate sweats while performing a great deal more than does the unconditioned or unfit person.[5] As part of your Prevent-System always remember that there is a definite relationship between salt loss and body temperature. In heat prostration (or heat exhaustion), however, the temperature may remain at normal, but the athlete has other complaints. In graph form here's what to look for in your prevention system:

[4] D.G. Moyer, "Sideline Observation," *Journal of the NATA* 5, no. 3 (Fall 1970), p. 22.

[5] J. Kral, "Sweating and Fitness," *Aerospace Medicine* 39, October 1968, pp. 1101–4.

HOW TO READ
SYMPTONS OF SALT LOSS

Percent of Salt Loss	Athlete's Complaint	Body Temperature. When This Occurs
5	Weariness	Normal
10-20	Very tired Lacks desire Lacks energy	Normal
30	Dizziness Nausea Headache	Normal
40	Cramps in abdomen and limbs	Normal
50	Circulatory collapse	Normal

Figure 4-4

Watch for drug users!

This point alone is worth the price of the book! Many drugs are used and misused, some of them by prescription. We're concerned with *antihistamines.* These drugs, used for allergies (hay fever, etc.), change the blood chemistry and affect the vasomotor system. *They suppress the sweating mechanism* and that's when heat and humidity close in on the athlete. Heat stroke is inevitable! To prevent the problem check with *all* athletes about drug intake. Consult their records to determine previous users and what the prescription is. Warn against antihistamines and other drugs being used in hot weather.

Peak performance in football depends on the player's natural defenses working normally. Where there is interference with the thermal regulatory center (the hypothalamus) in the brain, for example, a host of reactions are set into motion. "Two percent of the body weight is available for normal sweating. When this amount is used up the shut down of sweating becomes your alarm signal. Venous pressure goes up, cardiac output goes down, and heat finds no outlet through the normal cooling system of the skin." [6]

Prevent-System Procedures for Heat Stroke

When the regulating mechanism (hypothalamus), which triggers heat loss is not functioning adequately, the athlete becomes progressively more susceptible to heat stroke, in the form of sun stroke, heat cramps, or heat exhaustion (heat prostration) in direct proportion to the response of his physical conditioning, the length and intensity of his workout, the clothes he wears, his physical condition, and the environment temperature and humidity to which he is being subjected.

Heat stroke may quickly be fatal. The following signs may be precursors to death no matter whether they appear on the playing field, in the trainer's room, or in the hospital. These signs are: *fever, lost consciousness, warm and dry skin, headache, confusion, dizziness, lack of coordination, and faintness.* Particular preseason conditions lead to heat stroke. All members of the football squad should be made aware of the fact that heat stroke may be brought on by easy summer living, getting too fat, being overweight, working the summer months in air conditioning, or switching to a different climate and overworking without making the necessary acclimatizing transition.

To help prevent heat stroke issue lightweight whites for hot sunny and muggy days. Give salt tablets before practices and games. Permit controlled water drinking during practices and games. Stop all water drinking if cramps begin. Cancel out practices and games or practices on hot humid days (more about this later). Wear lightweight caps with bills to keep sun off face and head. Cut down calisthenics, have more stretching exercises. Between practice sessions have boys strip to trunks for dry towel rubdown and to don dry T-shirts. The athletes' diet should be low in fat, high in protein. Supplement with vitamin C and the bioflavanoids.

[6] Article from Becton-Dickinson Products publication entitled "Man, Sweat, and Performance," December 1969, p. 5.

Higher temperatures cause the human heat regulating apparatus to go into a state of malfunctioning because *body heat is not lost.* Normal methods of dissipating heat by conduction, convection, and radiation are inhibited or lost when air temperatures rise above 82°F. This leaves only sweating and evaporation as a heat regulator. If the ability of the sweat glands to function in cooling the athlete is inhibited, dehydration and vasomotor collapse become a possibility. To prevent this influence of the external environment on the athlete, here are some procedures as derived from many interviews with coaches, trainers, team doctors, and from experience.

The prime rules for countering heat injury are: (1) Don't play a tired athlete in hot weather; (2) Schedule games to avoid hot areas; (3) Stick to temperatures and altitudes to which your athletes are adapted. If a game has to be scheduled in a warmer, moister climate, or if you hit a hot spell in your own zone, get your boys acclimatized with regular short workouts. This may take weeks. During workouts keep them in lightweight whites (shorts, T-shirts, and sneakers). Have a dry change of clothing available when the boys become soaked with sweat. Schedule games and practices for the boys' sake and not for the spectators, officials, or administrators. *Salt your boys down!* Administer salt with water, sugar, and vitamin C. Give three five-grain tablets with each meal and two before a practice session or game. The various new commercial drinks in cans may be used to wash the salt tabs down. That's their greatest value other than adding potassium.

When humidity is under *70 percent,* and the temperature goes up to 90°F, watch the boys closely for the danger signs. Give them a rest period on the hour. Ten to fifteen minute breaks are effective. *When humidity is* over *70 percent* and the temperature is over 90°F, CANCEL ALL PRACTICE SESSIONS! If you don't, you're not using the Prevent-System. You're asking for trouble and perhaps an ungodly fatality that may dog you the rest of your days. If practice is an absolute must, practice only in *very short* sessions. *When the temperature is over 100° F* simply refuse to let your boys play because it may cost one or more of them his life or his future health. Athletic action at high temperatures, especially football, regardless of humidity, brings on exhaustion, prostration, and vasomotor collapse. *When two or more boys appear exhausted* check the entire squad immediately. If the squad shows similar signs and symptoms *cancel the practice or game.* The point is: never mind saving face! Save the boy! He's much more important then a game any day!

In order to adapt to hot temperatures athletes need four to eight weeks of preseason conditioning before the official season begins. Prior to that, in the year-round training program, they should run, run, run!

Wind and endurance should be built in by having the athlete progressively increase the length of his windsprints until he can make a steady mile in six minutes or less. This lessens the dangers of heat prostration or heat stroke during practices or games but it's still not infallible. Another tip: Keep constant check on body weights. Watch that chart in hot weather! Any athlete who shows a consistent 2.5 percent or more weight loss per session should be referred to the team physician.

One observant coach said: "During hot weather we *just go through the motions of a play.* We use no hard hitting action during the run-throughs or practice periods. We do permit moderate water-drinking." Said another coach: "During hot weather we have very few daytime games under the sun. We book a well-lit police-protected ball park for those cool evening hours." This coach maintains a free flow of substitutions during the game, and in this manner the first squad gets a rest and does not dehydrate too fast.

Emergency Care of Heat Stroke

There are characteristic signs and symptoms in heat stroke or heat prostration. The skin is warm and dry. Oral temperature zooms to 105°F. Muscles become weak, fatigued, and go into spasm. This is particularly emphasized if an athlete is given a little water too late! (Remember that too much water is not good either. Sodium chloride metabolism may become disorganized due to body salt dilution.) The athlete passes from lassitude into unconsciousness and death may be the aftermath if emergency care isn't begun immediately.

The objective of prevent procedures in heat stroke is to reduce body temperature, replace water and lost chlorides gently, alleviate shock, and get the blood vessels of the body to constrict. For this purpose I use the following techniques:

1. *Cold tub bath.* Immerse the stricken athlete to his neck in cool water. Place an icebag on his head. Add ice to the water as his body temperature declines. This may be done in a reclining whirlpool bath, a bathtub, or the local river or crick.

2. *Cold pack (alternative).* Wrap the nude athlete with a cold wet sheet. Place him on a bed covered with plastic sheeting. Spray or sprinkle him periodically with cold water, or provide a cold air douche with a fan. (Bounce the force of the fan against the wall so that the breeze is indirect but cooling.)

3. *Cold water enema.* Insert the lubricated tip or nozzle of the enema tube into the athlete's rectum. Have him hold as much cool fluid as he can retain without discomfort. To each water bag container add two tablespoonsful of salt to make a weak saline solution.

LOW EFFICIENCY

Humidity	Air Movement	Temperature	Sweat	End Result
high 70%+	very little	High 80°F+	Little or none	Prostration, vasomotor collapse
-70%	very little	85°+	Partial	Possible heat exhaustion
70%	very little	80-90°	Excess sweat	Heat exhaustion begins
-70%	low	90-100°	Heavy sweat followed by none	No sweating
70%+	None	100°+	Extreme and then none	No sweating followed by death. Don't subject team to workouts. Cancel practices. Work only short periods.

HIGHER EFFICIENCY

Humidity	Air Movement	Temperature	Sweat	End Result
Low -70%	Moderate	60–80°	Little or none	Exhilaration
-70%	Moderate	85°+	Sweating	Good workout
70%	Breezy	80–90°	Sweating	Good workout
-70%	Breezy	90–100°	Sweating if using water	No problem but tired
70%+	Moderate to Breezy	100°+	Sweating if using water	Tires easily. Less efficient. No big health problem

Figure 4-5. *Predicting an athlete's efficiency by humidity/air movement/temperature.*[7]

[7] J.V. Cerney, "The Training Room Scale and What It Can Tell You," *Sports Trail,* 1964, p. 131.

Set the above Prevent-System immediately into effect while waiting for the team physician to get there. (This procedure has to meet his approval, of course.) He may administer digitalis, oxygen, or give plasma intravenously. If he believes antibiotics to be vital these, too, may be administered. While all this is going on, *make certain that the athlete's feet are elevated* above the level of his head. Block up your training table or cot. Here's another emergency measure to add: Wrap his lower extremities from foot to hip with three-inch cotton elastic compression bandage.

Prevent-System Procedures for Heat Exhaustion

The danger signs in heat exhaustion are marked. Body temperature is subnormal, respiration is rapid, and pulse feeble. Prostration may come on slowly but in some athletes it develops rapidly. There is weakness, dizziness, faintness, and nausea. The skin is pale and cool. The problem may resolve to partial or total unconsciousness. The point here is that heat prostration results from excessive heat in enclosed quarters, and this can happen to a football player in the confines of a hot cramped bus or a boiling hot training room. As such "heat prostration" should be differentiated from "sun stroke" to assure the proper therapy.

The complicating factors here are excessive heat, closed quarters, lack of ventilation, fatigue, low vitality, and nutritional deficiencies. Sometimes previous injuries to the head play a role in the heat exhaustion phenomenon. I wasn't aware of the latter until after ruling out all other possibilities on a few athletes I found that their tight helmets were contributing to misleading signs and symptoms. Each of the boys had had previous skull trauma. New, well-fitted helmets changed the whole pattern and that's the way it was.

Treatment for heat exhaustion revolves around keeping the athlete in a cool shady place while administering *hot* drinks! The athlete may be given a warm bath (95°F) for twenty minutes followed by mild friction in the bath or shower. Finish with a cold water shower. Repeat the bath process daily (ten minutes) until the athlete is totally recovered. He should have no solid foods other than soup and crackers. He may have cracked ice and ginger ale, but no milk!

WEIGHT LOSS AND OTHER WARNING SIGNS

What Your Training Room Scale Can Tell You

When you want to check out the values of your conditioning program, and you want the facts on a particular boy, turn to that diagnostic agent the training room scale. Inanimate as a scale may be, it speaks loudly. Its story is packed with the kind of information that takes know-how to evaluate. Here are some tips to help you.

By watching fluctuations in weight gain or loss, by watching peaks, lows, and plateaus, you can learn to adjust and understand matters such as the effects of conditioning, of endocrine cycles, which influence both male and female athletes, of emotion factors, humidity, staleness, salt loss, "midnighting," and many other factors contributing to weight loss or gain at the wrong time. With your training room scale making characteristic information available, you begin to understand previously inexplicable behavior on the part of the athlete. For this purpose your training room scale can be your number-one help in making a diagnosis of the problem. How it does this is told briefly in the following. Read this material slowly. Then reread it. Give it some thought. Note how some of the thoughts you have had on the matter begin to click into position as they did for me. The moment this happens you will begin to appreciate that training room scale as something more than an indicator of avoirdupois. Fifteen rough categories are listed below. They indicate possible reasons why an athlete may lose or gain weight during an athletic season. Keep the list in mind especially when you are worrying about a particular boy or even an entire squad's showing consistent weight loss.

The Big Fifteen Possible Causes for Weight Loss

1. *Poor conditioning.* Early season weight losses are greatest. The less physically fit the boy the greater the loss. The fatter the boy the more he will lose until he levels off. "Soft living exhaustion" is a preseason hazard and football players who spend the summer with soft foods, drinks, cars, and general soft living, or spend it working in air conditioned areas are among the first to pass out with heat exhaustion and heat prostration in initial football workouts. The fact that a boy looks great when he shows up for practice doesn't mean a thing until he has proven himself out on the training room scale. Weigh him and watch him.

2. *Weather conditions.* Humidity plays a strong role in weight loss by sweating. To demonstrate the importance of sweating, and how it shows up on the training room scale, I set up the following chart (see Figure 4-6). Note how temperature and humidity play a compelling role in weight loss. Note also the Prevent-System procedures offered.

3. *Overwork*

4. *Glandular changes* (endocrine cycle)

5. *Physical weakness and exhaustion*

6. *Rigorous workouts* under the best of conditions

7. "*Midnighting*" (nighttime job)
8. *Improper sodium salt balance*
9. *Playing while injured*
10. *Emotions*
11. *Disinterest* in football
12. *Dietary deficiencies*
13. *Drug taking*
14. *Postural imbalance*
15. *Conflict with the coaching staff*

Warm weather brings on weight loss due to *free perspiration.* Raising internal body heat through athletic action sets the sweat glands flowing to release heat through the skin. If body metabolism adapts to weather conditions the weight loss levels off with no repercussions. If there is a high external temperature, a high internal body temperature due to athletic action, and the humidity increases over 50 percent there is going not only to be weight loss but other physical problems.

Prolonged workouts in moderate heat with moderate humidity will result in heavy weight loss. *This is water weight!* The athlete's metabolism drops and he may lose as much as eight to eighteen pounds. Example: a 188-pound boy losing 8 percent of his weight loses fifteen pounds. This same boy showing a 18 percent loss will drop thirty-three pounds. Subject this same boy to prolonged workouts in moderate heat with high humidity and he's going to suffer. Other factors complicate the heat and humidity problem but the basic pattern remains the same. Remember that all weight loss is not water. Some of it may be protein and fat; therefore, consideration has to be given to other factors than those mentioned above. If the following are added to heat and humidity you can expect trouble. They are: practice sessions starting with a crash program and full gear; failure to give salt rations and failure to check out the dietary and sleep habits of the athlete; elongated daily practice sessions on warm, muggy days; refusing to permit the athlete to have water during workouts on warm, muggy days; not knowing in advance about possible physical defects.

Place the weight chart immediately near the training room scale. Instruct all squads to enter the exact weight before and after workouts. Maintain a rigid control on these entries and discuss the necessity of keeping these weights recorded. Do this during the preseason talk. Don't make them feel, however, that you are going to use the chart to spy on them. Each chart should cover a week. Make certain in charting weights that you have all the facts at hand before coming to any conclusions about

Temp.	Humidity	Effect on Athlete	Weight Loss	Suggestions
65°F	50%	Athlete exhila-rated	5 lb.	He feels great. Let him work.
65°F	70%	Sweating--may chill.	6 lb.	Work boys in light weight clothing. Put them under wraps when resting.
70°F	65%	Sweating and gets hot.	5 lb.	Don't start the season wearing full equipment.
85°F	60-65%	Sweating but "feels OK."	6 lb.	Watch the pro-fuse sweaters closely; they may begin to show exhaustion signs.
85°F	75%+	Begins to tire for no appar-ent reason.	8-10 lb.	Get the boy out of wet gear. Replace with dry light-colored clothing only. (No dark colors.)
95°F	65%	Tires even with salt and water.	8 lb.	Shorten practice time.
95°F	70%+	Tires fast despite salt and water re-tention.	12 lb.	Cut practice time.

Figure 4-6. *Weight scale key for trainers (for a 188-pound athlete).*

95°F	65%+	With no salt or water: exhaustion, collapse.	1-2 lb.	Cancel practices and games. Dehydration, fever, and possible death.
100°F	65-70%	Tires fast, exhausted.	10-18 lb.	Cancel practices and games.
100°F	70%	Quick exhaustion, death	10-23 lb.	Cancel practices and games.

***Figure 4-6**—(Continued.)*

a boy going stale. If all things are equal and the athlete has good food, plenty of sleep, no drugs, and has a controlled exercise program, his weight reports will tell a dramatic story.

Guidelines for Weight Loss in Well and Poorly Conditioned Athletes

The following factors are laid out in brief. They point to specific phases contributing to weight loss in the well-conditioned athlete as well as in the unconditioned athlete. Associate these factors with the foregoing chart on heat and humidity and the Big Fifteen of possible causes for weight variables, and see what you come up with in your personal Prevent-System. Keep all factors in mind when making an evaluation of the weight chart.

WEIGHT LOSS IN THE WELL-CONDITIONED ATHLETE:

1. Depending on his size and condition, an athlete will demonstrate a consistent loss of two to eight pounds of water per workout. Normal athletes will show the same amount replaced each day. Loss goes out in sweat and is replaced by food and beverages overnight.

2. There will be heavier weight loss in the normal athlete when the air is hot and humid.

3. If a squad of well-conditioned boys, not just one athlete, demonstrates progressive weight loss check your coaching staff. Look for the fuel that is burning them up with anger, dissatisfaction, frustration, or for any other emotional problem.

4. When weight loss continues at midseason look for training or handling problems. At this point a boy's weight should level off to a plateau on the chart. He should lose less water weight in a day. In fact, under normal circumstances he should show an overall weight gain.

5. Compare the weight losses by the day. The amount of weight loss not only indicates the amount of water loss but also points up how much the kid is putting into the game.

6. Weight loss during workouts may indicate an inadequate diet or a diet deficient in the amount of calories necessary to meet the physical requirements of football stress. The boy cannot operate on reserves for long.

7. Secret or public attempts to make weight by using crash diets, steam baths, or drugs will often be brought to light by exhaustion sweats during workouts, which show up plainly on the training room scale.

8. Discounting the average daily weight loss through sweating, the athlete should lose no more then two pounds per week.

9. After the initial weight loss there will be a gradual weight gain as muscles develop, as indicated, but any weight loss occuring at this time may possibly be due to staleness. Check the Big Fifteen causes of weight loss before coming to your conclusion.

WEIGHT LOSS IN THE UNCONDITIONED ATHLETE:

1. The inadequately conditioned boy demonstrates a progressive weight loss in normal circumstances with no stress factors from humidity, heavy gear, coaching needling, etc. This amount will be no more than two pounds per week until he hits his leveling off period if he ever manages to get there.

2. If weight loss in the unconditioned athlete continues after the second week, suspect any one of the Big Fifteen causes.

3. Overweight athletes will continue to lose weight until they reach a plateau and level off. This will indicate their peak-condition weight and should be recorded as such and compared each season.

4. The greater the fluctuation of weight in the unconditioned athlete the higher the injury rate!

5. Where weight loss variations show on the weight chart but the boy appears to remain the same, look for the reason why an alert boy is trying to "fake out" the weight chart. He must have a reason for falsifying the entries!

The Tape Measure: Aid to the Weight Scale

At the preseason athletic examination measure all the athlete's body and extremity parts. Records of these, with your training room scale records, can be used in checking out physical and weight changes, as well as muscle changes following illness, dietary problems, injury, or changes resulting from the effects of conditioning itself. Remember that added girth doesn't always indicate muscle. It may be fat. It may be swelling. A tumorous mass may be present. When comparing extremities, for example, indicate whether one of them has hypertrophied or atrophied. Coordinate all measurements with your training scale of findings and you will come up with information that is highly pertinent not just to the prevention program but to your team physician when he needs the information. The fact is, when you consider your tape measure and the weight scale you'll find basic information giving you explanations for things you hadn't thought about or couldn't put your finger on before.

Tips from the Trainer's Table on Water Drinking

Certainly the body must replenish its water losses after athletic action but this must be done by careful water assimilation without side effects. Here are some points to remember:

1. An athlete should not drink ice water when he is heated up by practice, warm-up, or competition. In fact it's wise to forbid him to drink ice water at any time. He may get a headache almost immediately. He may vomit. In his hot stomach the cold water is an irritant and may be expelled, but only after it has caused abdominal complications.
2. Do not permit the athlete to drink before weighing out.
3. Run a check on all water supplies (bacterial count, chlorination, etc.) of all towns, cities, or rural areas where your teams will be competing. Do it before you permit your boys to drink it! The one time that you don't may be the one time the whole team lands in the hospital.
4. A change in water may result in diarrhea.
5. Tainted water may result in "summer flu" or dysentery.
6. Sipping very hot water sometimes relieves a headache. I have found this especially effective in those boys allergic to drugs.
7. Hot salt water may be drunk to cause vomiting and clear out the original irritant in the stomach. Follow the vomiting of salt water with scalded milk or cold ginger ale.
8. Dispense water *only* in individual throwaway paper cups for obvious sanitary reasons.
9. Avoid the use of mechanical water buckets on wheels. Water under pressure may contribute to horsing around and to a number of consequences including injury to the sinuses, eyes, and tender tissues of the throat. Most of all the mechanical water bucket is a source of contamination since its hoses and nozzles are completely exposed to offensive bacteria and possible tetanus and they *never get sterilized.*

10. Use industrial wipes on the floor when water gets slopped. Never use a towel! In this way, other boys will not be contaminated by the debris that toweling picks up when it is used in this manner.

Danger Signs: When to Pull a Player

Nobody makes an exact diagnosis from the sideline according to David G. Moyer, medical director and team physician at Lafayette College, and he has set up a series of guidelines that signal when to pull a player from the lineup or from the field. Dr. Moyer advises to watch for the player who is slow returning to the huddle, the player with a broad-based gait, belly out, shoulders back, and head sagging. He suggests watching for the boy who is breathing uncommonly hard. Under these circumstances the athlete is vulnerable to new injury. Dr. Moyer espouses letting the players know of the necessity of communicating their problems and describing fully any injury if they have one. He points out extreme behavior to watch for. For example, look for the player who can't get settled and bounces around when the play is dead, or the one who doesn't align well in formation or huddle. Watch for manic behavior, over-vocalization, and aimless and confused behavior. At secondary school level watch for crying, vocalization, fighting, errors in social judgment, etc.

Coughing or hiccoughing after a blow to the abdomen may suggest ruptured organs and hemorrhaging. The boy with his wind knocked out could possibly have a lung puncture. Dyspnea (labored breathing) and cyanosis (dark blue-grey discoloration of the skin) in a well-conditioned athlete may presage trouble. Vomiting and incontinence of urine and feces spell out trouble.

In Dr. Moyer's Prevent-System when there is the slightest doubt about the athlete's problem remove him from the field and get him to the locker room, field house, infirmary, or hospital immediately. A quick glance from the sideline is not enough. You must know the athlete so that you can read those danger signals properly.[8]

Know your athlete! Interpret the danger signals he presents.

Dr. Barry B. Monzello also stressed the necessity to "know your athlete" at the Sixth Postgraduate Conference on the Medical Aspects of Sports. He told his audience that anyone skilled in the observation of emotions could prevent athletic time loss due to injury. He said that there are certain danger signals you can look for: the quarterback who panics,

[8] D.G. Moyer, "Sideline Oberservation," *Journal of the NATA*, Fall 1970.

the pounding headache that develops just before a game, the halfback who slips and falls just before being tackled, etc.

There's even a humorous aspect to all this. Coach Earl (Red) Blaik, now deceased, liked to tell a story about his trainer. Tough little Rollie Bevan had been with Blaik many years. Said Blaik, "One of my backfield men went down. I thought he was starched. Rollie ambles out on the field. Instead of giving the kid a whiff of ammonia he sticks his toes in the kid's ribs. He says 'Up hero! The grandstand now knows who you are. Take your bow!' Charley jumped up. The crowd roared. Charley hadn't been knocked out and Rollie knew it." [9]

FIELD CONTROLS

A Vital Part of the Prevent-System

There are many factors that point to the excellence of a coach, such as his insistence on timing, speed, form, coordination, and position play; his insistence on the athlete's willingness to play, on teamwork, sportsmanship, and good clean play; his insistence that all participants learn and adhere to the rulebook; and his discouragement of everything that increases the possibility of hazard. These factors help to form the framework of injury prevention. Field controls are another valuable part of the Prevent-System. Only a few methods of prevention through field controls are dealt with here. I consider them major ones.

That Good Front Four

When all is said and done, at amateur level or at professional level, that front four (or five) is the best prevention a backfield ever had! The basic success of a team lies in its line. The best linebackers, the greatest quarterbacks and cornerbacks, halfbacks, and fullbacks are ineffective without them. If that front four doesn't hold, the play is clobbered, the quarterback or other ball carrier gets racked up. That front line not only protects the play, it also is a major factor in the injury Prevent-System.

At the professional level the big bad front four get paid to stop the opposition and cause organized mayhem. According to Deacon Jones of the Los Angeles *Rams*, "We're a bunch of animals kicking and clawing and scratching at each other. Going into the Pit I like to slap the guys' helmets. It shakes them up. When I get to the man with the ball I hit him as hard as I can. If I can hit a man hard enough so he has to be carried

[9] Earl Blaik, personal interview with the author.

Give that
QUARTERBACK "COVER"
to prevent injuries
STOP "BLITZING"
TECHNIQUES and
RED-DOGGING
(at high school level)
Cerney

Figure 4-7

off the field, I'll be glad to help him off."[10] This is the attitude of the professional, but this kind of attitude is neither permissable nor affordable in the amateur leagues. In any league, however, that front four is vital in saving backfield injury.

Developing a Sound Policy on Substitutions

When weather conditions are hot and humid, when athletes are not in the best of condition, or when the opposition is tough, *use substitutes liberally* if you would prevent injury. Injury prevails when athletes tire. Never permit exhausation to contribute to this kind of disaster. Athletes should be instructed to take themselves out of the game when they are tired or for less serious injuries. All they have to do is signal. Maintain sufficient reserves and substitute them as the regulars tire. Don't gamble with limping players. That limp may be the prelude to something much more serious. Pull the boy out and have him examined.

Game Scheduling: Play In Your Own League

Coaches are fast becoming aware of the necessity to schedule games for the athlete and not for the convenience of spectators, officials, or school authorities. Too often coaches rue the day they scheduled and played games out of their class, or at altitudes and temperatures foreign to their players. To determine what coaches had to say on the matter of game scheduling and injury prevention, I queried fifteen of them. They came up with the following important "don'ts." Some of them repeat what I have previously discussed, but they bear repetition. Here they are.

1. *Don't* schedule or play "premier" games or even half games if the athletes have not had at least four or more weeks of preseason practice time.

2. *Don't* send your boys out to practice or to participate in games if their gear is inadequate to protect them against injury.

3. *Don't* develop irrational rivalries so that the stands, as well as the gridiron, become involved in civil war. If this happens, cancel the game until sanity is restored.

4. *Don't* book out-of-season "All-Star Games." Stick to the sanctioned schedule. It's your guarantee against losing boys in an unnecessary exhibit in which the only concern is vanity and/or money.

[10] P. Zimmerman, "The Front Four," *Pro Quarterback* 1, no. 4, February 1971, pp. 22–23.

5. *Don't* run the boys directly from the conveyance to the gridiron in away games! Transportation, housing, and practices should be arranged so that there is a rest period before a game. Travel tensions, cramped quarters, and inadequate facilities (especially at high school level) prepare even the best athletes for injury.

6. *Don't* permit less then four days acclimatization time when playing in an unusual climate or altitude. If yours is a northern school, for example, avoid scheduling games in the hot areas of the South, or, as an alternative, provide at least four days to two weeks acclimatization time so that the team's physiological status is adapted. The team should not be subject to the microtraumas of climate and altitude that lead to more serious injuries.

7. *Don't* be the small school that attempts to "knock off" a larger school. Admittedly this has happened, but it's unsusual. It does make the headlines. What is more apt to happen, however, is a bad shellacking in which a squad of good small-school boys are overwhelmed by an unending river of talent from a larger school. When a team is outmanned, and thoroughly defeated, it indicates failure to use the Prevent-System. It's more than defeat. It's demoralizing and physically dangerous. This kind of defeat can be prevented by more judicious game scheduling.

THE TRANSPORTATION PROBLEM

Prevention *has* to be used in all aspects of football or any other sport. For example, the type of transportation a team uses should be carefully considered before the team gets on board. In 1970 two college football teams (Wichita and Marshall) were killed in crashes of chartered airplanes. Someone forgot to use the Prevent-System to check out the vintage and quality of the planes used. When booking flights, use only the most responsible flight services. Don't pinch pennies any more on transportation then you would on good gear. Those players mean everything!

Here are some prevention tips for the transportation problem. In using your football Prevent-System efficiently:

1. Use only bonded reputable common carriers. Where possible avoid the use of private conveyances of all kinds.

2. Inform parents of liability laws and the responsibility they assume when they chauffeur the children of other parents.

3. No student should be permitted to drive. In all transportation, no student of the school will be permitted to drive a private car, bus, or

other vehicle to transport team personnel, cheerleaders, the band, or other persons.

4. All team members must be required to travel as a group.

5. Parents cannot take their own children home from a game unless they have specific permission from the athletic director.

6. Travel releases or waivers of liability must be signed by parents or legal guardians. If the parents will not sign waivers the youngsters will not be permitted to travel with the squad, cheerleaders, band, etc.

7. Check out in advance the eating places at which the team will stop enroute. Place food orders in advance.

8. Avoid out-of-state games where possible.

9. Carry all possible available multiperil insurance. This should cover all aspects of travel as well as the game itself, which some insurance companies exclude.

Returning the Injured Via Air

A return trip with injured can present a preventable problem. For example, illness of one kind or another may break out. Here are a few of the prevention factors necessary for injured athletes making air travel.

Asthma. Although asthma is not common with athletes, when it *does* occur, the boy should NOT be permitted to travel until his attack is terminated.

Chest Injuries. Keep a supplementary (portable) oxygen tank and mask on board for athletes with chest injuries who are being flown back to the school or to their home town. If there are any indications of pulmonary edema while in flight, get the plane down for emergency care of the boy. Hit the nearest air strip as fast as possible for immediate hospitalization.

Contagious diseases. Athletes with known cases of contagious disease should not fly. Anyone who manifests symptoms and signs while on board should be reported to the local airport or to the local health authorities on landing. Other passengers have to be protected.

Hernias. Seat belts and air pressure changes may aggravate a hernia. Make certain that a hernia developed during an away game is well strapped and padded or maintained with a proper brace before taking off in the plane.

Time Zone Fatigue

More and more time is being spent by athletes in air travel. Longer distances are being spanned in jets and these juants can be exhausting.

Because of the overlapping zones the natural rhythms of the body and mind are changed. Time change factors, plus differences in environment and altitude play a remarkable role in athletic performance. This was noticed by Dr. Max Novich, orthopedic surgeon and former boxer, when he took the A.A.U. boxing team to Russia. They flew to Moscow on February 6, 1970 for a return match with the Russians. (The Russians had beaten the U.S. squad earlier at Las Vegas on October 25, 1969, 6–5.) What was remarkable, according to Dr. Novich, was the fact that international travel, with time changes, played havoc with the American athletes. In Las Vegas, William Hawthorn earlier beat Kukamov. But in Minsk he was no match for the same Russian. U.S. boxer Ruiz beat Hromov at Vegas. In Moscow Hromov swarmed all over Ruiz who was without his usual pep. According to Dr. Novich, the time difference, new food and clothing, etc., require time for adaptation if players are to attain maximum performance.

To prevent "time zone fatigue" the American Health Service suggests this: (1) get as much rest as you can before departure; (2) allow a full day at the destination to adjust to the new time cycle; (3) if a full day's allowance isn't possible take a flight that arrives after dark so you can sleep all night; (4) if you can't sleep go out and exercise; (5) watch what you eat and drink. Eat simply.

THE GRIDIRON AND THE BLEACHERS

Guidelines for Preparing Better Turf

The prevention factors to keep in mind when considering natural grass turf are as basic as the choice of the sod or seed best for your area and the use to which it is put. Here they are.

Engineer and prepare the field competently for drainage, contour, best growth, etc. Use only durable, attractive, acclimated turfgrass which is best for your territory. Give the turf constant maintenance. Seed, provided the seed supplies the needs of the sport. For example, grasses for the putting green don't and won't work on the football field. *Poa trivialis* (shallow-rooted type) would provide no traction for football cleats if cleats are used. Colonial bent grass gives poor footing. Clover makes for slippery footing. Uganda grass may prove to be a prima donna needing an excessive amount of personal care. Use grasses that multiply their coverage and whose runners or rhizomes heal scarred areas quickly. Avoid slow growing turfgrasses such as the gems or zoysias. Remember that bermuda grasses sleep after the first frost and enjoy the warm weather. Bluegrass recuperates better in spring and fall. Make certain that the athletic department budget allows for fertilizer and water. When you present your request to the school board, base your argument on the fact that good turf is a safety factor. It's the athletic mattress that prevents a host of injuries. A good turf on the gridiron or on other fields is indeed a vital factor that the athletic director must keep in mind.

Turf can be a carrier of parasites. To prevent the invasion of chiggers and other parasites dust the field with sulphur in July and August. If any clothing is invaded it should be processed in the laundry with special repellents. Here's how to do it: Put clothing through the regular wash. Rinse in clear water. To the rinse water add benzyl benzoate. Soak for another hour. Then run the uniforms through the dryer without additional rinsing. This application is good through at least two launderings. If benzyl is used as a repellent for chiggers it remains in the mesh of the cloth for four or more washings. I have found, however, that some boys are allergic to benzyl, and I prefer the lesser of two evils, which is having the players dust sulphur powder on their ankles and legs before going out on the turf.

Safer Bleachers and Stands

A safe sports environment encompasses the safety of spectators as well as athletes, so bleacher seats play a role in the Prevent-System, too. Running a regular inspection on permanent and temporary bleachers is part of the athletic director's periodic tour of duty. It is especially vital that he check out the condition of temporary bleachers. Lack of attention to bleachers, their maintenance, and their construction may lead to injury and the dangerous possibility of a negligence damage suit.

Although folding or collapsible bleachers have replaced the old portable type, there are still many antiquated bleachers in use in the United States. It is these antiquated types which demand replacement or constant surveillance. For safety's sake the athletic director can call upon local county or city safety engineers, the sheriff's office, the state police, or the state fire marshall, to inspect and/or condemn them. Guarding against the possibility of injury makes regular inspection of bleachers a must. Most of the accidents which occur each year on the "portables" are usually the result of carelessness in erection or installation, or a lack of thorough inspection of the foundation material upon which the bleacher stands. To point out some of the possible dangers in bleachers the following checklist should be used.

Foundation supports. These should be placed only on solid and level areas. Never place a portable bleacher on concrete blocks. Pour concrete footers for bleachers erected in the open air.

Bolt A-frames rigidly. Fit the risers in only after the A-frames have been rigidly bolted. All risers must be secured and well-fitted. Be sure there are no broken weld joints.

Run a continuous check on footboard supports. Inspect the ironwork that braces the footboard. Check for rotting, breakage, loose screws, or bolts. Make certain that the footboards are lapped, strong, and without defect. Be certain that they are strongly supported.

Check all seats. Seats should be free of cracks, knots, breaks, slivers, rotten areas, chipped paint, nails, loose lag screws, jutting bolts, and chewing gum and spilled cola drinks. Seats should be cleaned before each contest. Check the strapirons that maintain the seat. Watch for loose screws and bolts. Then put up a rail on the back of the top row. A strong backboard is needed to keep people from tumbling backward. This should further be supplemented by heavy rabbit fencing or other wire fencing to keep children from falling through.

Maintain strong side rails. To keep side rails from being used as chinning bars, reinforce the openings with additional posts. Then close them in with chicken wire. Close off *all* unprotected areas where there is a possibility of a spectator slipping and falling.

Keep all wood and metal painted. The life of the structure is lengthened by constant painting and varnishing. Do not paint or varnish over rotten areas or other areas of potential disaster. Check the firmness of all boards with an ice pick. Stab the board. Pick at it. Determine its solidity. If it is the least bit suspicious, replace it immediately. Don't wait until tomorrow!

Use every cross brace. Too often in the race against time the tendency is to skimp on getting all the braces in place. Lock all cross-braces and then check the bleacher for possible sway. All braces must fit over the risers snugly and be in proper position. Check and recheck for loose bolts, rods, bars, struts, or stringers.

Do not permit portables to remain outdoors all year round.

Do not loan out your bleachers.

Do not borrow bleachers. Inefficient and careless handling, plus the problems of careless transportation, tend to cause damage which can lead to spectator injury.

Buy only the best bleachers.

Police the bleachers constantly during games. Use local police, Booster Club members, etc., before, during, and after game periods to prevent fights and keep youngsters from running up and down. Keep the Prevent-System functioning at all times!

Instruct the student body and parents on bleacher etiquette.

Never overload a bleacher. Know and maintain the approximate seating capacity.

Keep the stairway open at all times!

Keep your bleachers clean at all times. That ounce of prevention in cleaning up spilled coke, ice cream, etc., may prevent a costly fall. Stadiums and gyms are public places with public responsibilities. Clean all footboards and seats with a strong germicide. Remove grease, chewing gum, popcorn, candy wrappers, and other dirt after each game.

No bleachers should encroach on the sidelines or be immediately behind the goal posts.

In other words, eliminate every possibility of being accused of negligence by an enterprising attorney who would build a case against you.

Guidelines for Fire Inspection Checkpoints

A complete building examination (of the stadium, gymnasium, locker, shower, training rooms, etc.) should be made yearly by an accredited fire marshall. This should be done specifically before the indoor season begins. Outdoor facilities should be surveyed by the board of education representative. This inspection may prevent injury or death to many.

There are fourteen significant checkpoints on which to maintain surveillance in your fire inspection.

1. Limit attendance only to the maximum established for the facility.
2. Make certain that all doors open out!
3. Check all stands and bleachers for security.
4. Do not permit people or equipment to extend into the aisles.
5. Keep all stairs and floors dry and uncluttered.
6. Use uniformed police or firemen at all games.
7. Use parents (Booster Club, Dad's Club, etc.), as ushers to prevent exits from being crowded to stop running and to keep the aisles clear.
8. All outside approaches to the playing areas should be free of snow, ice, water, mud, or other hazards including automobiles, athletic equipment, bicycles, etc.
9. The entire facility should be stringently examined for all possible fire hazards and other sources of hazard like (bad wiring, storage, oil, a heating plant, solvents, fuel cans, spray cans, etc.).
10. "No Smoking" signs should be posted prominently on the inside of the stadium whether it is "fireproof" or not. Post them also in the locker room, toilets, storage rooms, and training room.
11. Have the fire marshall provide a set of rules and regulations for protection of everyone concerned in emergency situations.

12. Develop a program for the handling of mass casualties (see the end of this section).

13. Set up first aid stations.

14. The athletic director should control and coordinate the entire program of fire prevention.

Concession Stands

A concession stand is certainly a money-maker and can be a method of raising funds for the school when managed by a faculty member or by members of the Booster Club or P.T.A. Foods and beverages, however, can be sources of infection, and cause poisoning and the public spread of disease.

To curb contamination in the concession stand, run a health check on those who will be serving or making the food. Send them to the county health officer for examination. They may be innocently spreading diseases like skin disease, flu, colds, tuberculosis, and more to others. Keep vendors in clean uniforms. Maintain complete sanitation. Wash down all facilities with germicide detergent and deodorize. At least a day in advance exterminate all bugs and rodents on the premises, as they are carriers of disease. Then air the premises thoroughly.

Do not use questionable foods or oils. If there is a possibility of rancidity of vegetable or animal fats, throw them out! Don't gamble! Throw out hamburger that has an obnoxious odor or wieners that are slick to the touch. Inspect and control outside commercial vendors. In contracting outside vendors reserve the right to eject dirty operators with inferior products.

Do not use food that has a high probability of being poisoned. Notorious sandwich fillers such as chicken salad, tuna, and ham salad, are quick to spoil. Botulism and the salmonella organism are deadly; sell only boiled, packaged or bottled drinks, such as newly boiled coffee, pasteurized milk in individual containers of current date, and carbonated beverages in their own sealed containers. All other drinks are subject to spoilage and contamination resulting in violent stomach disturbances and they may cause a bad name, if not a lawsuit, for the school.

The First Aid Station: An Athletic Department Must

Emergencies directly and not directly connected with team play may occur in the stands or otherwise at any athletic contest, and it is the school's duty to see that the best of available facilities are provided to render first aid. The first aid station should be in a convenient location and kept open for all events. It should be marked with large letters and be accessible from the outside as well as from the inside of the building or stadium. It should be kept scrupulously clean. The person or persons in charge of this station should be completely trained. First aid supplies should be completely adequate to serve the needs of the doctor or other trained personnel. (A phone call to your team physician will get you a list of the inventory needed.)

Management of Mass Casualties

Too many school administrators are convinced that their facilities for spectators are adequate, that there is no danger in the stands, and that disaster is an impossibility in their school or stadium. Mass casualties *can* and *do* happen, however, as in the case of collapsing stands in Pennsylvania in 1964. Spectator injury is a possibility at any athletic contest. Such injury may be on a minor scale or it may be a major string of casualties or deaths. The thought of such a disaster produces nightmares for any administrator and his athletic department, and to solve this problem there should be in your Prevent-System a plan of action to cope with such a possibility. In the United States today there are many stands and other facilities in high schools and small colleges that should long since have been condemned. There are untold numbers of fire-trap schools and untold numbers of other potential disaster areas that exist because of administrative laxity.

It is just as necessary to have a plan of action for spectator welfare as it is to have one for the welfare of the athlete, and despite those who would pooh-pooh the possibility of mass casualties, the problem remains. There is always the possibility of stands collapsing, of explosions and fires, of skylight glass dropping, or of riots. It can all become starkly real and horrible at the wrong time and the chaotic examples of such disasters leave a raw and violent memory. It is a moral as well as physical responsibility for the administrator to insure against such disaster. He should do so by every means necessary. When an administrator considers mass casualties occurring in *his* school, gymnasium, or stadium (frightening as it is) he has to consider the following:

1. Recognize that a mass problem is always a possibility.

2. Set up an inspection program that checks out every possible area where a dangerous condition could exist and that evaluates every measure that can be used to correct the possible danger.

3. Make all necessary first aid preparations for such an eventuality making sure all personnel are alerted to what has to be done in an emergency.

4. Special personnel should be trained for particular mass casualty

duties. These people should be of such character that they will not join in mass hysteria or panic.

5. Local area hospitals should be checked out as to their capability for handling mass casualties and agreements should be arrived at on emergency handling.

6. Red Cross, Civil Defense, and morticians should be contacted about the availability of mobile equipment for transporting the injured.

7. All school personnel should be put through classes on emergency duties, just as for a fire drill or for fire control.

8. Check with the local medical association and the associations of other professions to see whether they have a plan as to how they would handle survivors, how the injured would be removed and treated.

9. Consult with the local police and fire departments on their plan of action in an emergency.

10. Work out an emergency program with the local Civil Defense.

11. Check out all possible legal involvements and complications.

12. Check out all liabilities from the standpoint of insurance coverage.

13. Wide exits should be part of all existing facilities. All doors should open outwardly.

14. Crowd control should be planned and practiced. In addition to police, parent volunteers, cheerleaders, and band members should be trained for such duties.

15. All personnel should be trained in all aspects of riot control.

16. Parking facilities can be a hazard and necessitate complete control.

17. Rising out of the ashes of disaster should be quick rebuilding and repair. For this possibility there should also be a master plan. Everything, for the school administrator, should be black on white long before the danger even occurs. This is the Prevent-System at work!

Planning and setting up a program against such a possibility is the ounce of prevention that is so vital at the right time. There should be a blueprint for action, and this holds true for the little red schoolhouse as well as it does for the mammoth buildings that grace the universities of the nation. Thousands upon thousands of human beings can be packed into the concrete giant called a stadium, and a football game can become more than a Saturday afternoon spectacle in one flaming moment of disaster.

In planning the methods of prevention designed against mass casualties, it should be remembered that calamity sparks changes in people's personalities. Social inhibitions are lost. Fear lifts the corners of their personal controls when there is the least possibility of getting hurt. Fear, sweeping through a group, can and does result in an enormous tragedy even though no true physical danger exists. The big unknown in any blueprint for disaster is the human being. Every effort should be made to control him in a time of emergency, to help him, and to provide for him, as a prevention against further injury at an athletic contest. For this reason the administrator of any school, large or small, must be concerned with the possibility of mass casualties. He has to insure that every effort is made to check out fire hazards, conditions in the stands, exits, etc. Mass casualties can never be excused or shrugged away by saying "It can't happen here." It *can* happen! It *has* happened! And it can happen again, and every available method should be used to prevent it.

Public Address System

The public address system can be a highly valuable adjunct in the prevention program, when used with forethought. The athletic director should designate a number to be used for all doctors when requests or messages are being voiced on the P.A. Public proclamations for a doctor tend to inspire fear in the football squad as well as in the stadium. The P.A. should be immediately available for use in emergency or for summoning aid. It may be used to calm a crowd or to issue instructions during an emergency. It may be used to direct personnel to areas of conflict or other difficulty. If private telephone stations are not part of the school facilities, the public address system may be used by the athletic director to place guards and other personnel at vantage points at a moment's notice.

Police Protection

Every athletic contest is a public occasion. As such it often necessitates police aid indoors or out as well as for everything from outdoor parking to maintenance of the law. Off-duty firemen, police in uniform, private police, etc., may serve in this capacity. The athletic director should discuss with the police in advance all areas to be controlled and the type of controls to be used in the prevention of injury to the athlete and to the spectator.

Duties of Police at Games and Contests

1. Police will handle all traffic before and after games.

2. They will be ready and equipped to handle all adverse crowd behavior and will eject the unruly.

3. They will be schooled in riot control.

4. They will cope with all problems of liquor and gambling.

5. They will assist in emergency situations.

6. They will promptly come to the aid of school personnel who are defending themselves or school property.

5

TREATMENT TECHNIQUES

Strategy Covered:

- *Neck injuries*
- *Shoulder injuries*
- *Upper arm injuries*
- *Elbow injuries*
- *Forearm injuries*
- *Hand injuries*
- *Thorax injuries*
- *Back injuries*
- *Spine injuries*
- *Abdomen injuries*
- *Pelvis injuries*
- *Hip injuries*
- *Thigh injuries*
- *Knee injuries*
- *Shin and leg injuries*
- *Ankle injuries*
- *Foot injuries*

NECK INJURIES

The neck is highly vulnerable to injury in football. Current headgear contributes to injury and provides little or no protection for the cervical area. Shoulder padding leaves the side of the neck exposed. Any injury affecting the neck sooner or later affects the brachial and cervical nerves as well as the vertebral arteries. Neck muscles become involved because they act as a splint that maintains the position of the head.

Brachial nerve injury may occur as the result of a referred blow when a player lands on the hands, elbows, or shoulder. When the neck is injured and the brachial nerve becomes affected, the shoulder, arm, and hand are also affected. The vertebral arteries which ascend the spinal column to the brain are also involved. Any pressure on these arteries from rotation of a cervical vertebra, for example, may cut off blood supply to the brain resulting in lack of coordination, imbalance, lack of go-power, and dizziness. Neck injuries, in turn, may affect the entire nervous and vasomotor systems.

There are characteristic times when neck injuries occur in football. They are:

When the defensive player anticipates contact and ducks his head to one side. This is a normal reflex, but it's at this time that an observant offensive player may throw a fist, forearm, elbow, knee, hip, or head block into the slot. He may spear him with his face guard.

When a player drops his head to avoid oncoming impact. When the head goes into chin-to-chest position the back of the neck yawns open. In this exposed position the neck is open to attack, whether purposeful or accidental.

When a player looks away at the wrong time. The face and neck are exposed to trauma when a player looks away. The player should remain in a state of tension from the opening whistle until the last whistle terminates the game.

When the player's arm is suddenly jerked. When a backfield man is running with the ball with his arms flying, his elbow becomes a convenient handle to be grabbed and yanked. When the ball-handler is tackled low and wide, his arms may be forced back resulting in extension and abduction of the shoulder muscle and joint structure. Such a grab may also pull at the musculature of the neck.

When an end is running with his arms and chin up anticipating catching a pass. He may run into a horizontally extended arm ("clothesline").

When a player tackles with his eyes closed.

When the ball carrier is hit high and low simultaneously and the head is whiplashed.

When a player is hit from the rear.

When the faceguard is used as a handle to snap the head and neck.

Football fatalities have been directly linked to head and neck trauma. According to the Thirty-Eighth Annual Survey of Football Fatalities, there were twenty-three direct fatalities in 1969. Eighteen were at high school level, three on the sandlot, and one each in college and professional football. In 1968 there were thirty-six deaths. Twenty-six were in high school football, five at college level, and one in professional football. According to the survey, the direct fatalities since 1960 have been caused by head and neck injuries. Carl S. Blyth, Ph.D., of the University of North Carolina, noted that nineteen, or 84 percent, of the 1969 deaths resulted from head and neck injuries. The investigators urged proper conditioning exercises to strengthen the neck and condemned the practice of "spearing" and "cross-body blocking."

Some doctors feel that most serious neck injuries result from "spearing" and head-on tackles (driving the chin down into the chest). Cervical collars help prevent these injuries, though such collars do have their weaknesses. They protect against abduction and extension injury, but do nothing for flexion. But neck injuries result not just from playing techniques but also from poor conditioning, poor equipment, and failure to remember the vulnerability of the neck.

Prevent-System Procedures for Neck Injuries

To prevent neck injuries, start your prevention program in the preseason screening. Squad eliminations begin long before the practice sessions start. Here are some Prevent-System techniques to follow:

1. *Eliminate the skinny-necked kids immediately.* Channel them into other sports until they develop.

2. *Instruct the player to never drop his head on a play.* Dropping the head is an invitation to neck injury. "Keep it bulled" is the way the coaches put it.

3. *Protect old injuries* with commercial pads, ring collars, or toweling. The torticolis-type of adhesive tape strapping may also be used where the neck is easily subject to reinjury (see neck taping techniques).

4. *Check the helmet daily.* Neck injuries begin too often with the helmet and face guard. The posterior edge of the helmet is hard and nonadaptable. Remodel and pad it. Getting "dinged" on the crown of the helmet blasts the helmet down on the neck, or, forward and down on the nose.

5. *Develop weight-training programs, isometrics, isotonics, and calisthenics for building the neck.* Resistive exercises are excellent for this

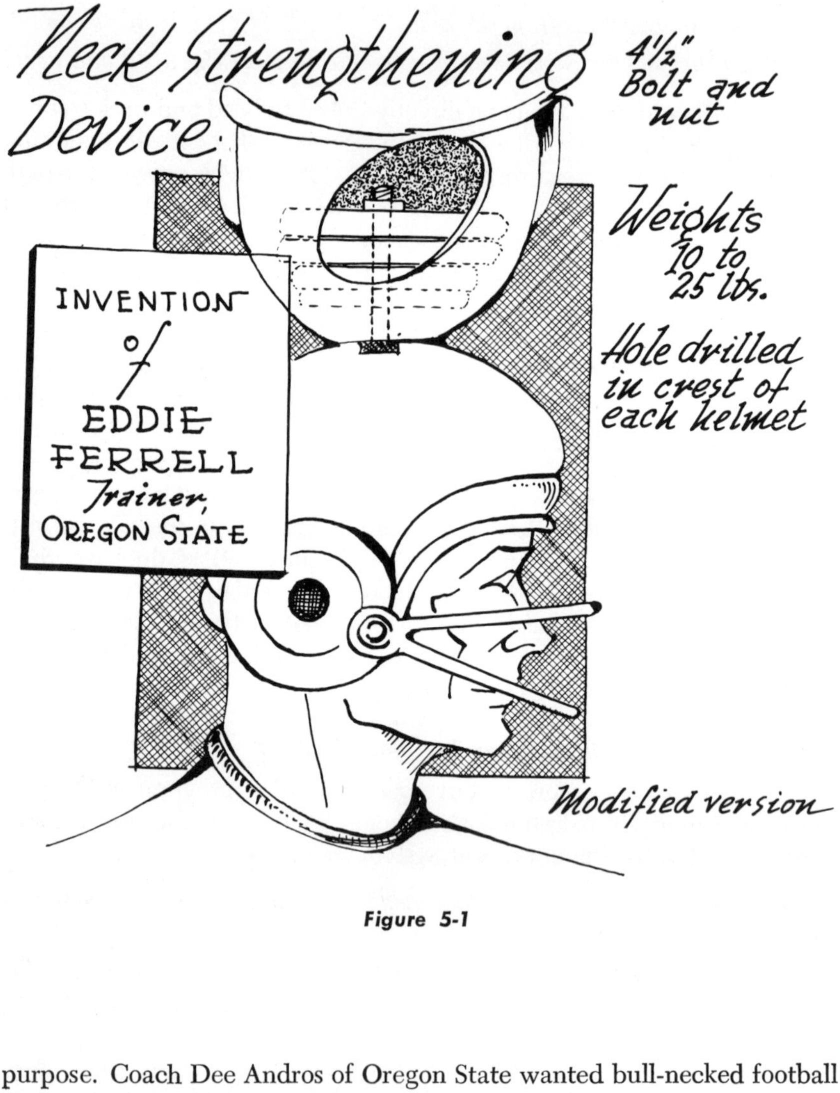

Figure 5-1

purpose. Coach Dee Andros of Oregon State wanted bull-necked football players. Trainer Eddie Ferrell was assigned the job. Ferrell came up with a real neck-muscle builder utilizing old football helmets. He bored holes in the tops of two helmets, stuck a six inch piece of half-inch pipe through the holes and locked the helmets top to top. Inside the upside-down helmet he placed a set of weights. Players with neck injuries, or skinny necks, wore these two hours a day. Weights started at ten pounds and went to twenty-five. I tried it. It worked.

6. *Enforce rigid field rules against spearing* in which the helmet is driven into the chest, stomach, head, neck, or kidneys of an opponent.

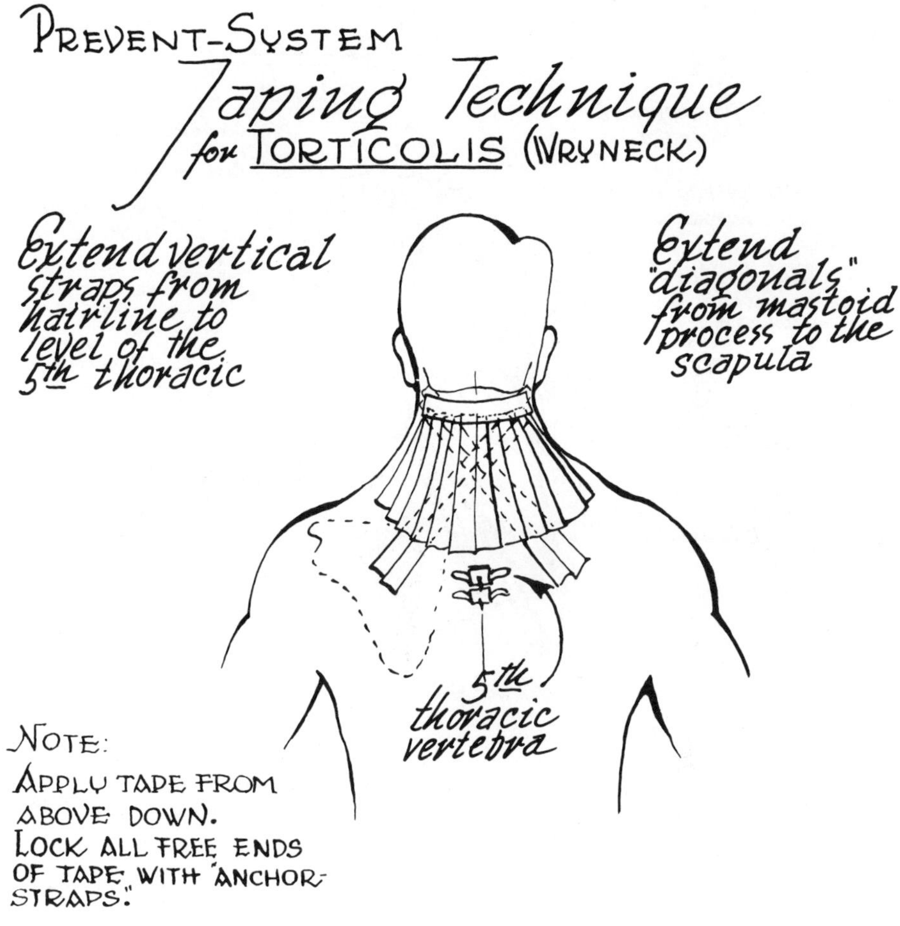

Figure 5-2

SHOULDER INJURIES

Shoulder injuries are never local. For example, an athlete falling on his shoulder "point" may have a direct contusion on the deltoid muscle, but he may also have an injury to the acromion process. Also, as a result of this trauma, the humerus may be dislocated from its socket. Sprain may occur in and around the acromioclavicular joint. The clavicle may be dislocated or even fractured. There may be an involvement of the cervical vertebrae and cervical nerves that make up the brachial plexus. When an athlete falls on one elbow or hand, there may be injury to the hand,

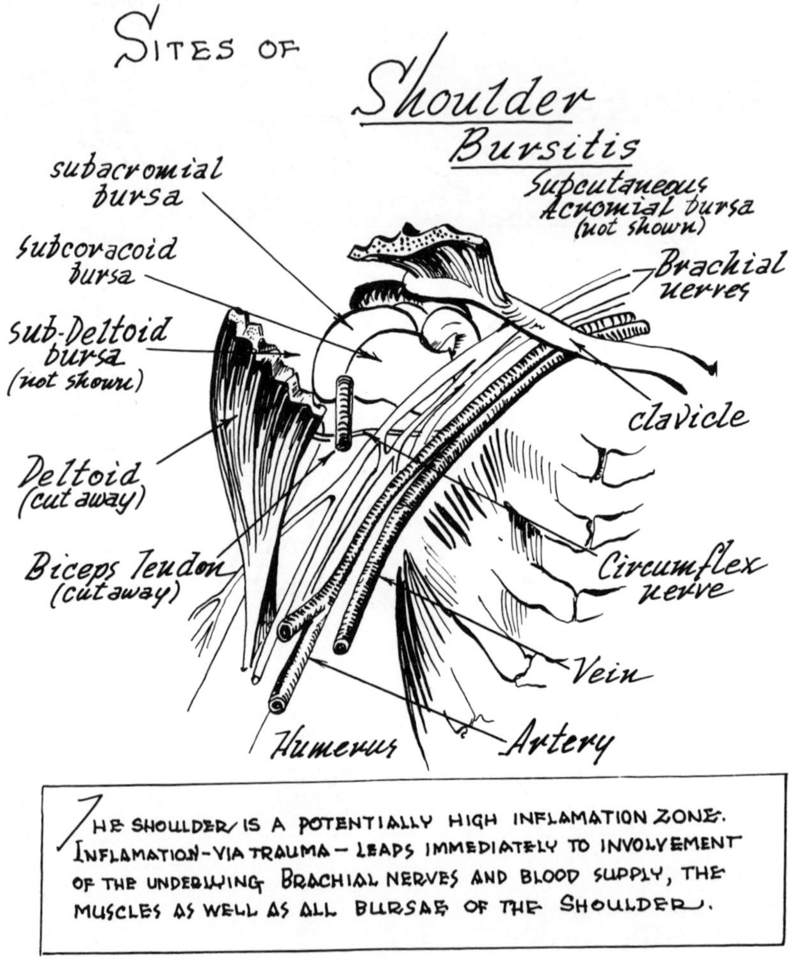

Figure 5-3

wrist, or elbow, and because of the referred impact, a shoulder dislocation may follow. When a player tackles low and wide, the arm may be forced back, causing too much extension and abduction which results not only in pain but also in destruction to local tissues. *No shoulder injury is ever local* and this is a point worth repeating.

Protective gear for the shoulders must therefore be the very best, but, sadly, the best available gear could be better. It is not designed for the athlete in motion. It is not dynamic. It is nonconforming. Because of these shortcomings, the Prevent-System techniques for shoulder injuries must begin with teaching how to tackle and how to tumble so that no stress is brought to bear on the shoulder.

Shoulder injuries in football are usually in the following groups: (1) contusions, (2) acromioclavicular joint injury, (3) separation (sprain, dislocation, subluxation), (4) clavicular fracture, (5) strain (internal rotator cuff injured when the arm is pulled or jerked), (6) nerve impingement (the brachial nerve, in which the hand swells painfully for five to ten minutes with weakness following, and painful swelling develops in the deltoids), (7) "knocked-down" shoulder (injury to shoulder and neck with spasm occuring in the rhomboids, trapezius, and cervical erector spinae muscles with unilateral pain.

Prevent-System Procedures for Shoulder Injuries

In all shoulder injury prevention efforts there are six important steps to follow:

1. Get a complete medical history of all previous shoulder and neck injuries. Try to determine how and why they happened as well as when.

2. Have the trainer run his "Athletic Examination" and study his current findings.

3. Eliminate any boy from the lineup whose bones and soft tissues demonstrate an area of potential future damage.

4. Develop a special restriction harness for chronic shoulder dislocation in the athlete who has high playing potential. Preserve him (see the taping techniques that follow).

5. Teach all football men how to tumble. Assign all football players to the gymnastic squad. Tumbling is one of the best injury preventives I know. In my Prevent-System it's *the* way to avoid shoulder injury. Teach players how *not* to fall on their hands and elbows.

6. Set up a muscle-building program immediately. A suggested weight-training program follows.

Weight Training Techniques

(a) *Press.* With the back straight, grasp a barbell in each hand with palms in toward the thigh. Pull it up to the chest, then press overhead. Lock the elbows, lower the weight to the chest, bend at the hips and lower the barbell to the floor (ten repetitions).

(b) *Straight arm forward raise with dumbbells.* Alternate left and right.

(c) *Lateral raise with dumbbells.* Lift directly to the side in unison, arms straight, while leaning forward at right angles from the waist.

(d) *Curl with dumbbells.* Press dumbbells overhead and lower to the shoulders before repeating the curl. Handles should point from front to back.

Taping Techniques for the Shoulder

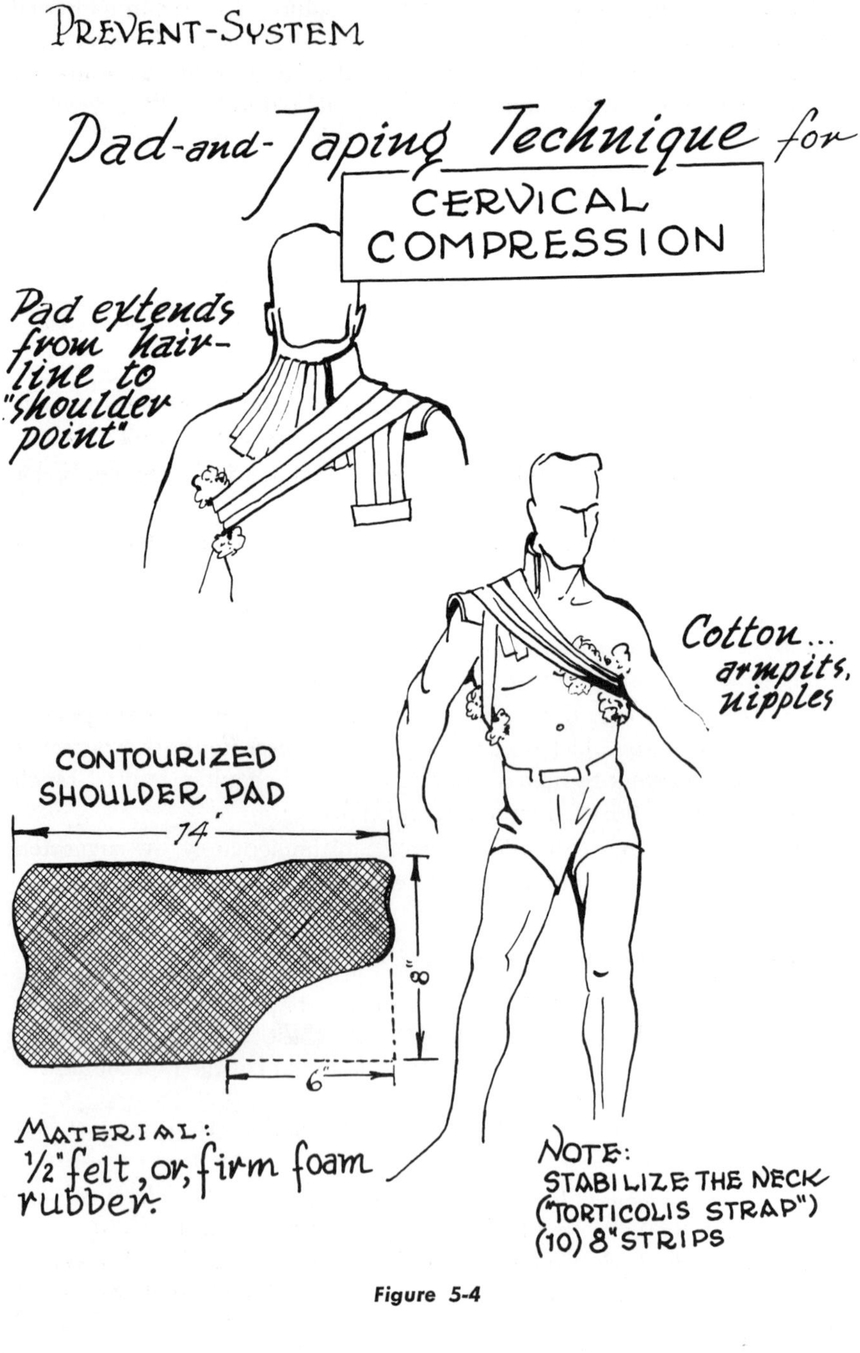

Figure 5-4

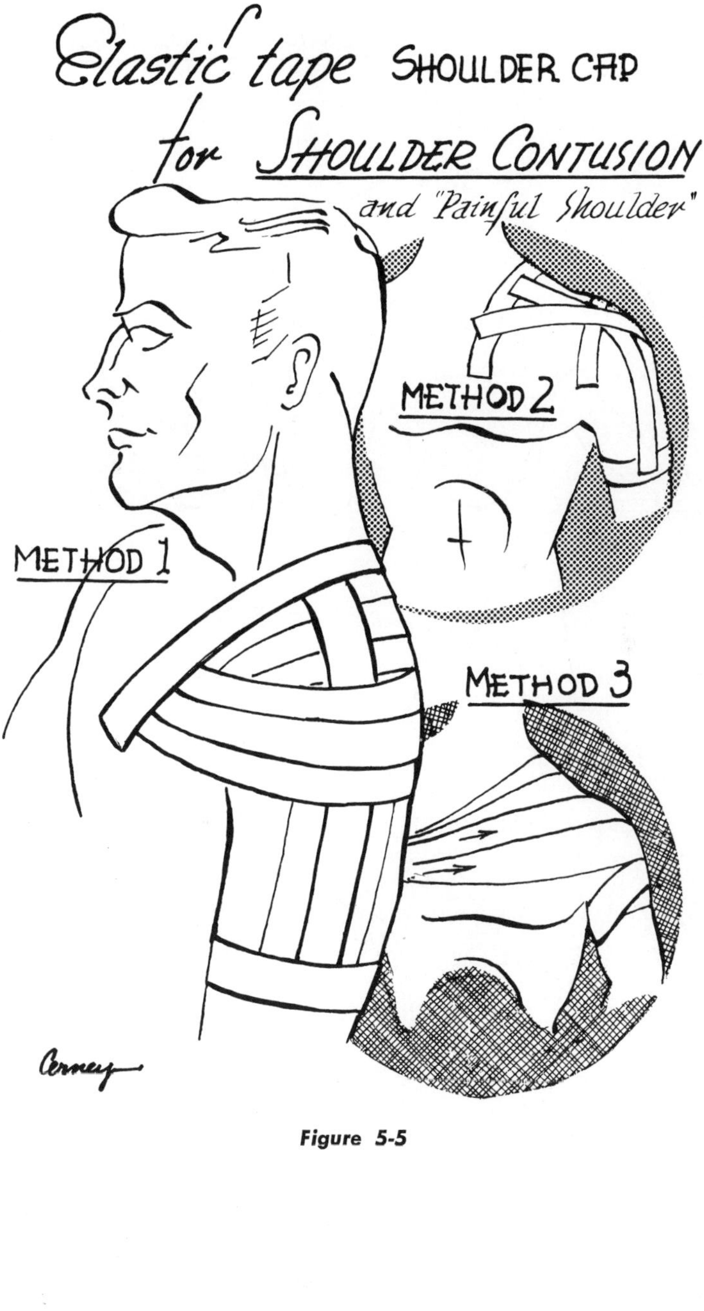
Elastic tape SHOULDER CAP
for SHOULDER CONTUSION
and "Painful Shoulder"
METHOD 1
METHOD 2
METHOD 3
Cerney

Figure 5-5

PREVENT-SYSTEM Taping Technique for WEAK SHOULDERS

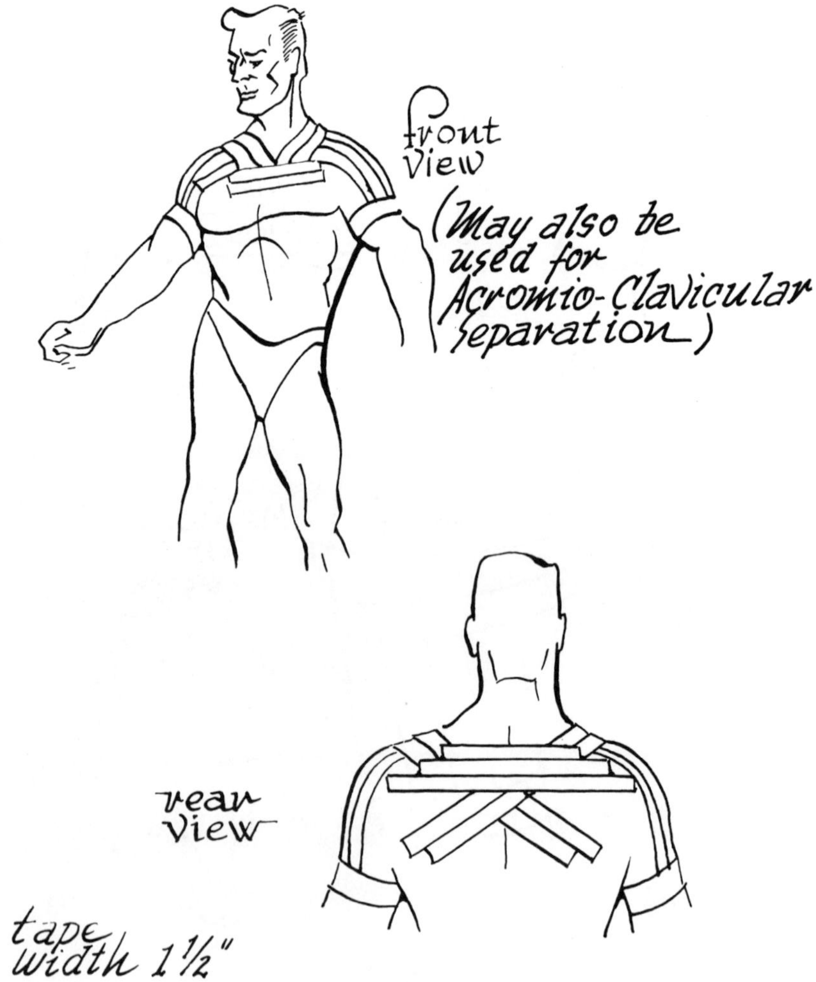

Figure 5-6

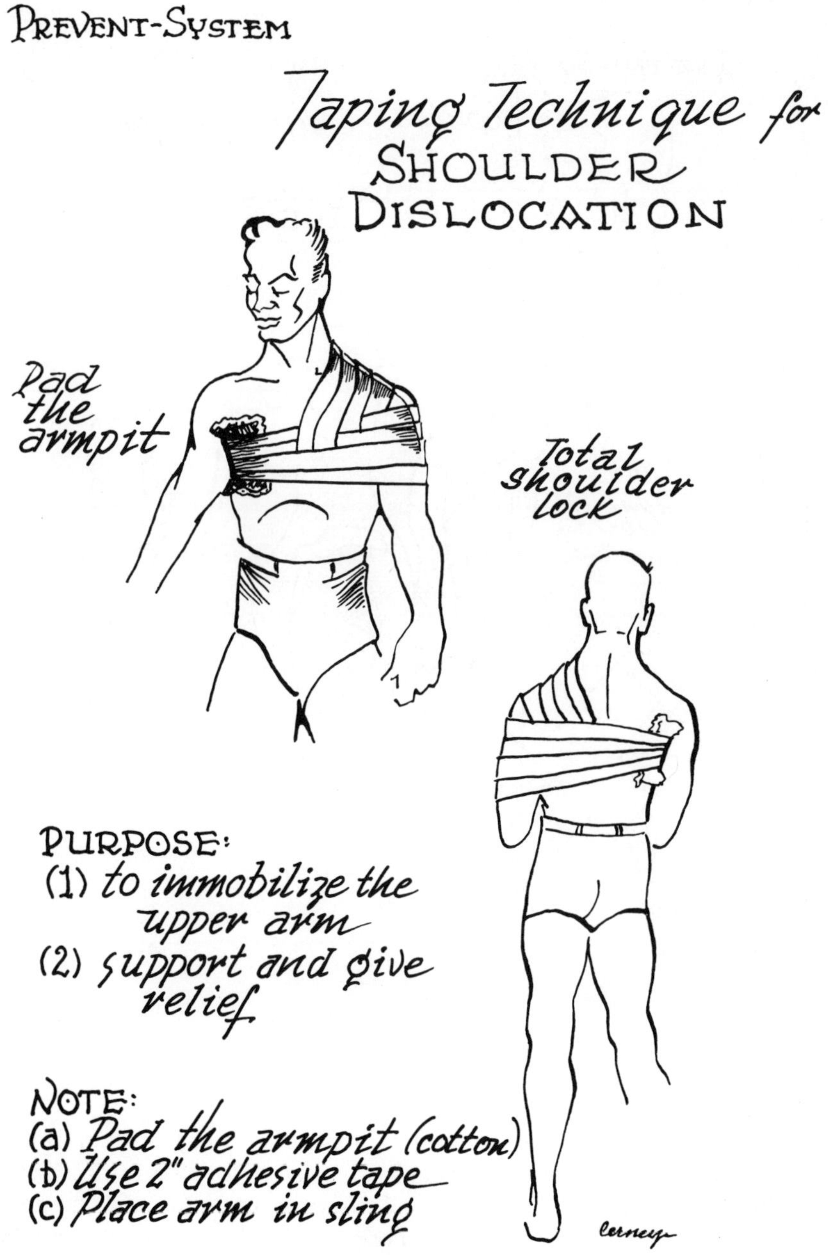
PREVENT-SYSTEM
Taping Technique for SHOULDER DISLOCATION
Pad the armpit
Total shoulder lock
PURPOSE:
(1) to immobilize the upper arm
(2) support and give relief
NOTE:
(a) Pad the armpit (cotton)
(b) Use 2" adhesive tape
(c) Place arm in sling
Cerney

Figure 5-7

Taping Techniques for the Upper Arm

Figure 5-8

UPPER ARM INJURIES

The upper arm is seldom injured in football. It may sustain bruises and deep muscle contusions which can convert to myositis ossificans, but this is unusual. Why are there so few upper arm injuries? The upper arm tissues are well developed and flexible. Muscle tissues are large but pliable. They move and adapt to trauma by rolling with a blow. They are not fixed. The best prevention for injury to the upper arm is a well-developed musculature. For this purpose I prefer a weight-training program.

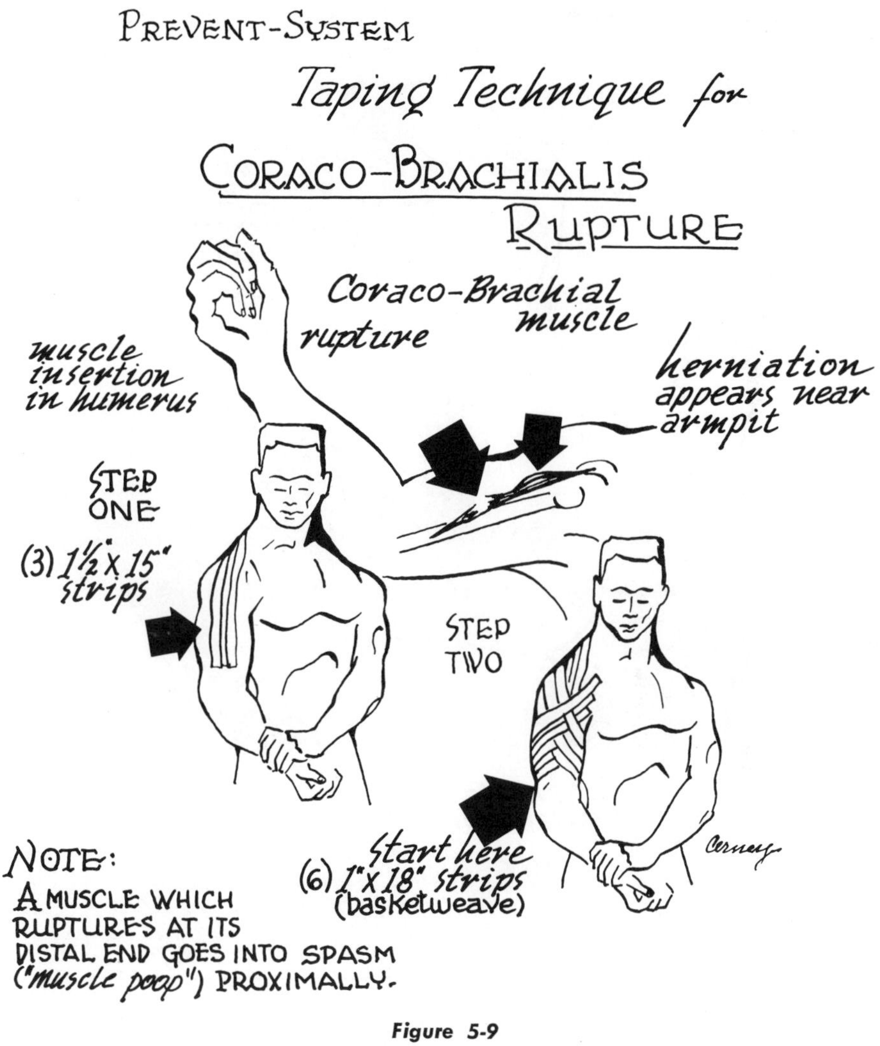

Figure 5-9

Weight Training Techniques

(a) *Curl with dumbbells.* Press overhead. Lower to the shoulders and repeat. Point the handles front and back and press vertically from the deltoids.

(b) *Rowing.* With the legs straight, lean forward while holding the barbell. Lower it until barbell is just above the floor. With the upper torso parallel to the floor, bring the barbell up until it touches the chest. Repeat ten times up and down in a rowing motion.

Taping Techniques for the Elbow

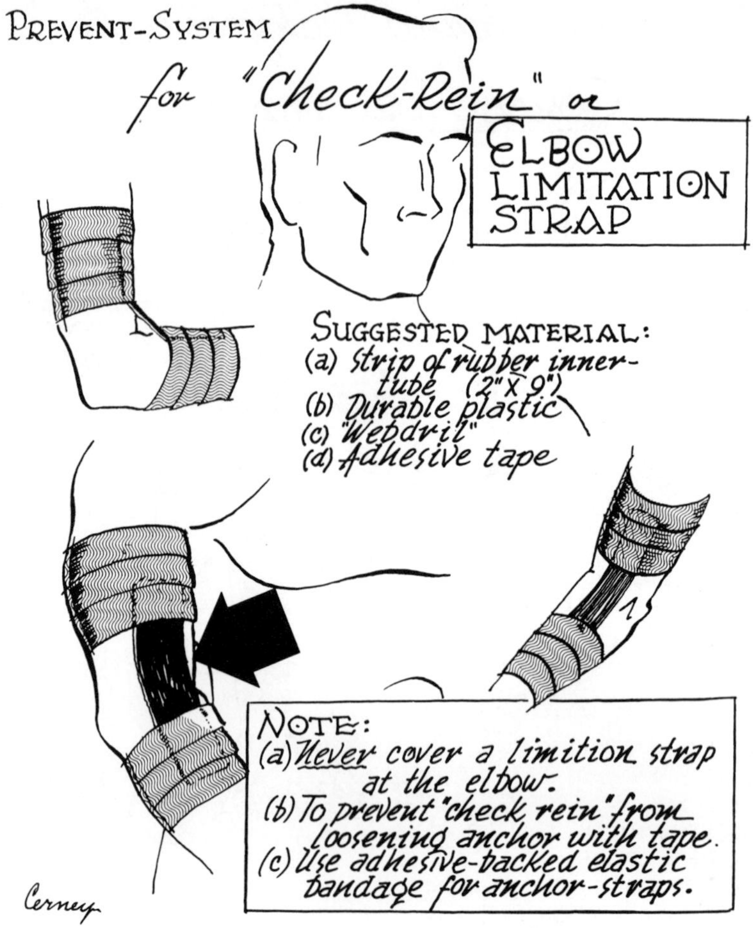

Figure 5-10

ELBOW INJURIES

The elbow, unlike the upper arm, is constantly in danger and constantly being hurt. Relatively unprotected, the elbow is almost completely open to attack. Self-injury is common and every football player has to know how to prevent the problem. Posterior elbow dislocations may occur when the player falls on an outstretched arm or when he sustains a posterior blow on the fixed or extended arm. Elbow sprain may occur when the joint is in hyperextension. The medial epicondyle may

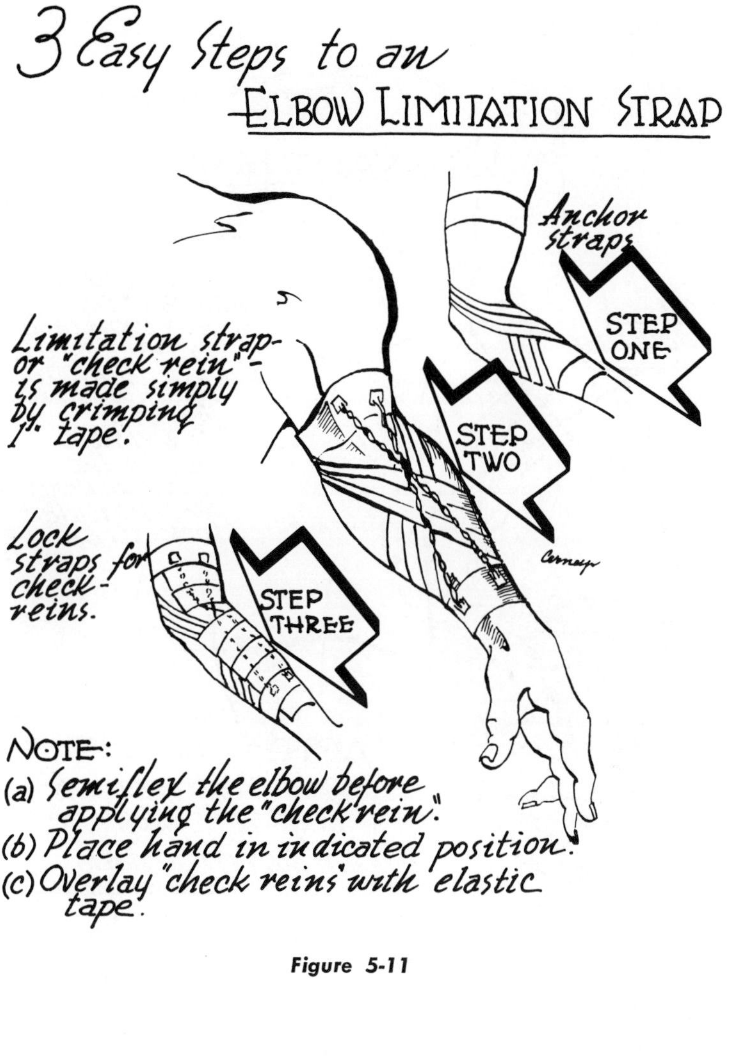

Figure 5-11

fracture when there is a lateral blow to the extended elbow with the hand extended or when the player falls on his outstretched hand not knowing how to tumble to take the blow "going away."

It becomes obvious that injuries such as these are the results of not knowing what to do with the upper extremities, not knowing how to take a fall, and not knowing how to use the elbows, arms, wrists, and hands as a springboard. *The prevention of these injuries lies in the art of tumbling.* The athlete should know how to land on his hands and come up running. Additional protection may be found in methodical warm-ups, the application of restrictive or limiting straps (adhesive tape) to old

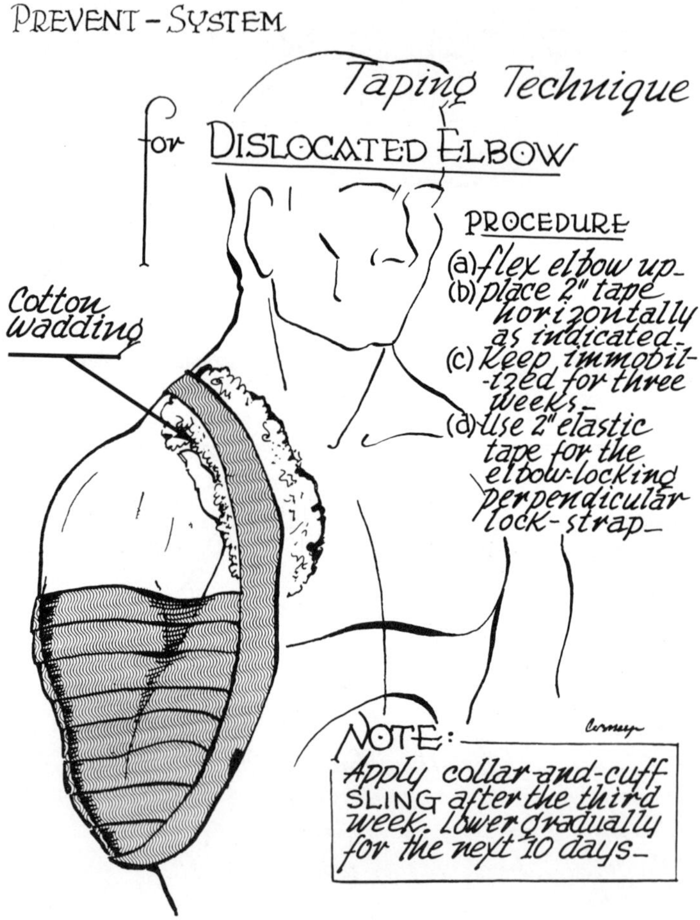

Figure 5-12

injuries of the elbow, or the use of elbow guards to prevent further possible fracture or contusion. Here are some weight-training procedures for strengthening the elbow.

Weight Training Techniques

Warm up the arms with presses before raising the dumbbells to a position behind the neck. Raise the weights to a straight arm overhead push. Keep elbows stationary. Do up to fifty repetitions as the arms improve.

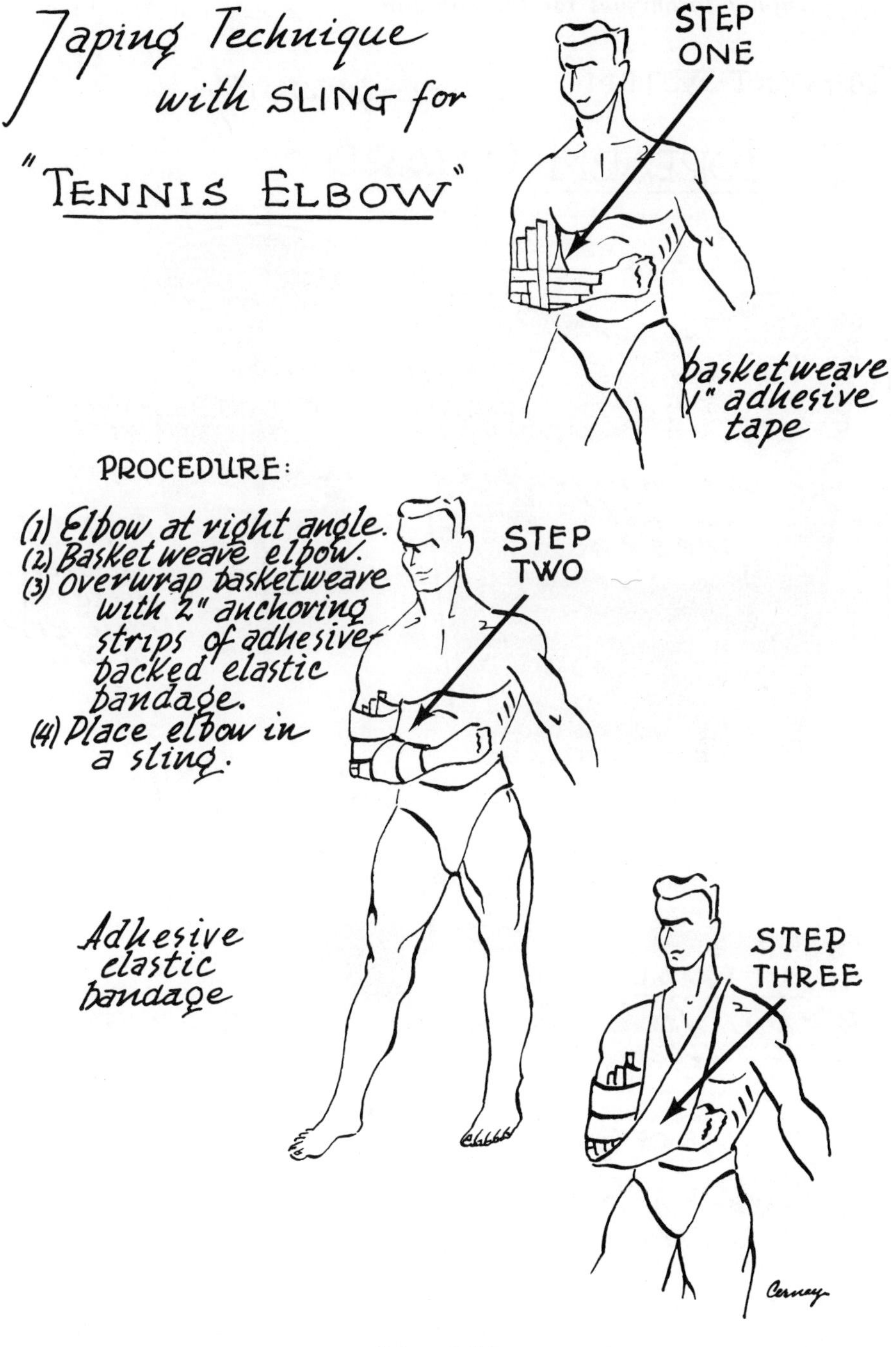
Taping Technique
with SLING for
"TENNIS ELBOW"
STEP ONE
basketweave
1" adhesive
tape
PROCEDURE:
(1) Elbow at right angle.
(2) Basket weave elbow.
(3) overwrap basketweave with 2" anchoring strips of adhesive-backed elastic bandage.
(4) Place elbow in a sling.
STEP TWO
Adhesive
elastic
bandage
STEP THREE
Cerney

Figure 5-13

Taping Techniques for the Forearm

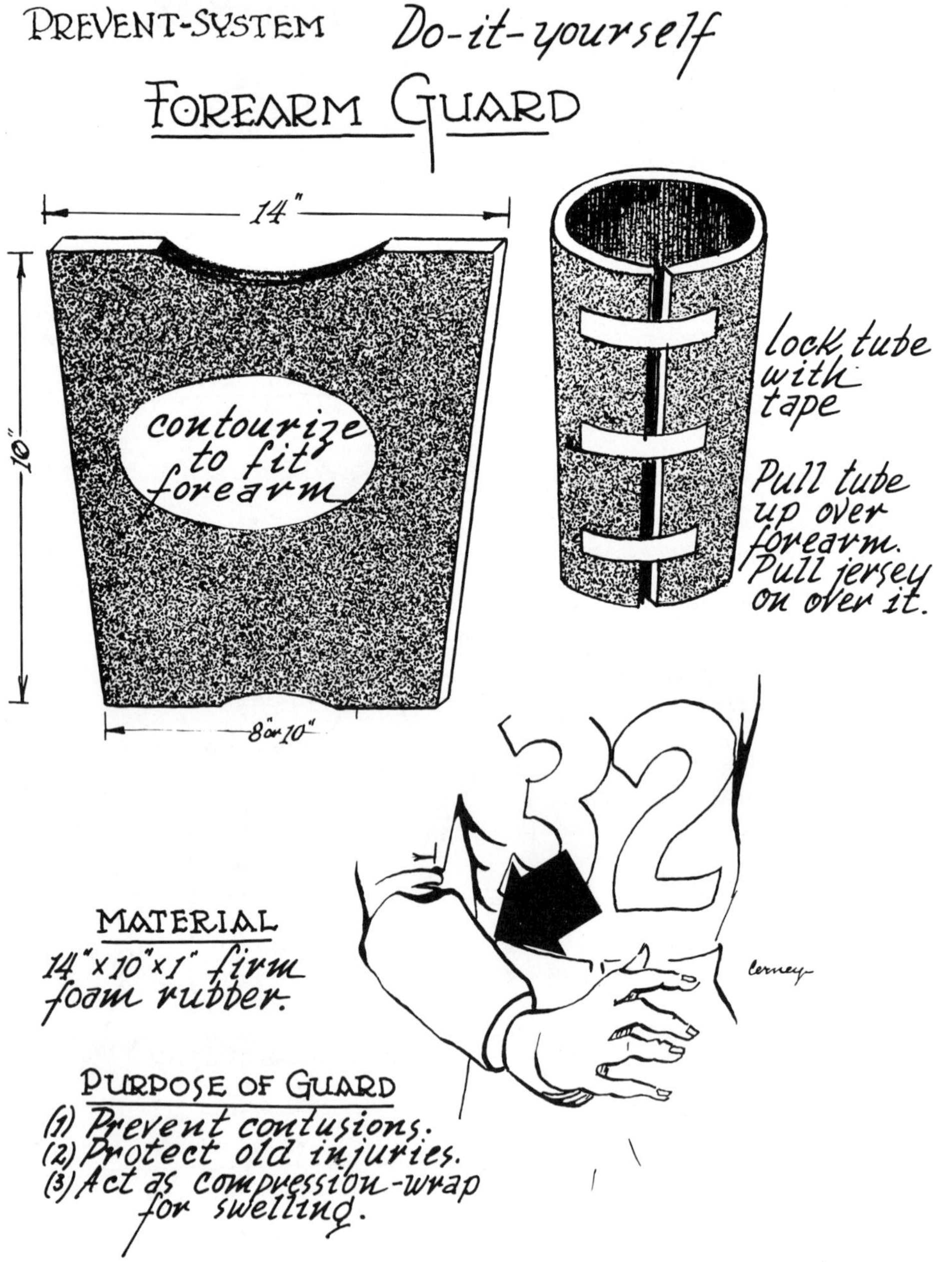

Figure 5-14

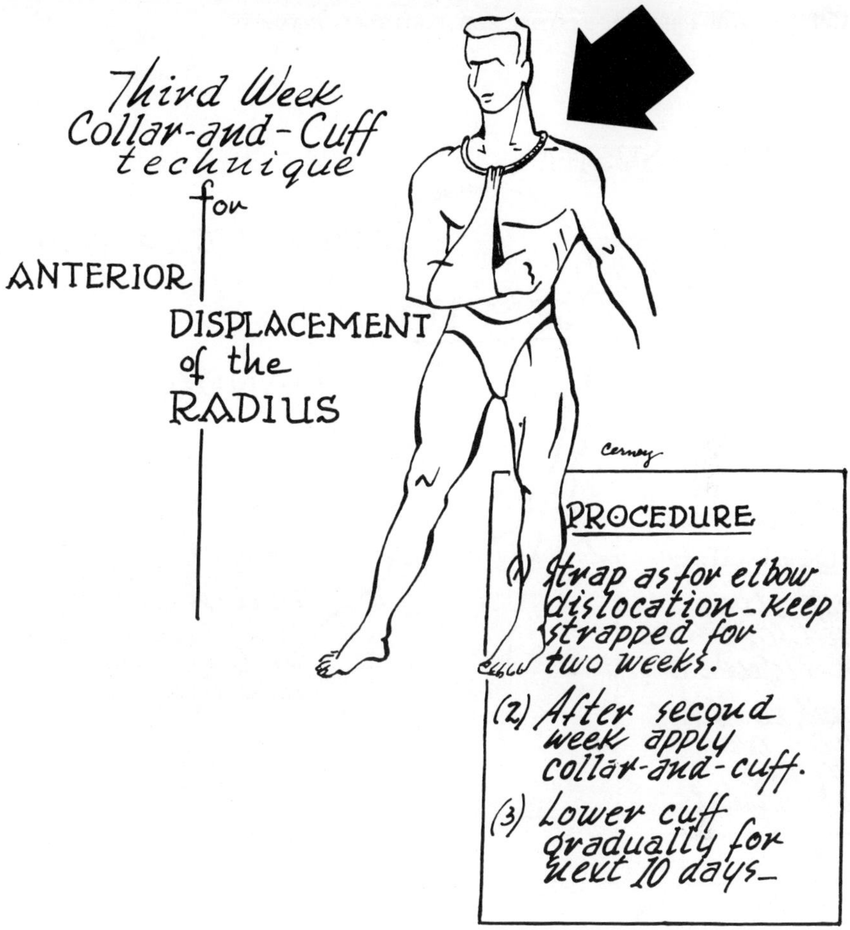

Figure 5-15

FOREARM INJURIES

Forearm injuries in football are usually confined to bruises and contusions, and armguards are the method of protection. Most forearm injuries occur in offensive blocking drills. A forearm may be contused by hard padding, helmets, judo chops, or blows from an opponent's forearm, helmet, facemask, fist, or foot. When padding on the forearm is used, the material should be washable and interchangeable. If felt, rubber, or other shock-absorbent material is not available, make your own padding by wrapping the forearm with newspaper. Lock the paper in position with cotton elastic wrap and spiral adhesive strapping to set it in position.

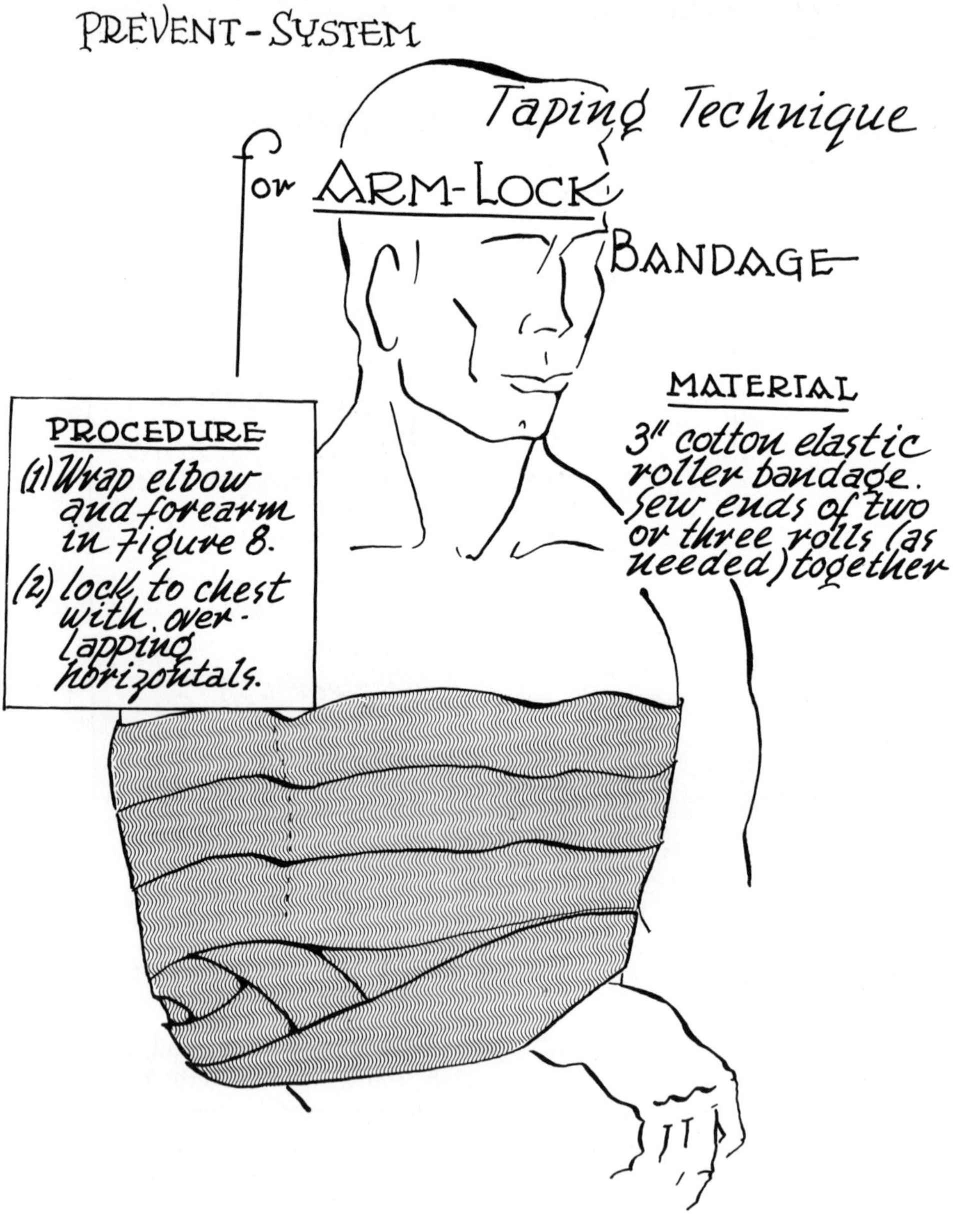
PREVENT-SYSTEM
Taping Technique
for ARM-LOCK
BANDAGE
MATERIAL
3" cotton elastic roller bandage. Sew ends of two or three rolls (as needed) together
PROCEDURE
(1) Wrap elbow and forearm in Figure 8.
(2) lock to chest with over-lapping horizontals.

Figure 5-16

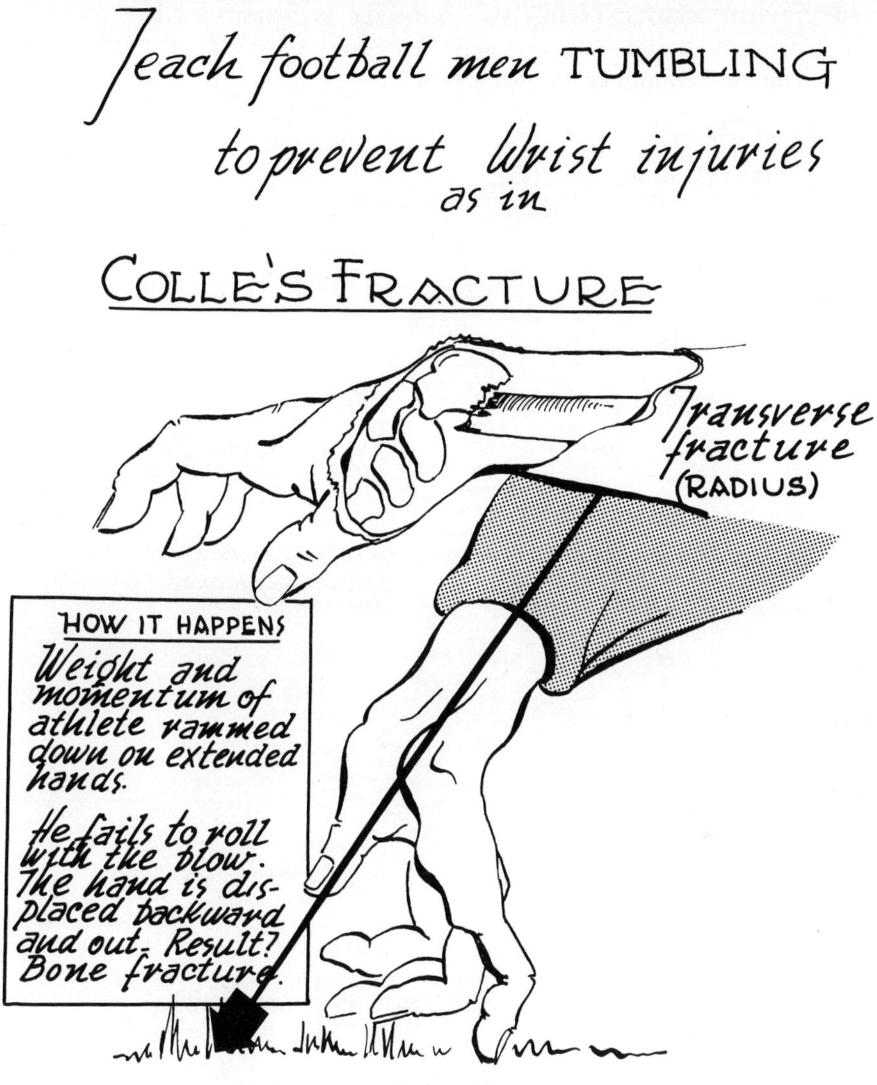

Figure 5-17

WRIST INJURIES

It is worth restating that the best injury-prevention technique for the extremities and their joints is tumbling. Teach football players to take a blow and disperse it. To take any jarring impact on the hands and wrist and elbow demands strengthening of the forearms. For this I suggest the following weight-training program. The forearm flexors and wrist are especially aided by the "wrist curl."

Taping Techniques for the Wrist

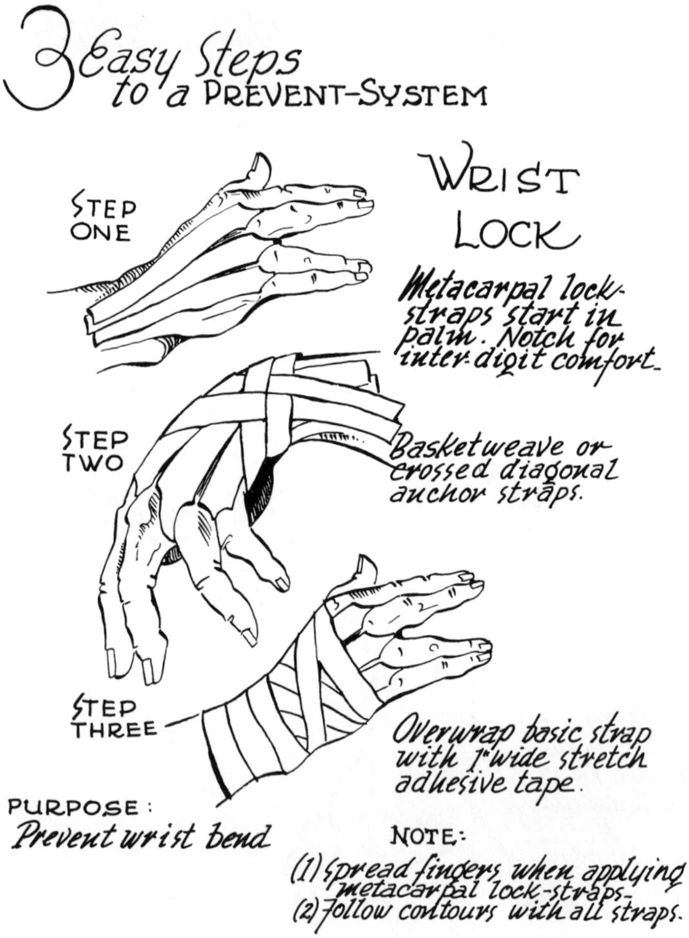

Figure 5-18

Weight Training Techniques

(a) *For flexors.* In seated position, grasp the barbell with the palms up. Place forearms on the thigh. Now work the wrist through all ranges of motion. Permit the barbell to roll down to the fingertips. Bring it back up into the hand. Repeat with palms down.

(b) *For extensors.* In standing position, with the barbell behind the neck, raise barbell to fully locked overhead position. Lower away and repeat. In supine position, holding the barbell at arm's length above the chest, bend the arms, lower the barbell to touch down behind the head. Keep the elbows up. Return in an arc to the starting point above.

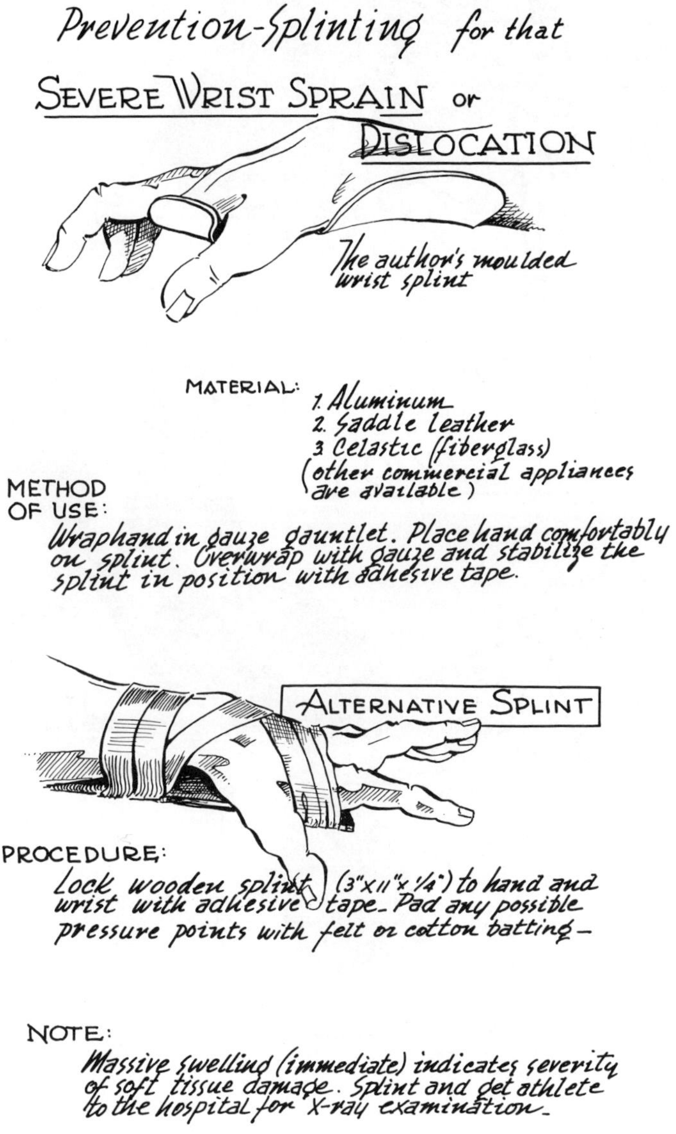

Figure 5-19

Special Note: *Use wristbands and adhesive strappings on an athlete only when there is actual bone, joint, or other soft tissue damage. Do not use them at the player's request, or permit him to use them unless he's a particularly valuable prima donna who needs them for psychological effect.*

Figure 5-20

HAND INJURIES

Hand injuries may include strains, sprains, fractures, dislocations, abrasions, blisters, pinches, excoriations, cellulitis, and penetrating wounds. Prevention procedures for the hand may begin with something as simple as wearing a pair of cotton workman's gloves in cold weather. Light leather gloves may be worn by linemen. Backfield men and quarterbacks can wear surgeon's latex gloves. Another valuable tool is the boxer's wrap, to which may be added foam rubber padding over the knuckles for warmth as well as protection.

Taping Techniques for the Hand

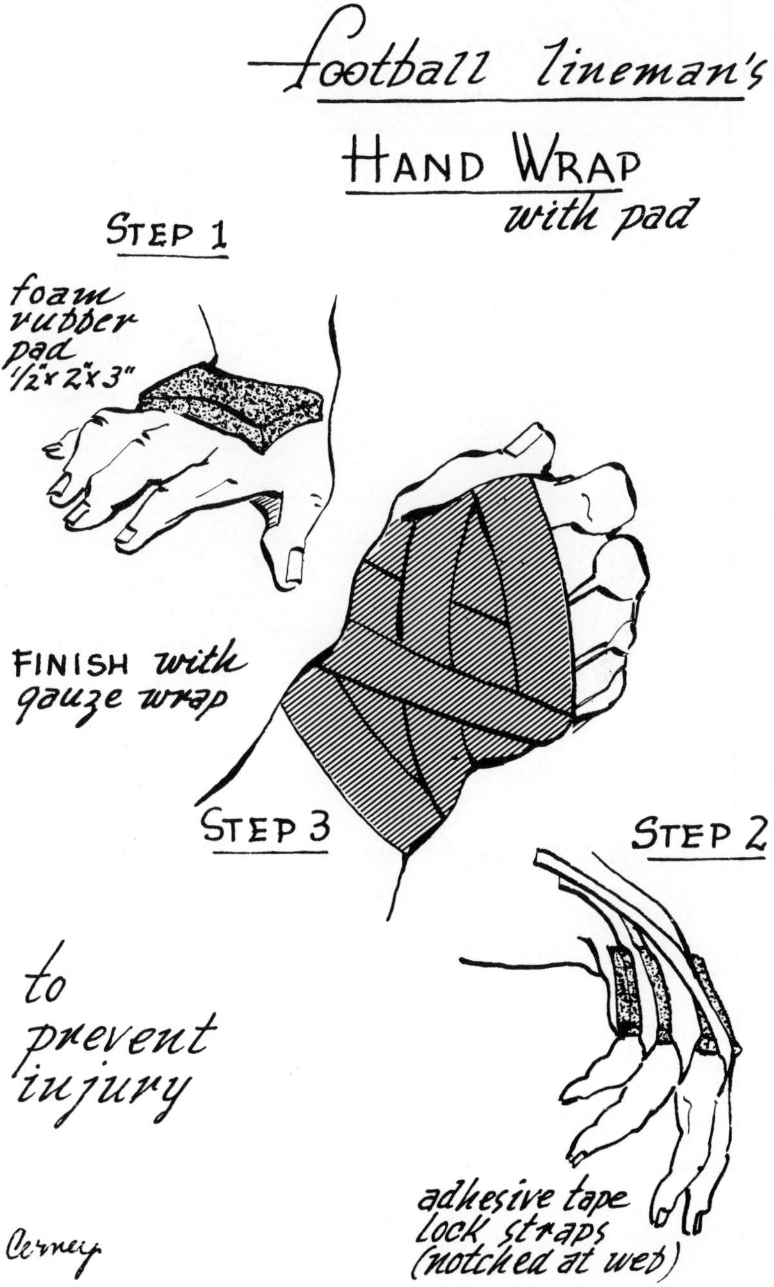

Figure 5-21

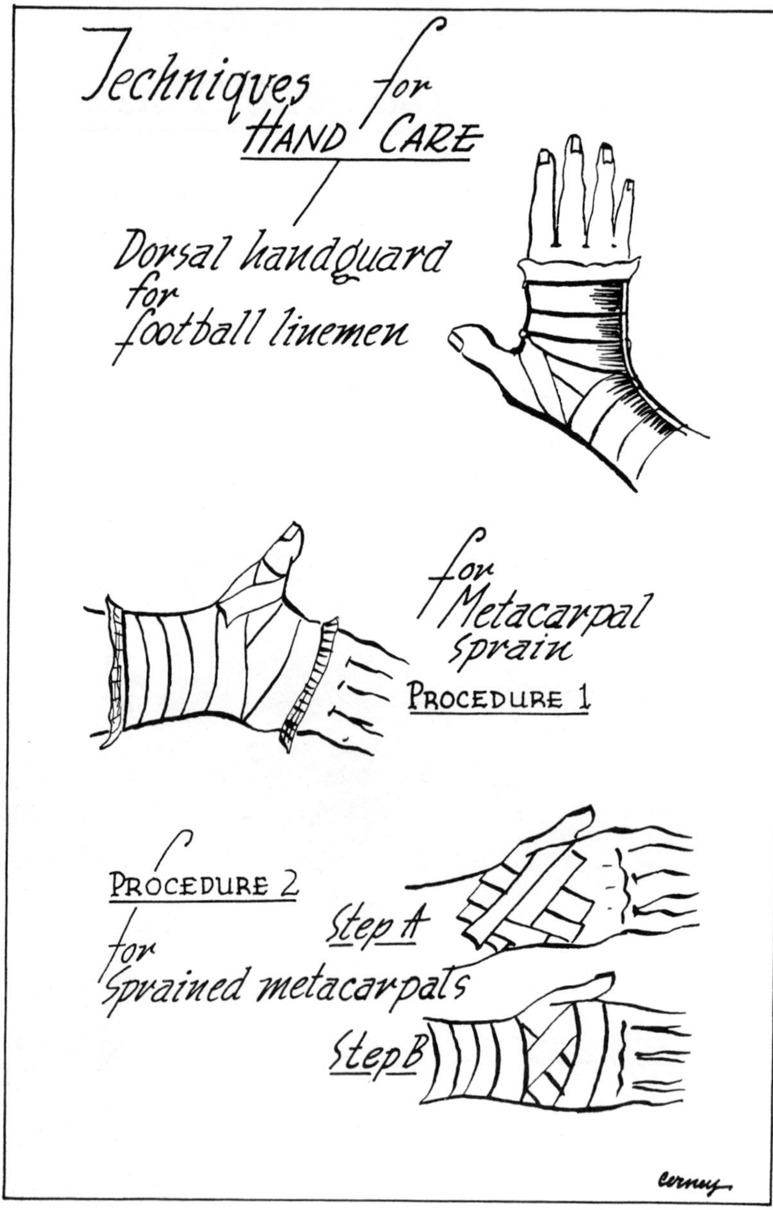
Techniques for HAND CARE
Dorsal handguard for football linemen
for Metacarpal Sprain
PROCEDURE 1
PROCEDURE 2
for Sprained metacarpals
Step A
Step B
Cerney

Figure 5-22

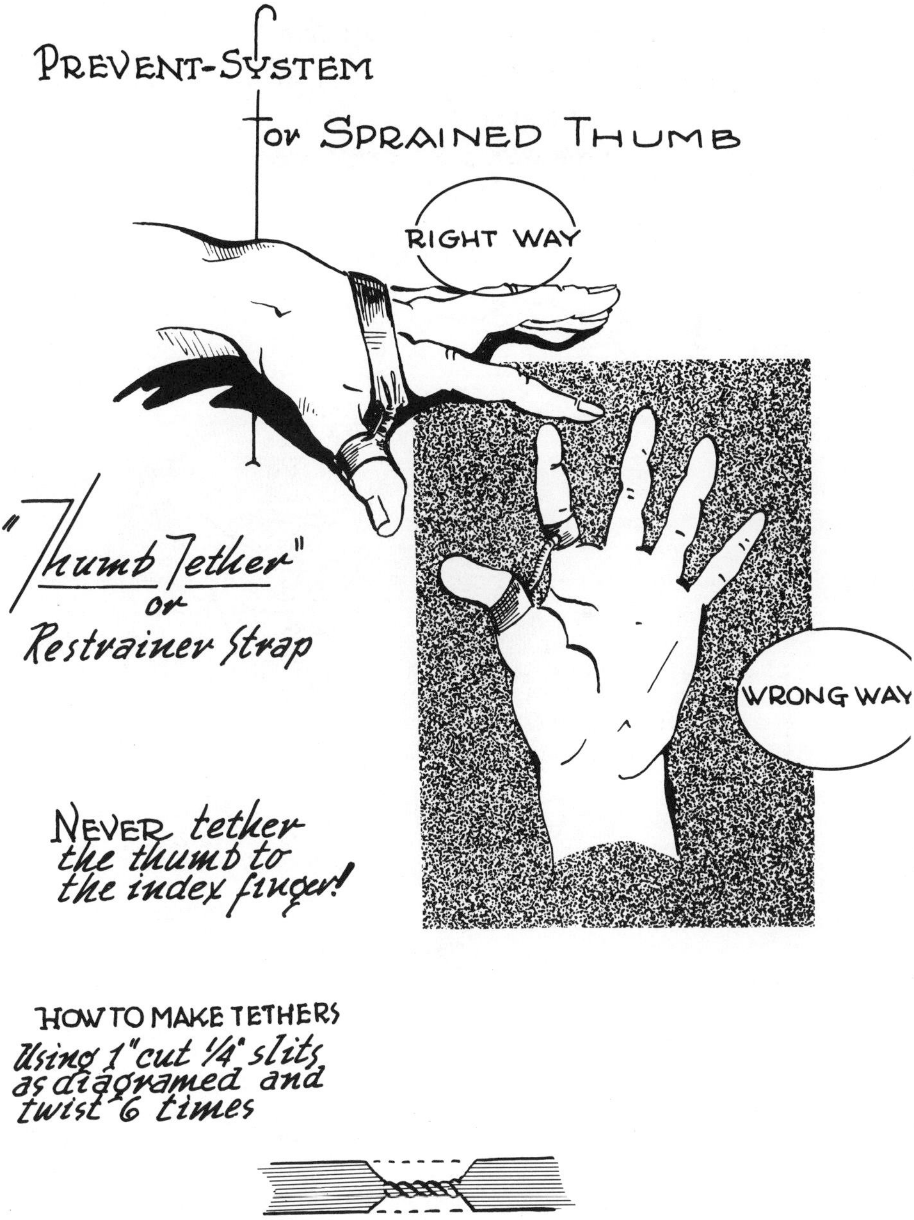
PREVENT-SYSTEM
for SPRAINED THUMB
RIGHT WAY
"Thumb Tether"
or
Restrainer Strap
WRONG WAY
NEVER tether
the thumb to
the index finger!
HOW TO MAKE TETHERS
Using 1" cut 1/4" slits
as diagramed and
twist 6 times

Figure 5-23

Taping Techniques for the Thorax

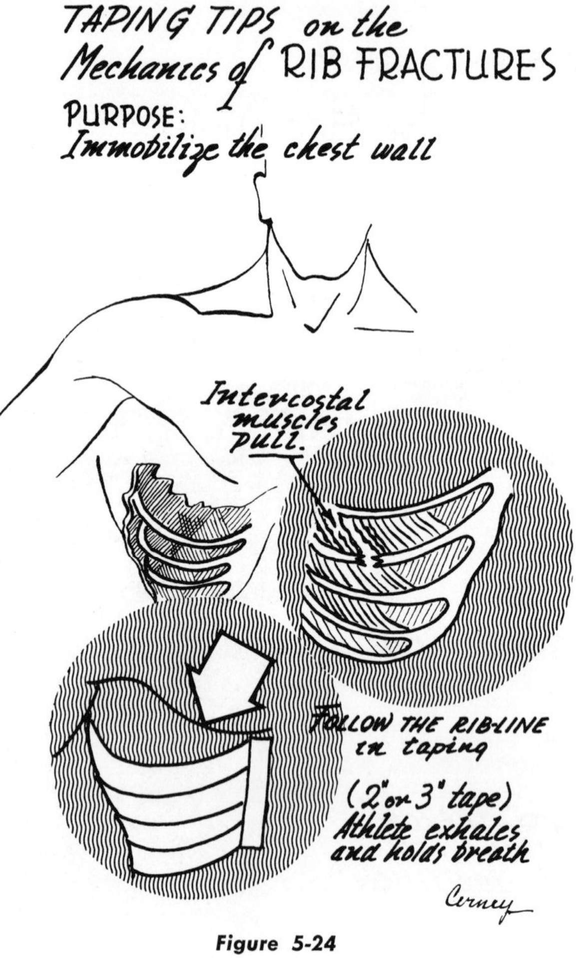

Figure 5-24

THORAX INJURIES

Injuries to the chest wall may occur as contusions, bruises, and abrasions. There may be intercostal muscle strain or rib fracture. Pain may occur in the chest as the result of ill-fitting shoulder guards. The clavicle may be fractured or dislocated from its socket in the sternum. Fracture to the clavicle may come as the result of a fall on the outstretched hand and arm, with the force of the fall referred up through the arm, shoulder, and acromioclavicular joint, along the clavicle and

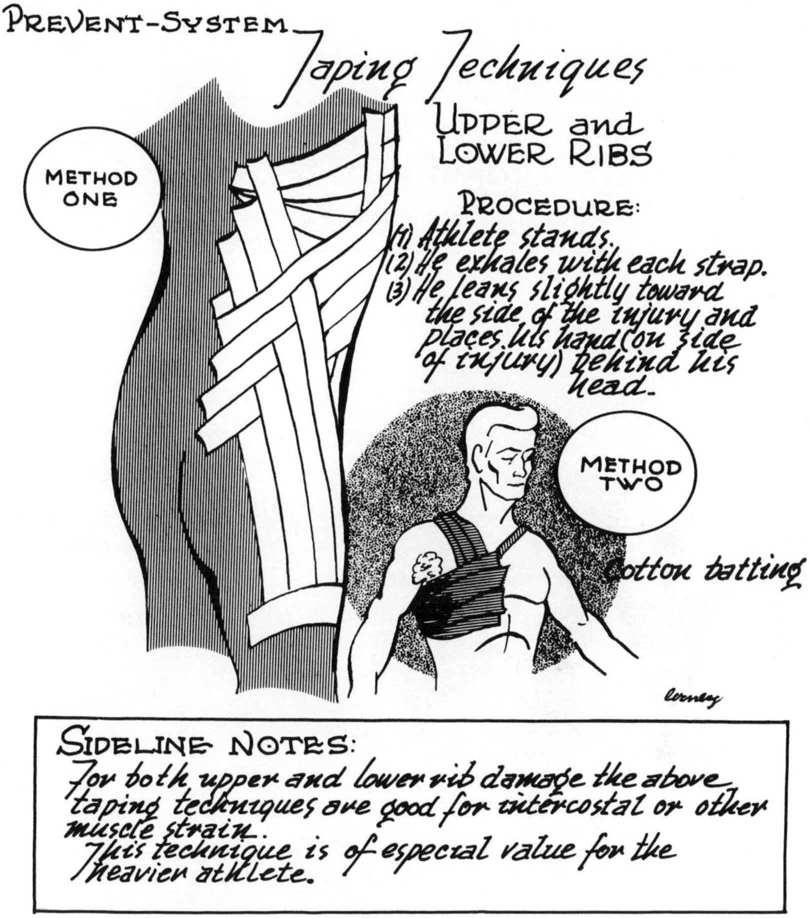

Figure 5-25

into the chest. It may also occur if a player lands ineptly on the shoulder point. A fall on the shoulder point may result from failure to control the body roll forward or backward.

There are not too many aids for the prevention of football injuries to the anterior and posterior chest wall. The first wall of protection for the thorax is the rib cage; it gives with trauma. The musculature is also a line of defense. To protect the chest wall further, the following should be taught: (1) how to tumble to take a fall; (2) how to scoop a football; (3) how to protect himself when blocking, tackling, and falling; (4) how to fall on a "loose ball" (fumble) and protect his ribs and belly; and (5) how to develop his chest muscles.

PREVENT-System Taping Techniques for the LOWER RIBS

METHOD ONE

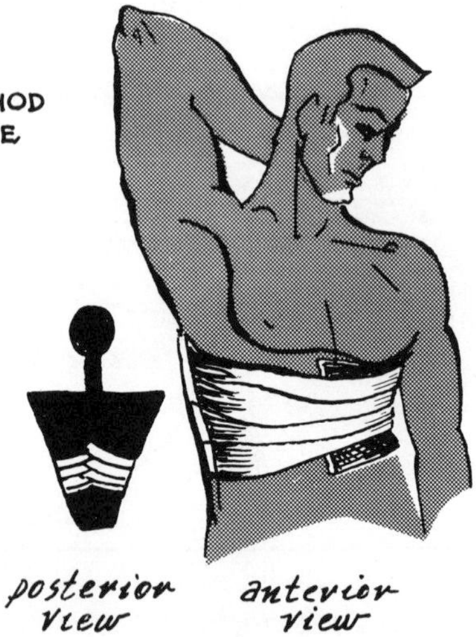

MATERIAL

(4) 3" adhesive tape strips around thorax-

(1) felt pad (1/4" x 7" x 15")

PROCEDURE

(1) Athlete standing
(2) He exhales before each strap is applied
(3) He leans toward side of the injury.
(4) Hand (on side of injury) placed behind head.

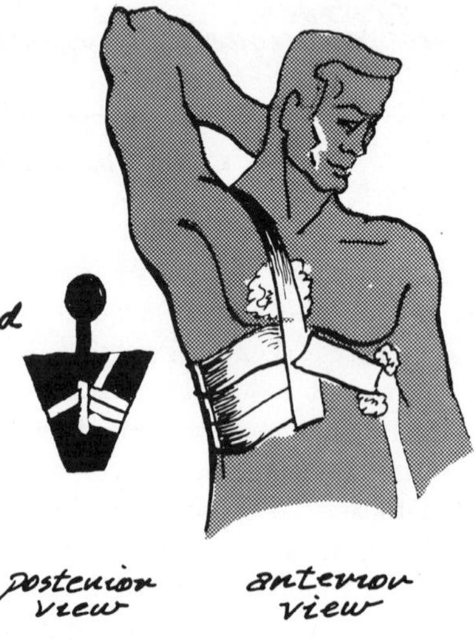

Cerney

Figure 5-26

PREVENT-System Taping Techniques

for INJURY to the STERNUM

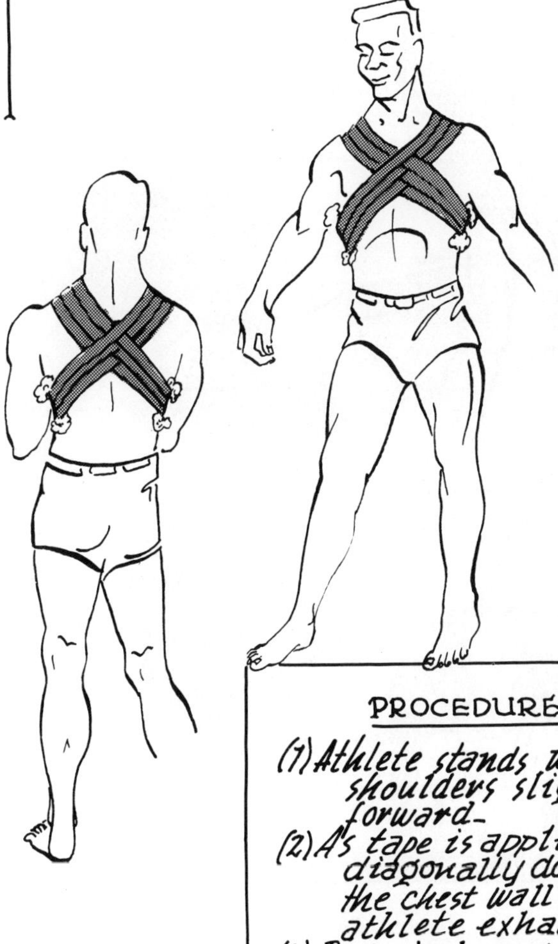

MATERIAL

cotton batting
1½" adhesive tape

PROCEDURE

(1) Athlete stands with shoulders slightly forward.
(2) As tape is applied diagonally down over the chest wall the athlete exhales.
(3) Pad nipples and ribs.

Figure 5-27

PREVENT-System using Elastic Tape
for
STRAINED
STERNUM
NOTE:
Elastic adhesive
tape provides
mobile control

Figure 5-28

BACK INJURIES

According to Dr. Vincent J. Turco, orthopedic surgeon at St. Francis Hospital, Hartford, Connecticut and team physician for the Hartford *Knights,* sports injuries to the lower back are relatively uncommon. "Back injuries account for about only 4 percent of all sports injuries." But he adds that "Minor back injuries—and most of them are minor, still seem to be a major catastrophe in the mind of the athlete." [1] Dr. Turco stresses prevention of such injuries and, when they happen, accurate diagnosis to insure a speedy recovery. For example, if a fractured transverse process on a vertebra is mistaken for a sprain or strain and the wrong treatment initiated, the disability may be prolonged and recovery slow. Instead of a few days disability, to everyone's surprise, the athlete may be out for the season.

When there is an actual low back compression fracture, Dr. Turco advocates a three-point hyperextension brace with ambulation and exercise to tolerance. The athlete should be barred from sports for six months to prevent reinjury. When there has been severe muscle damage in the low back, he calls for bed rest, analgesics, enzymes, muscle relaxants, and ambulation with a back corset for support. Disability, he indicates, usually lasts six months. Athletes are to return to the roster *only after full recovery* and to carry full protective equipment as well as corset and taping.

SPINAL INJURIES

From the surgical standpoint I can appreciate Dr. Turco's claim that back injuries are rare, but from where I have been standing at gridiron level in the midst of athletic injuries over the past thirty years, I've seen a lot of back injuries. They are definitely not rare.

As a result of direct blows, referred blows, flexion, torsion, or twisting in football, the athlete may get a contusion, sprain, strain, vertebral subluxation, a cervical myofasciitis (whiplash) of the neck, separated sacroiliac joints, muscle tearing, pelvic rotation, a "short leg" distorting low back muscles and cutting down efficiency, or any of a dozen other problems, and they're not that rare!

Particularly significant about back and spinal injuries is that the spinal cord and central nervous system is the body's control tower. Without it the football player could become paralyzed. The Thirty-Seventh

[1] V.J. Turco, "Back Injuries Are Rare," *Medicine in Sports Newsletter* 9, May 3, 1969, p. 2.

Annual Survey of U.S. Football Fatalities revealed that all thirty-six deaths due to football in 1968 were caused by injuries to the head, neck, or spinal cord. With statistics like these, even if back injuries are rare, they can be the worst injuries of all and must be scrupulously prevented. Some major back injuries are: arthrides after trauma such as osteoarthritis, fibrositis, calcified iliolumbar ligament calcification, adolescent wedging roundbacks, lipping and osteophytic formations on a traumatized spinal bone, sciatic scoliosis, structural postural posterior, anterior, and lateral curvatures, transitional and congenitally defective vertebrae brought to light by x-ray after low back injury, posterior defects in the sacral vertebrae, pseudoarthrosis at the sacral wings of the fifth lumbar, tilted pelvis due to an insecure lumbosacral junction following a tackling injury, posterior or anterior displacement of the fifth lumber on the sacrum called spondylolisthesis, spondylolysis, and spondylosis, and many other problems all in the back.

Prevent-System Techniques for the Back and Spinal Column

The preseason physical should include x-ray film of the pelvis and spinal column, as well as of the joint where injuries are known to have occured. This ounce of prevention is one of the most vital pounds of cure you can buy. If read properly, these films can tell so very much. They can tell you whether or not to put a boy back into competition, and they can prevent his becoming one of the fatalities in the annual United States survey.

Teach players to tumble to remove the impact of a fall.

Teach players peripheral vision procedures to spot, and be conscious of, lateral and posterior pursuers.

Teach players to maintain tension with absolutely no relaxation of any muscles, including the back, until the referee has blown the final whistle.

Teach players the necessity for physical therapy in the rehabilitation of new and old injuries to the back.

Weight Training Techniques

(a) *Upper Back.* Basic rowing and pullover exercises with the barbells may be used, or one-arm rowing with heavy dumbbells while the athlete leans forward with the torso parallel to the floor. Lying supine, use the bent-arm pullover for strengthening upper back muscles. Exhale while pulling over. Inhale while lowering the weight. Also do dumbbell presses while lying on a slanted board.

(b) *Lower Back.* Squatting exercises (only if the condition of the player's knees permit), combined with lifts from the floor may be used for this purpose. With legs straight, do a dead-weight lift. For additional stretch, stand on a low box.

Taping Techniques for the Back

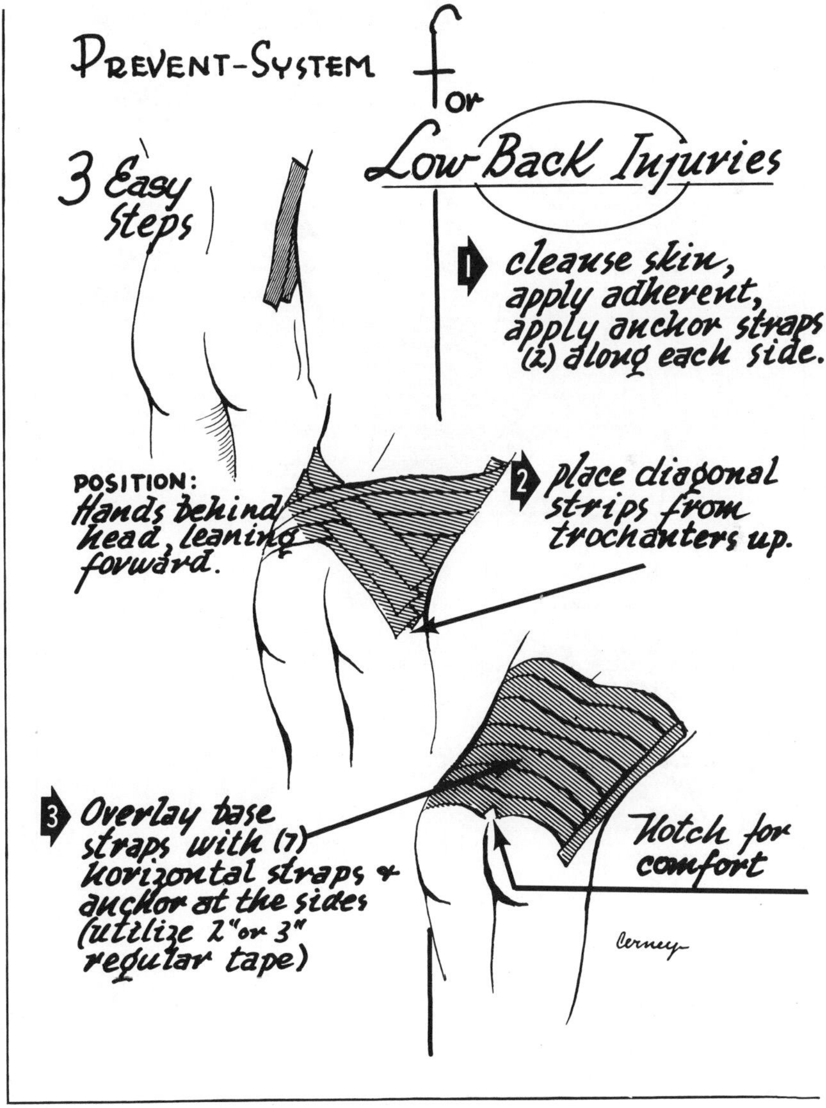

Figure 5-29

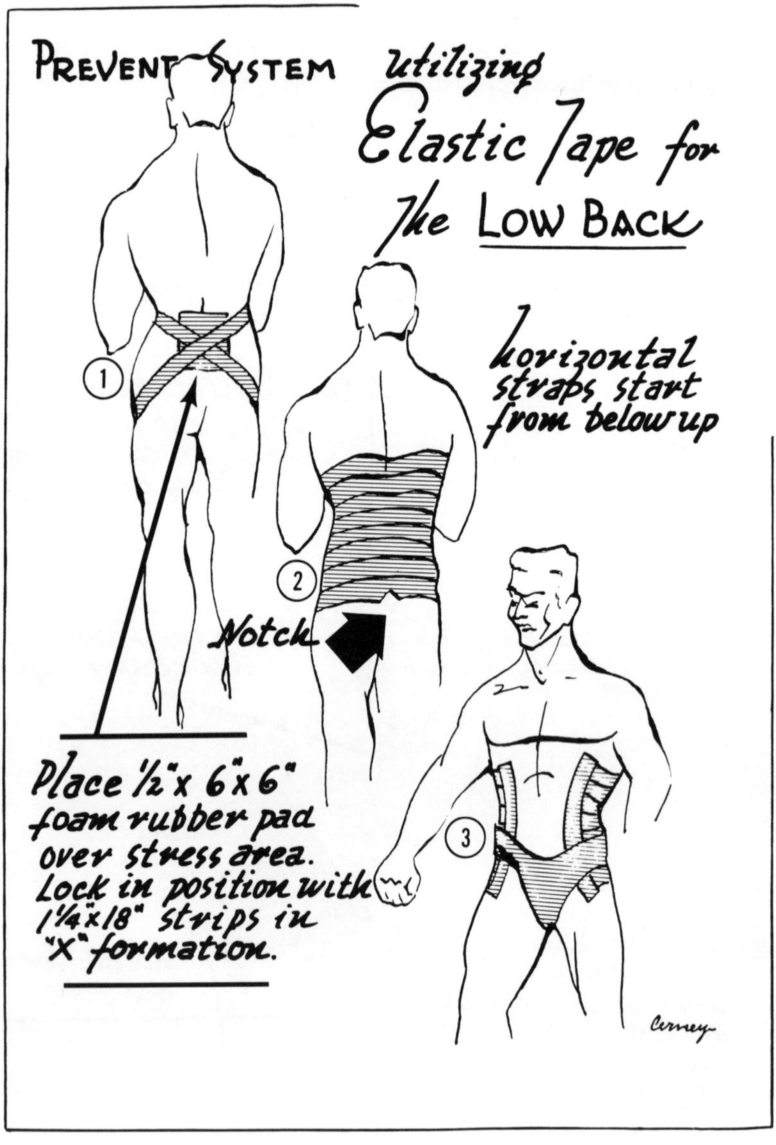
PREVENT-SYSTEM utilizing
Elastic Tape for
The LOW BACK
horizontal
straps start
from below up
Notch
Place ½"x 6"x 6"
foam rubber pad
over stress area.
Lock in position with
1¼"x18" strips in
"X" formation.
1
2
3
Cerney

Figure 5-30

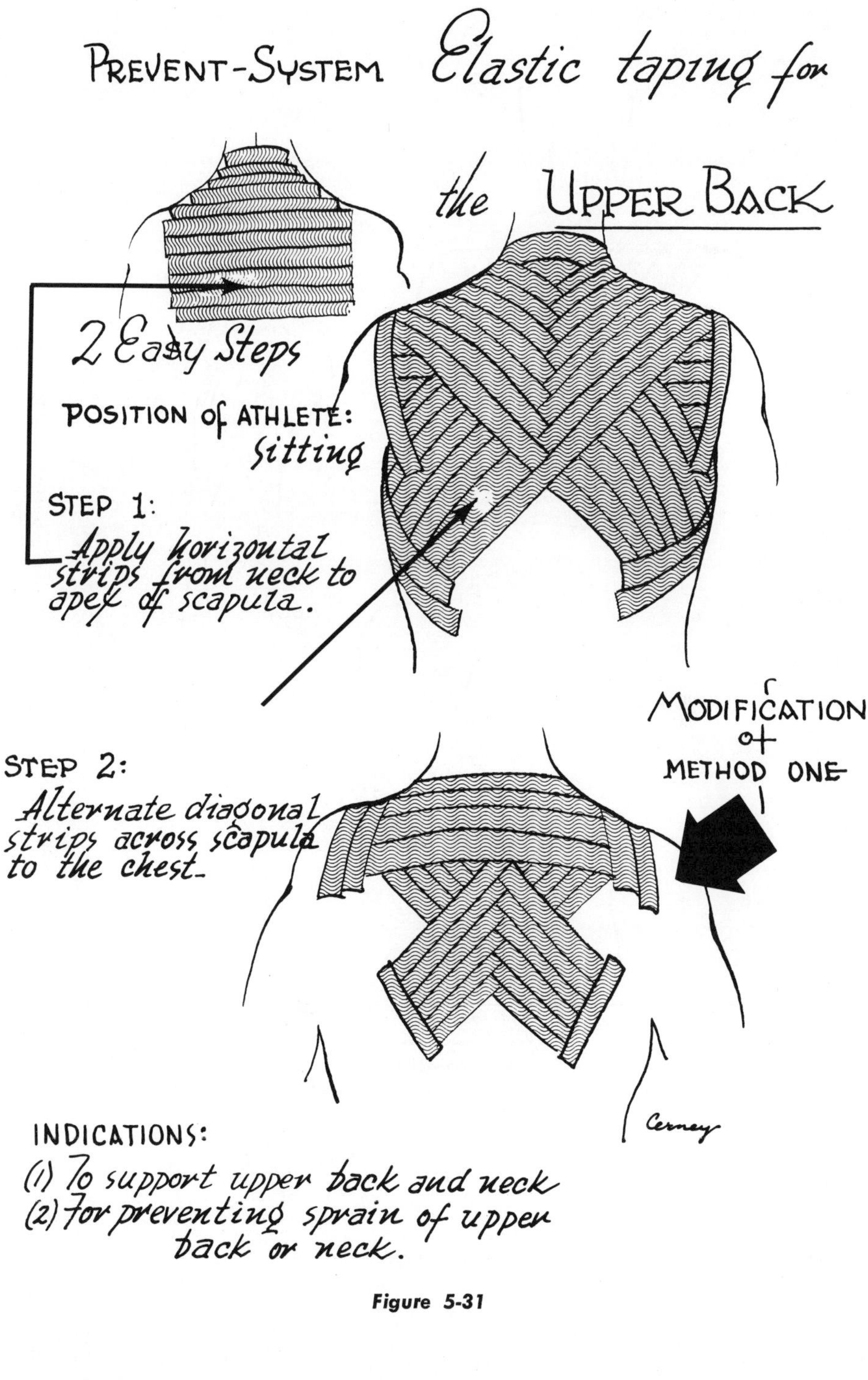
PREVENT-SYSTEM Elastic taping for the UPPER BACK
2 Easy Steps
POSITION of ATHLETE: sitting
STEP 1:
Apply horizontal strips from neck to apex of scapula.
STEP 2:
Alternate diagonal strips across scapula to the chest.
MODIFICATION of METHOD ONE
INDICATIONS:
(1) To support upper back and neck
(2) For preventing sprain of upper back or neck.
Cerney

Figure 5-31

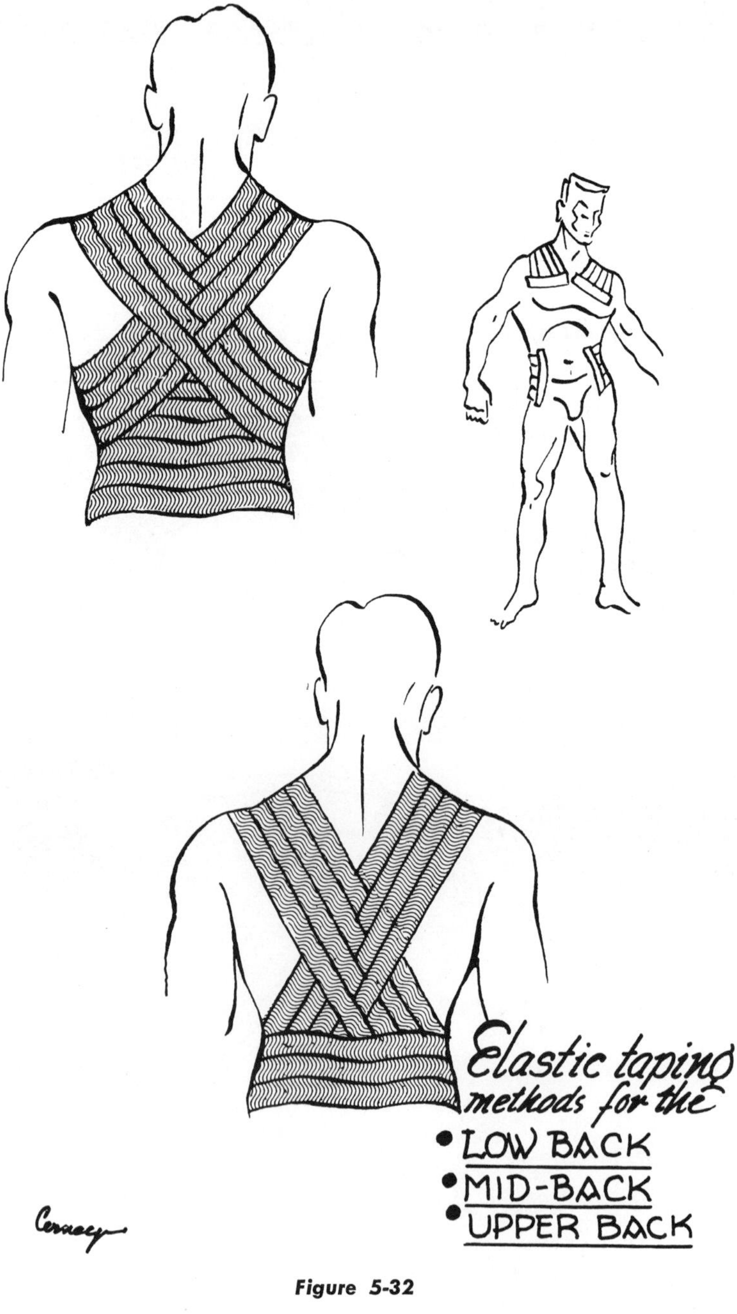
Elastic taping methods for the
• LOW BACK
• MID-BACK
• UPPER BACK
Ceraacy

Figure 5-32

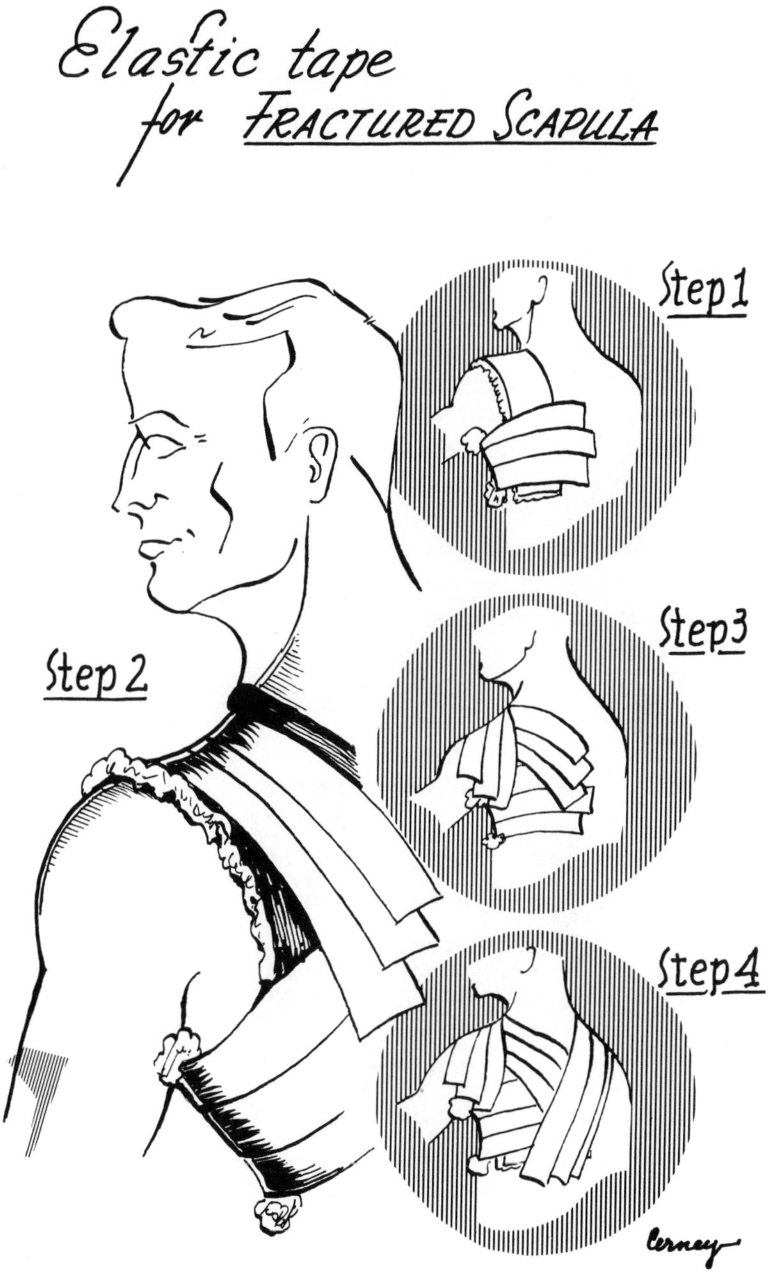
Elastic tape
for FRACTURED SCAPULA
Step 1
Step 2
Step 3
Step 4
Cerney

Figure 5-33

ABDOMINAL INJURIES

The more common injuries to the abdomen in football are *superficial contusions, muscle tears, hernia, splenic rupture,* and *loosened or "floating" kidneys*. The best protection an abdomen has is a strong musculature. For this purpose, calisthenics, weight-training, and rope climbing are the best procedures. Use the following excellent weight-training and taping techniques.

Weight Training Techniques

To work the abdominal muscles effectively, all weight-training exercises should incorporate leg raises or sit-ups. Weights may be attached to the head or feet as strength develops. Do not add weights until leg raises or sit-ups come easily after twenty repetitions. To increase the exercise work on an incline board. Raise the incline as power develops in the abdominal area.

Taping Techniques for the Abdomen

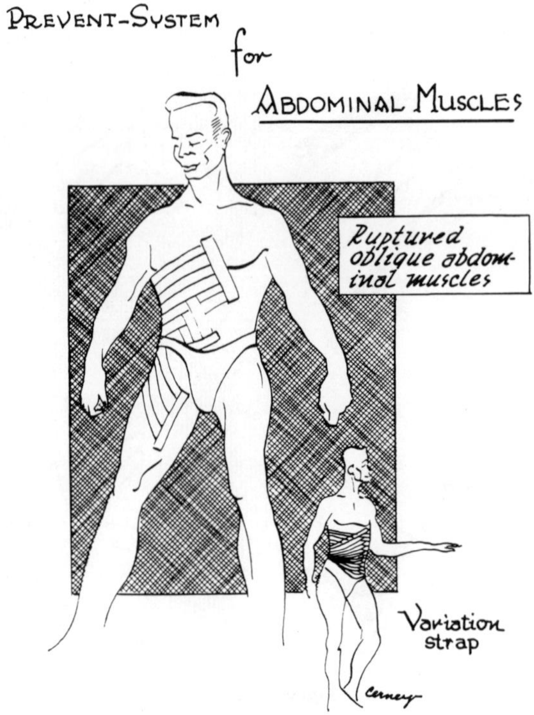

Figure 5-34

Taping Techniques for the Pelvis

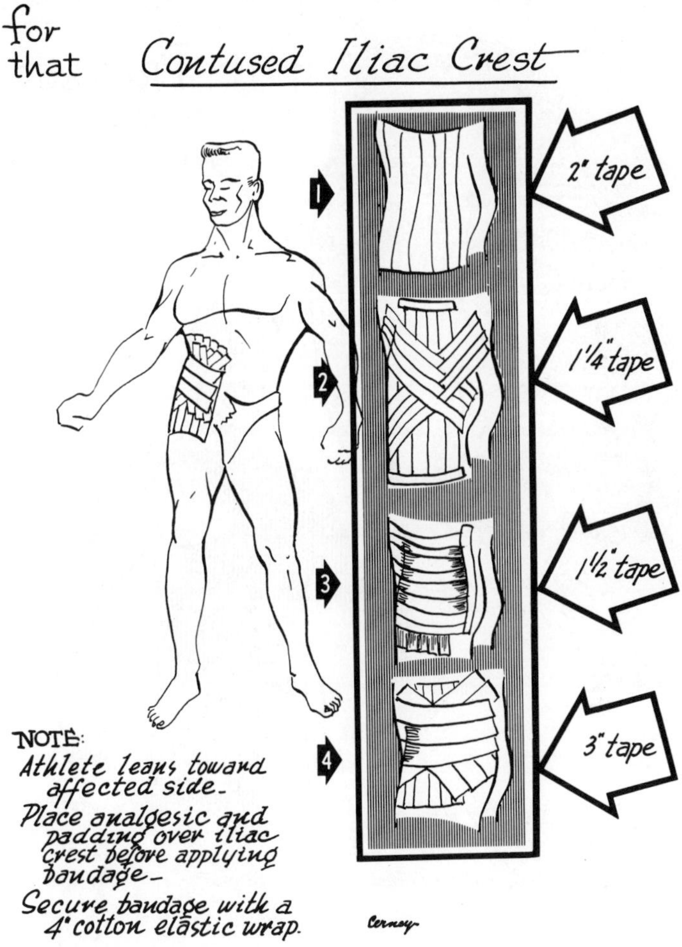

Figure 5-35

PELVIC INJURIES

Most pelvic injuries in football are from direct contact with other players. Such football injuries usually occur in "pile-ups" and on the "blind side" of the player. Contusions on the crest of the ilium may be complicated by large hematomas (trapped pockets of free blood). Such contusions may occur despite all kinds of padding. They may even result from padding which has shifted during action or is inadequate in its protective function. (See Figure 5-36.)

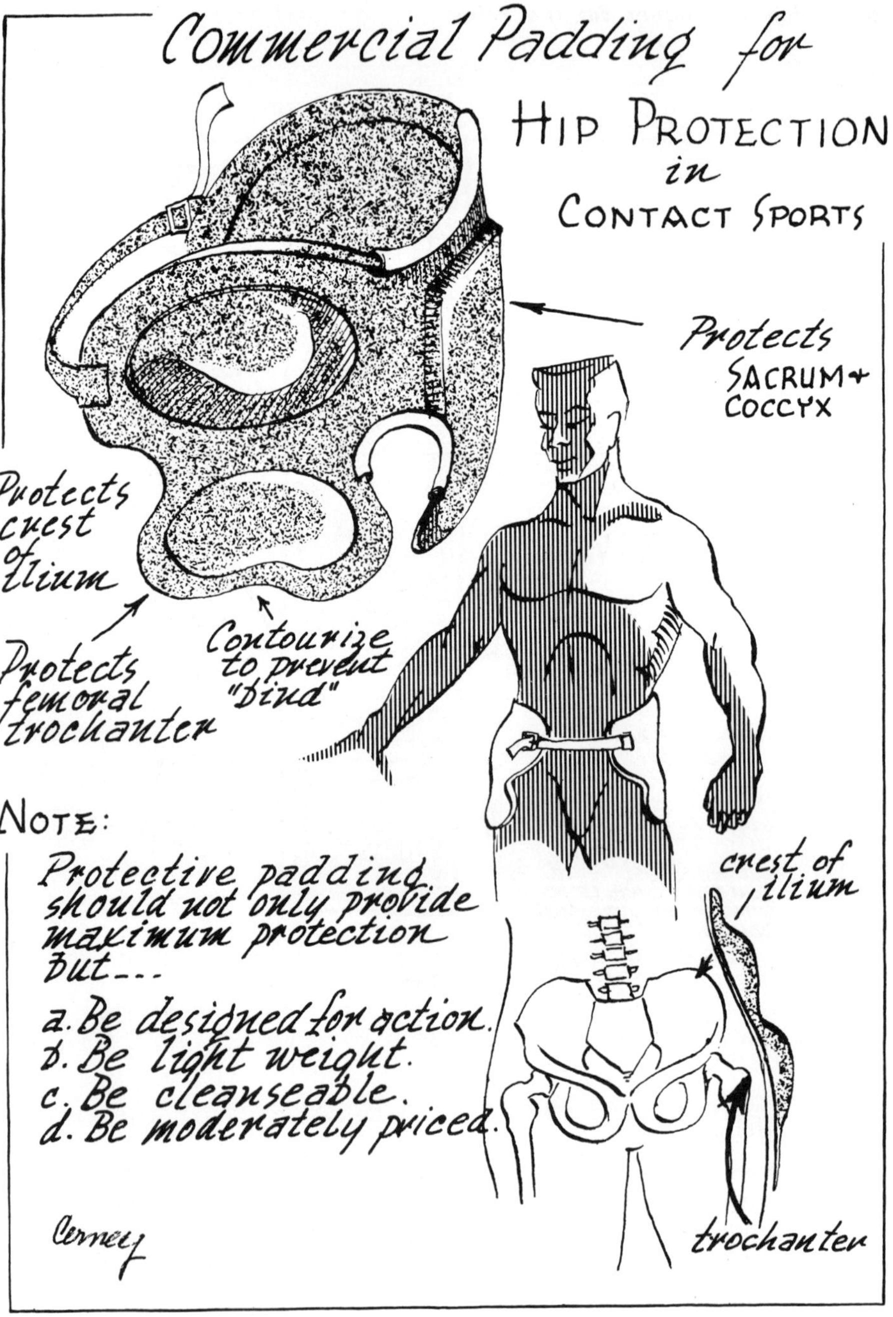
Commercial Padding for
HIP PROTECTION
in
CONTACT SPORTS
Protects SACRUM + COCCYX
Protects crest of ilium
Protects femoral trochanter
Contourize to prevent "bind"
NOTE:
Protective padding should not only provide maximum protection but...
a. Be designed for action.
b. Be light weight.
c. Be cleanseable.
d. Be moderately priced.
crest of ilium
trochanter
Cerney

Figure 5-36

HIP INJURIES

The great trochanter of the femur (thigh bone) may get contused. This happens more often to the thinner athlete who has not yet developed heavy thigh muscles. For the most part the thigh muscles protect this bony protuberance.

Taping Techniques for the Hip

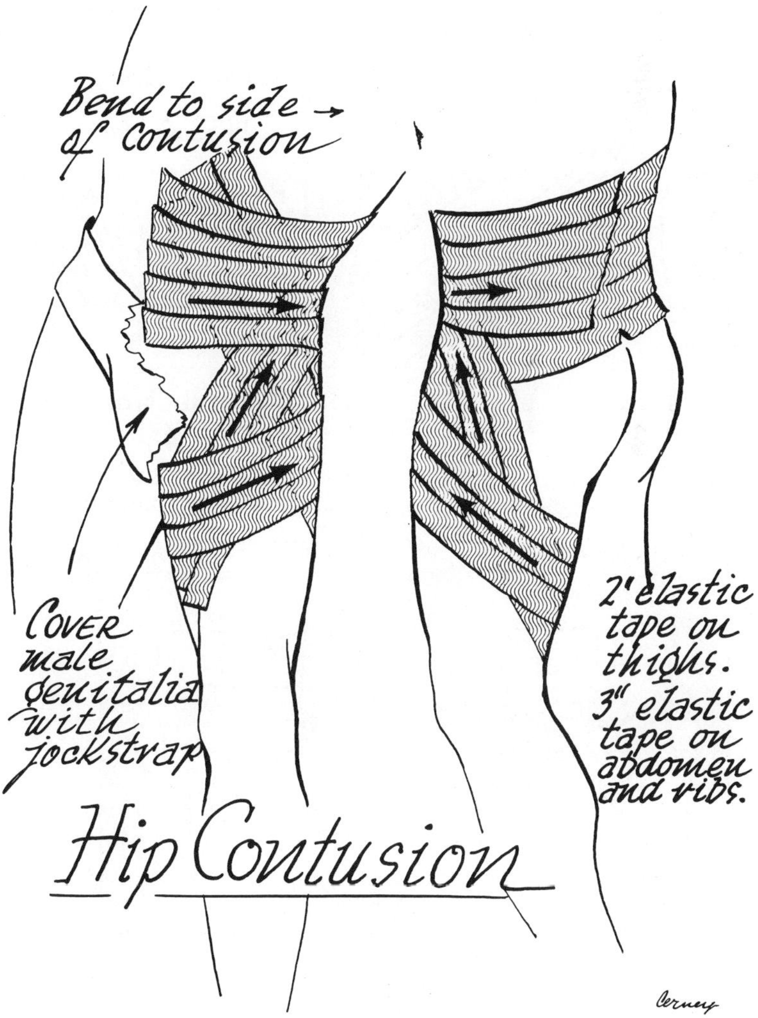

Figure 5-37

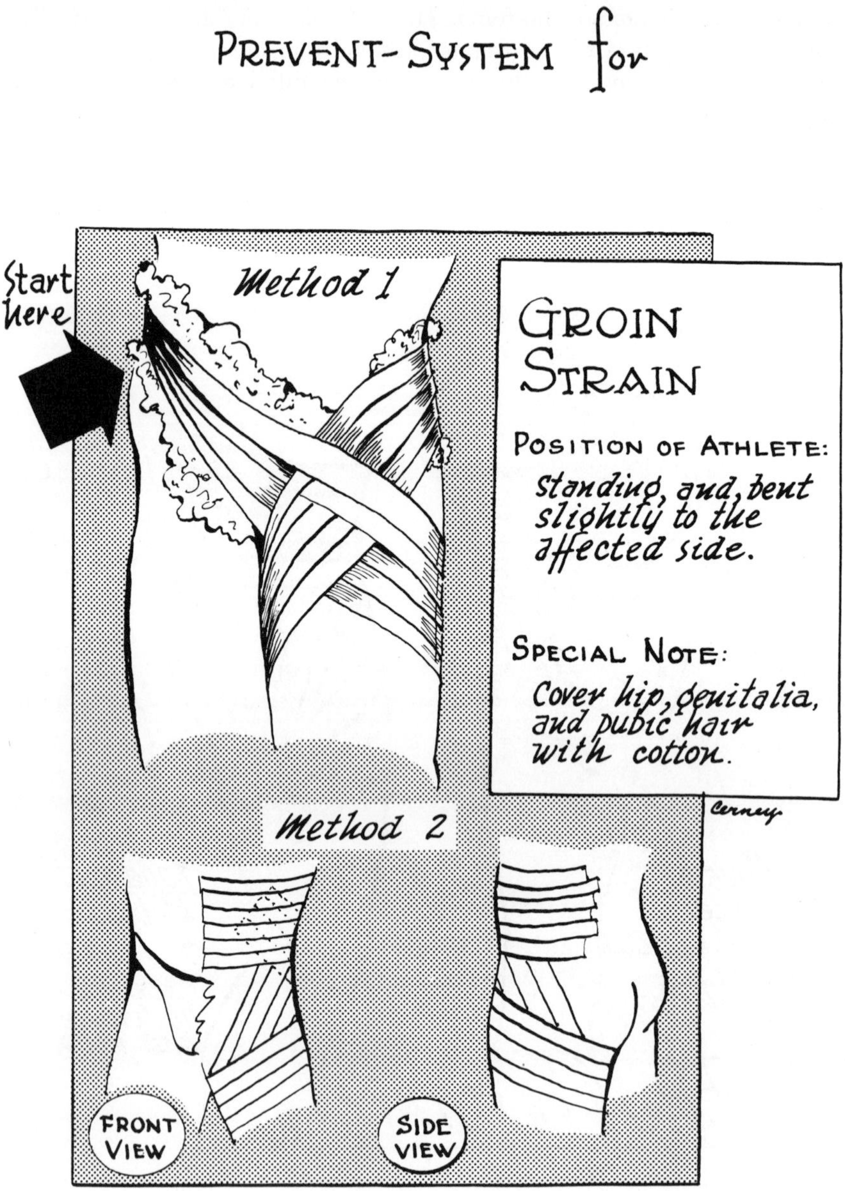
PREVENT-SYSTEM for
Start here
Method 1
GROIN STRAIN
POSITION OF ATHLETE:
Standing, and bent slightly to the affected side.
SPECIAL NOTE:
Cover hip, genitalia, and pubic hair with cotton.
Cerney
Method 2
FRONT VIEW
SIDE VIEW

Figure 5-38

THIGH INJURIES

Direct blows to the thigh may cause hematomas which may resolve, as they calcify, to myositis ossificans.[2] Shifted or inadequate padding, plus hard blocking, are the usual causes of thigh injury. Thigh injuries may occur when a player tries to block a kick. I have found that this injury is more apt to happen in soft and underdeveloped muscles that are not yet firmed out by rigorous training programs. Muscles have a preseason predisposition to injury. Therefore, the best protection for the thigh is development by preseason conditioning. Thigh muscles are the first to be affected in knee injuries; they are the "guardians of the knee." One of the first vital prevention procedures is to stop all early season croutching or squatting exercise. Elimination of such exercises is mandatory, especially for big men on the squad with heavy thighs. Special effort should be made to stretch the thighs in the warm-up, but *avoid knee-bends like the "duck walk,"* which tears tissue and can effectively kill a sports career in an afternoon's ill-considered "workout." Avoid fast starts in early season and fast starts coming up out of a crouched position. Thigh muscle "tears" begin with inadequate workouts. There is local stasis so if a direct blow occurs to this area, its condition makes it ripe for myositis ossificans.

Remember that a boy with a "pulled thigh muscle" is a bad commentary on the conditioning program. More often than not this boy already has a previous history of knee and thigh injuries. Injuries like this indicate an inadequate preseason physical examination and equally poor rehabilitation of those injuries. Make sure the trainer (at the team physician's prescription) initiates physical therapy for thigh muscle rehabilitation if an athlete has a record of thigh or knee injury.

Preventive padding for previous thigh injuries should be designed for muscle dynamics. To achieve this, avoid standard padding that slips into pockets in the pants or is suspended from a belt. As indicated earlier, the trainer should custom fit each player. The trainer should remove all possible blunt or trauma-producing edges from the pad. He has to skive felt padding down to a feather edge. When the preseason and athletic examinations and history reveal previous thigh trauma, start an in-depth investigation before permitting that boy on the field. Get anterior, posterior, and lateral x-ray films. Determine the status of each muscle with electrotherapy testing equipment. This could prove to be the best prevention you ever used!

[2] Myositis ossificans is an inflammatory condition of the muscle, complicated by the breaking of blood vessels and extravasation of blood into the local soft tissues, where it may become calcified.

Taping Techniques for the Thigh

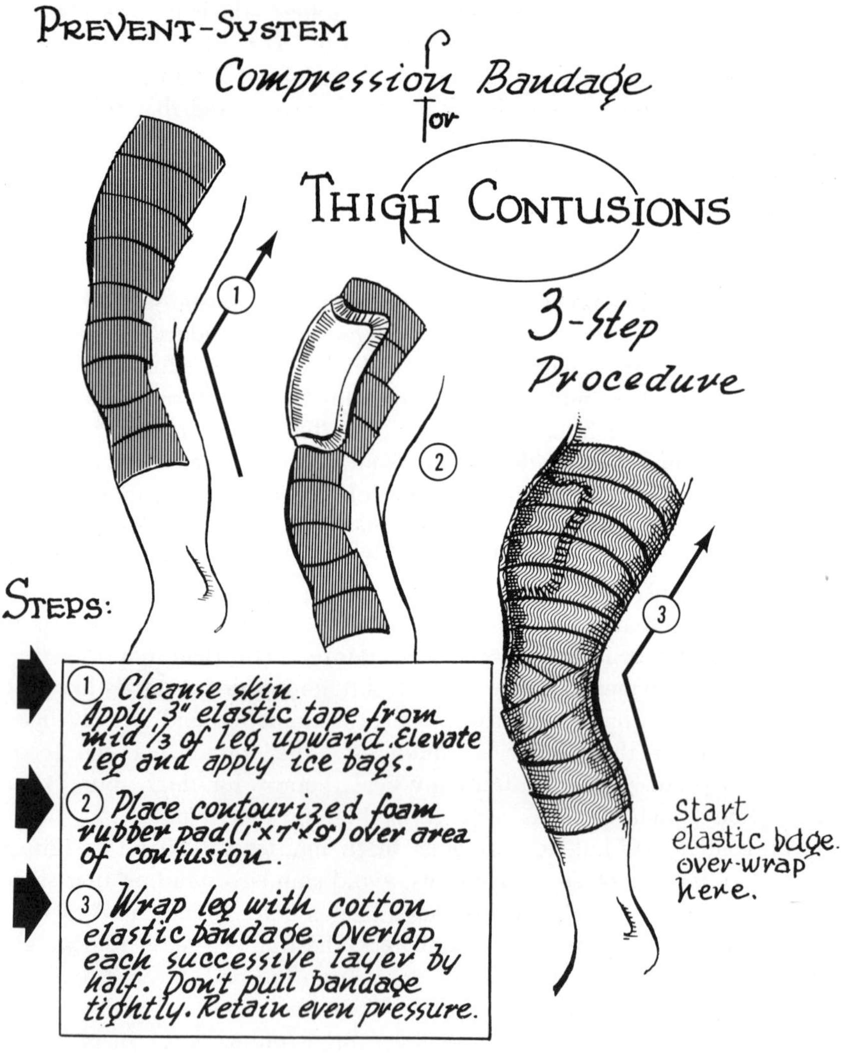

Figure 5-39

Weight Training Techniques

(a) *For Thigh Extensors.* With a 50-pound barbell at chest level and with the trunk erect, do a full squat (if there are no knee complications). Or, hold the barbell behind the body at the buttocks. Keep the feet close together and come up on the toes. Repetitions are increased as the

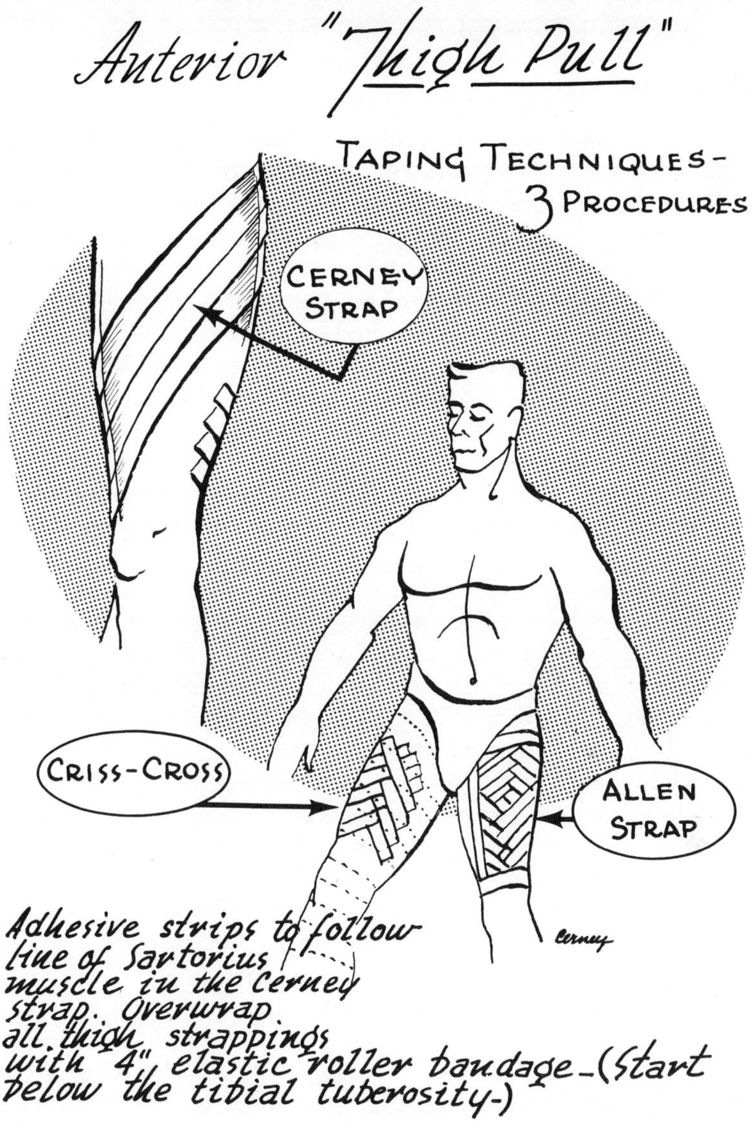

Figure 5-40

athlete improves. *Note: This exercise is not to be used by any football player with a knee injury or history of thigh injury!*

(b) *For Thigh Flexors.* While lying prone on an inclined board, curl weighted shoes on the feet up until they touch the buttocks. Then, while standing on one foot do the same with the opposite extremity. Bring weight shoes up alternately left right. Another method is to don weighted sandals, lie supine and make inverted bicycling motions with the legs.

KNEE INJURIES

The knee is an open target in football. Because of its shallow construction, this joint is highly vulnerable. The majority of knee injuries occur from direct impact. Less than 10 percent, to my knowledge, occur from the rear, and these are usually sustained when the foot is fixed to the ground.

Direct contusion to the front of the knee affects the patella, the tibial tuberosity, the bursae above, below, and behind the knee cap, and tendon attachments. A very vulnerable bursa is the suprapatellar bursa. Tackling or blocking may injure it because it is affected by any blow striking between the knee and the thigh padding. Noncontact injury to the knee may occur in "cutting" or a sudden change in direction while the athlete is running, resulting in torsion on the knee joint while one foot is anchored to the ground by body weight, cleats, or even the grasping hand of a tackler.

Knee injuries may occur from indirect sources such as poorly fitted pants with constricting leg bands. They may occur as the result of foot insecurity (broken arches etc.), or old injuries to the thigh. No matter what causes a knee injury, the end result never remains local. The thigh is immediately affected and it, too, merits specific care. Knee injuries may also begin with knee-bending exercises, with inefficiently applied taping or faulty pads, with previous inept surgery, with inadequate training, with inherent joint weakness because of a rotated pelvis, or even with a "short leg." Knee injuries may begin with fear of being tackled or with bad running habits. New injuries to the knee may begin when the athlete fails to report honestly about previous physical problems or injuries. The causes of knee injury are many, but their prevention lies mostly in education and understanding of all these causes!

There are many preventive measures you can take that will decrease the possibility of injury to the knee. Remember, the knee never forgets an injury. Because of this, there are no minor knee injuries. If a player has a history of multiple knee injuries, especially if he has no outstanding potential, drop him from the roster. For the school's sake, but most of all for the boy himself, dismiss him. Give him a managerial job if football is his first love. This is one of the first and best injury prevention methods you can use.

Here are some specific rules you can follow to prevent knee injury:

1. Maintain free circulation for the athlete's blood vessels and nerves. Allow no constriction of the leg by pants, ill-fitting braces, or poor tape jobs.

2. When adhesive tape is applied to the leg, make sure it follows and abets free-flowing muscle and tendon action.

3. Make sure the athlete's thigh muscles are conditioned. The thigh muscles are the watchdogs of the knee.

4. Use protective knee pads as standard equipment.

5. Use braces if the athlete has a history of previous injury.

6. Have surgery performed, at the recommendation of the team physician, when a player has a chronic history of cartilage or other joint problems.

7. Remember always to get a complete preseason examination, including a trainer's athletic examination, and maintain a meticulously complete history of your players' injuries.

8. Make sure the knee is 100 percent rehabilitated before sending the player back into action.

9. Have the players do preseason "high tire" exercises. Eliminate deep knee bends.

10. Restrain or eliminate players who insistently continue to make knee blocks.

11. Fit footgear properly. Too many knee injuries have their inception in inadequate footgear. No stationary cleated heels.

12. If a player has known trouble with his knees, teach him a four-point stance for greater security.

13. Insist on lots of running and a "keep active" policy at all times.

Always utilize a professional staff that has know-how in athletic injuries. For example, standard x-ray techniques may not always reveal the knee's true problem. The best of x-rays may be taken, yet an inadequate diagnosis or interpretation may be made, resulting in a player's being sent out on the field to the disastrous denoument of his career. Reliance on an x-ray interpretation of possible bone injury when only soft tissue has been damaged could lead to a poor diagnosis and continued problems for the athlete. The trainer can be a key man in this case. His examination can ascertain whether soft tissue damage exists and whether recuperation and rehabilitation is complete.

There are certain signs and symptoms of previous knee injury of which you should be aware. In addition to showing pain and swelling, the knee may lock or give way. Its motion may be limited. The joint may be painful to the touch. It may have a gravelly sound, or bony crepitus, or you might hear a clunking sound. The athlete may not be able to kneel. He may not even be able to crawl when he goes down. The shape of one of his legs may be different. He may be feeling weak or insecure, or may be unable to use his muscles in the affected leg. These symptoms point out the necessity to get the athlete in for immediate professional care and/or observation.

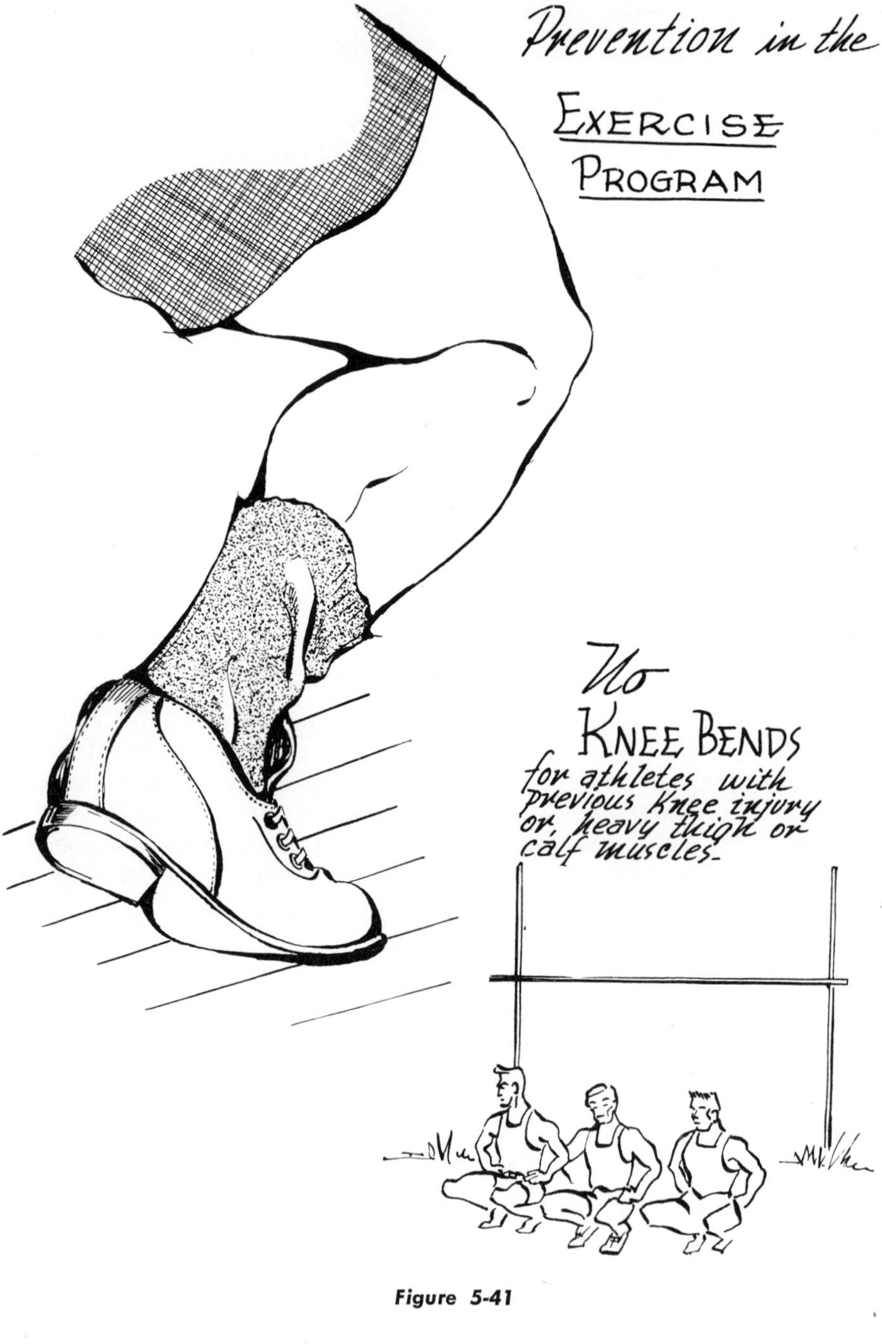
Prevention in the
EXERCISE
PROGRAM
No
KNEE BENDS
for athletes with previous knee injury or heavy thigh or calf muscles.

Figure 5-41

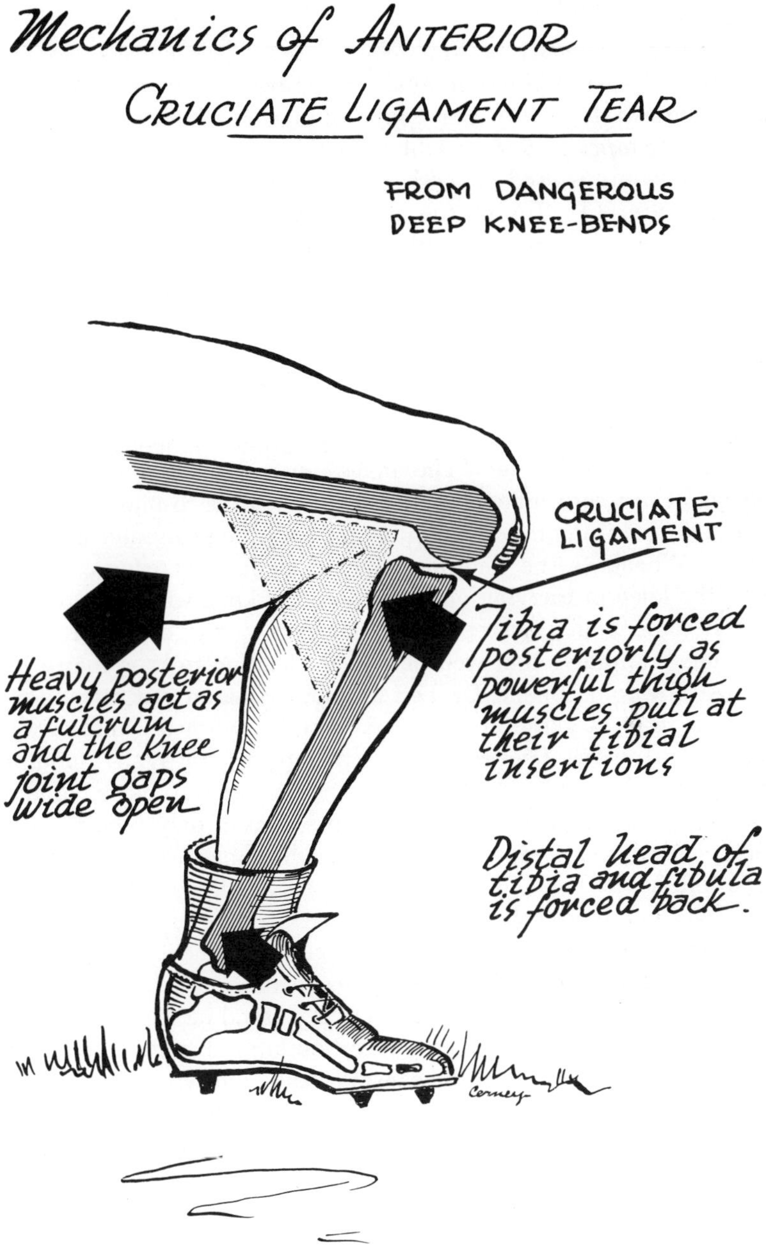
Mechanics of Anterior
Cruciate Ligament Tear
FROM DANGEROUS DEEP KNEE-BENDS
CRUCIATE LIGAMENT
Heavy posterior muscles act as a fulcrum and the knee joint gaps wide open
Tibia is forced posteriorly as powerful thigh muscles pull at their tibial insertions
Distal head of tibia and fibula is forced back.
Cerney

Figure 5-42

Taping and Wraps as a Preventive for Knee Injuries

At the University of Kentucky, trainer Chris Patrick has an angle to consider when it comes to ankle strappings as a method of preventing knee injuries. He says that he *wraps* all players who have no ankle injury history. He *tapes* only those athletes with a history of injured ankles. The same procedure is used for both game and practice time. His reasons for doing so are: (1) Taping the ankle puts stress on the knee joint and makes the knee more susceptible to injury. (2) The *wraps* give some support to the ankle, but more than anything they give compression control in the event that an ankle injury does occur. (3) The procedure at game and practice times is the same because more time is spent in practice sessions than in games, and the percentages indicate that ankle injuries are more apt to happen in practice. (4) Don't change from wraps to tape at game time. The player has enough mental adaptations to make.

Here's another view: "The ankle joint," said Dr. Joe Doller, former Chicago *Cardinal* trainer, "being very susceptible to injury, is commonly strapped, and if improperly applied, the strapping can interfere with knee action. Whenever the improperly-taped ankle joint cannot synchronize with the knee in carrying out its action, the knee will bear undue strain and become highly susceptible to injury . . . the overly tight or constricting strapping might well be a factor leading to knee injury." [3]

At Bowdoin College, Dr. D.F. Hanley indicated that his college hasn't lost a man for a game in five years who has worn his ankle wraps correctly. At Indiana University chief therapist John Wells, in discussing the relationship of ankle taping to knee injuries, reported that out of 11,098 ankles taped for the 1968 football season only nine knee injuries took place. Butler University had 962 ankles taped with only five injuries reported. Wells concludes from the twenty colleges reporting that the Big Ten Conference schools showed a marked difference with 2.53 percent more knee injuries when the ankle is taped than when it is not taped. "The general conclusion that must be reached from the evidence presented is that there is no general indication of a marked increase in knee injuries due to ankle taping. However, under certain predisposing conditions, the taped ankle may be one of the causes of knee injury." [4]

Reporting on the comparative effectiveness of ankle taping and ankle wraps to prevent ankle injuries in college football, James E. Simon, Ed.M. LPT, indicates that after a two-year test program there is little evidence to support many of the athletic fraternity's traditional procedures. He

[3] J. Dollar, "Reducing Knee Injuries by Proper Ankle Strappings," *Scholastic Coach* 25 (May 1956), pp. 40, 41.

[4] J. Wells, "The Incidence of Knee Injuries in Relation to Ankle Taping," *Journal of the NATA* 4, no. 4 (Winter 1969), p. 13.

says there appears to be little if any evidence available to support or reject the practice of ankle injury prevention through taping or wrapping. Expert opinion varies regarding the value of these common practices. A two-year study of their comparative effectiveness resulted in data demonstrating no difference in those techniques tested.[5] In a two-year study at Northwestern University, Doctors S.E. Reid and V. Swan indicate that with the advent of ankle taping, the knee had become the most common area injured, replacing the ankle.

With such conflicting testimonies at hand, you can form your own conclusions. Then, develop a Prevent-System of your own!

Taping Techniques for the Knee

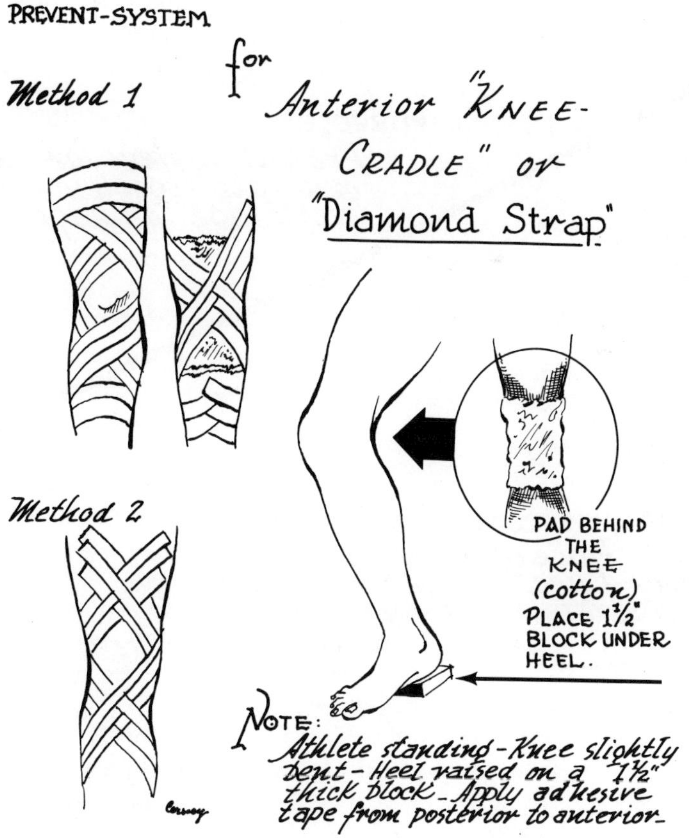

Figure 5-43

[5] J.E. Simon, "Study of the Comparative Effectiveness of Ankle Taping and Ankle Wrapping on the Prevention of Ankle Injuries," *Journal of the NATA* 4, no. 2 (Summer 1969), p. 7.

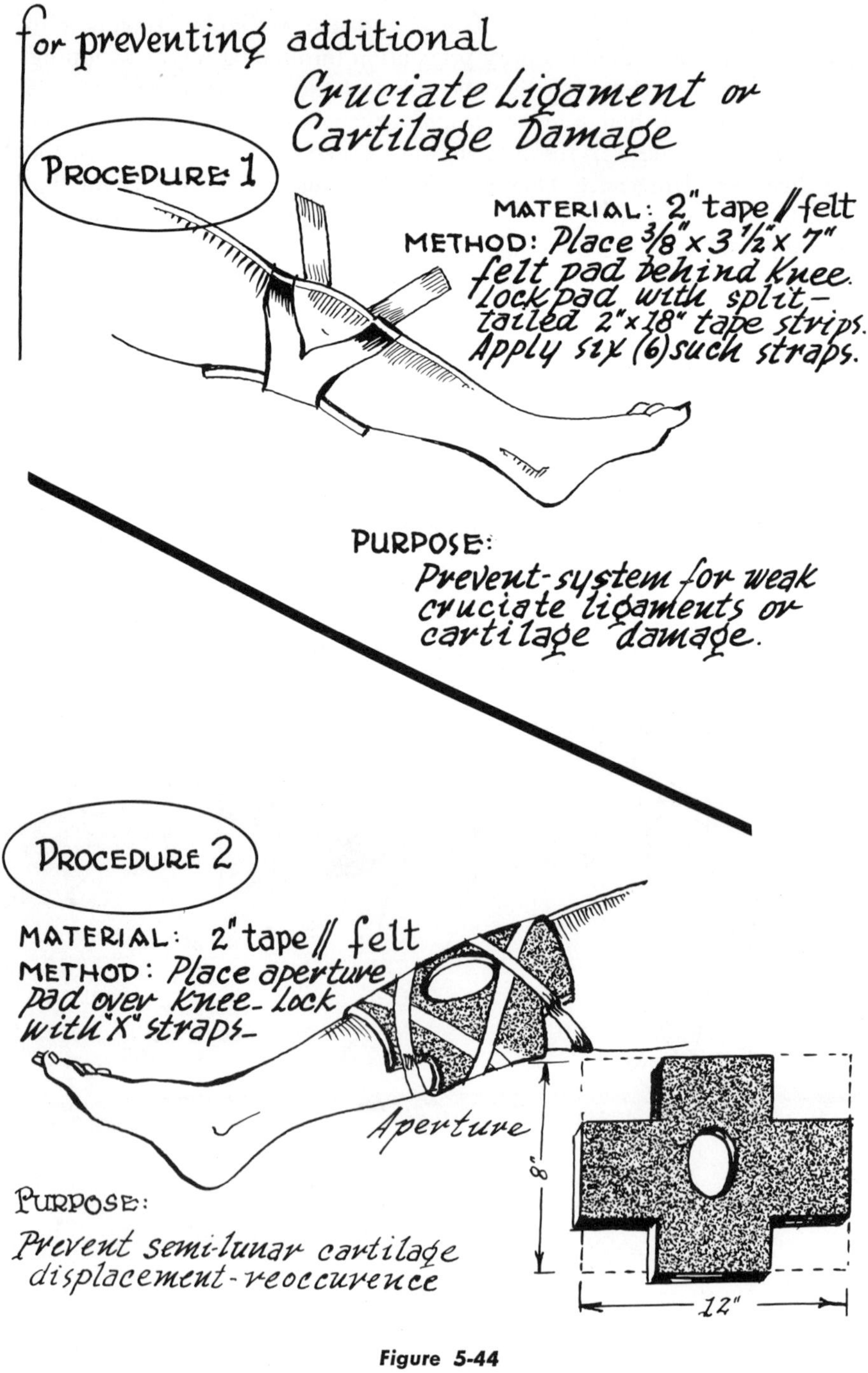
for preventing additional
Cruciate Ligament or
Cartilage Damage
PROCEDURE: 1
MATERIAL: 2" tape // felt
METHOD: Place 3/8" x 3 1/2" x 7" felt pad behind knee. lock pad with split-tailed 2" x 18" tape strips. Apply six (6) such straps.
PURPOSE:
Prevent-system for weak cruciate ligaments or cartilage damage.
PROCEDURE 2
MATERIAL: 2" tape // felt
METHOD: Place aperture pad over knee-lock with "X" straps-
Aperture
8"
12"
PURPOSE:
Prevent semi-lunar cartilage displacement-reoccurence

Figure 5-44

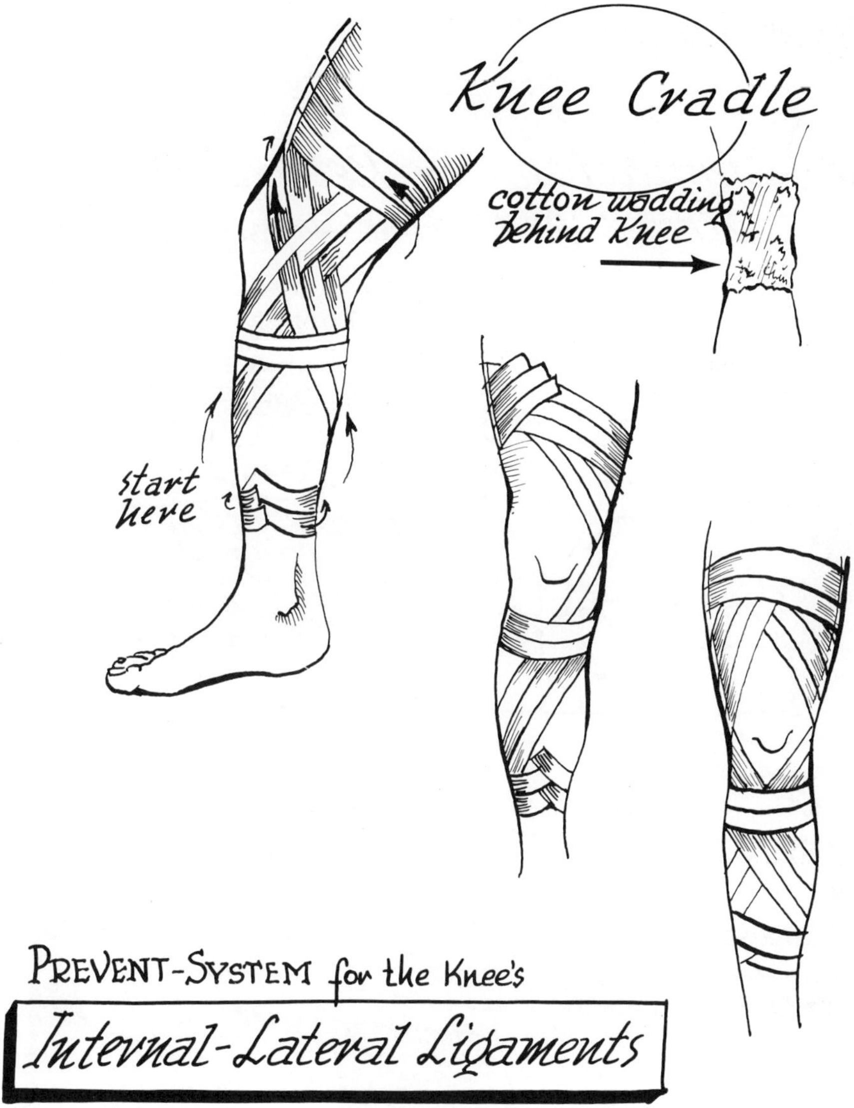

POSITION of ATHLETE:

Standing with knees slightly bent.
(Utilize 1½" width adhesive tape)

Figure 5-45

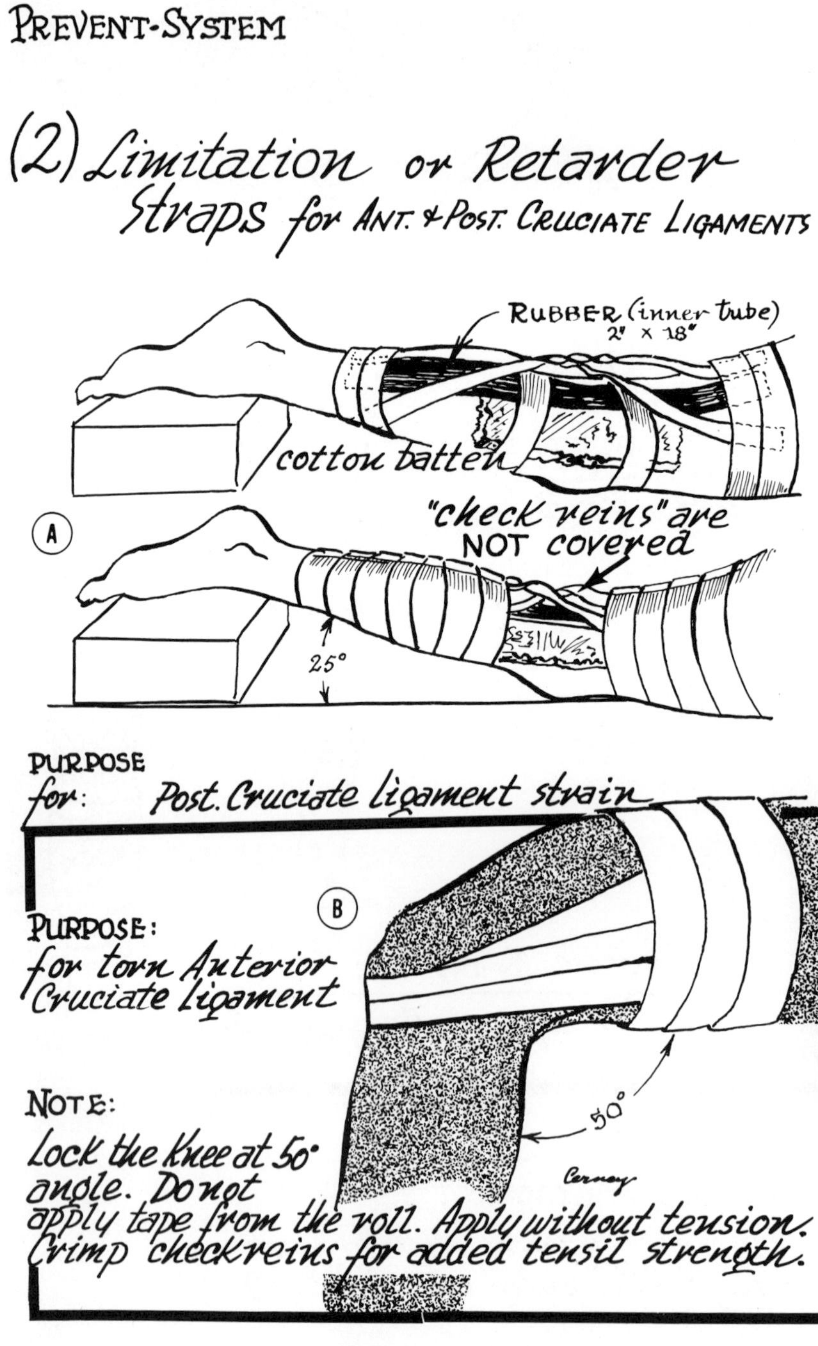
PREVENT-SYSTEM
(2) Limitation or Retarder Straps for ANT. & POST. CRUCIATE LIGAMENTS
RUBBER (inner tube) 2" x 18"
cotton batten
"check reins" are NOT covered
A
25°
PURPOSE for: Post. Cruciate ligament strain
B
PURPOSE: for torn Anterior Cruciate Ligament
50°
NOTE: Lock the Knee at 50° angle. Do not apply tape from the roll. Apply without tension. Crimp checkreins for added tensil strength.
Cerney

Figure 5-46

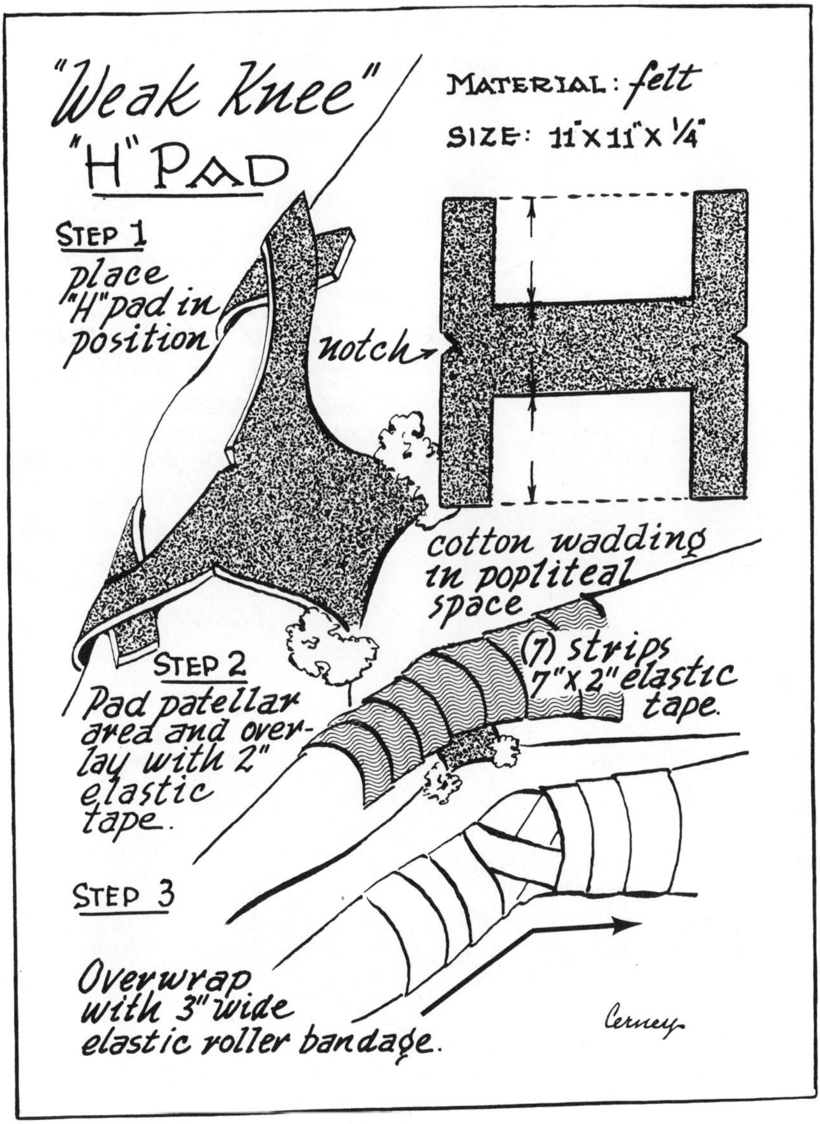
"Weak Knee"
"H" PAD
MATERIAL: felt
SIZE: 11" x 11" x 1/4"
STEP 1
place "H" pad in position
notch
cotton wadding in popliteal space
STEP 2
Pad patellar area and overlay with 2" elastic tape.
(7) strips 7" x 2" elastic tape.
STEP 3
Overwrap with 3" wide elastic roller bandage.
Cerney

Figure 5-47

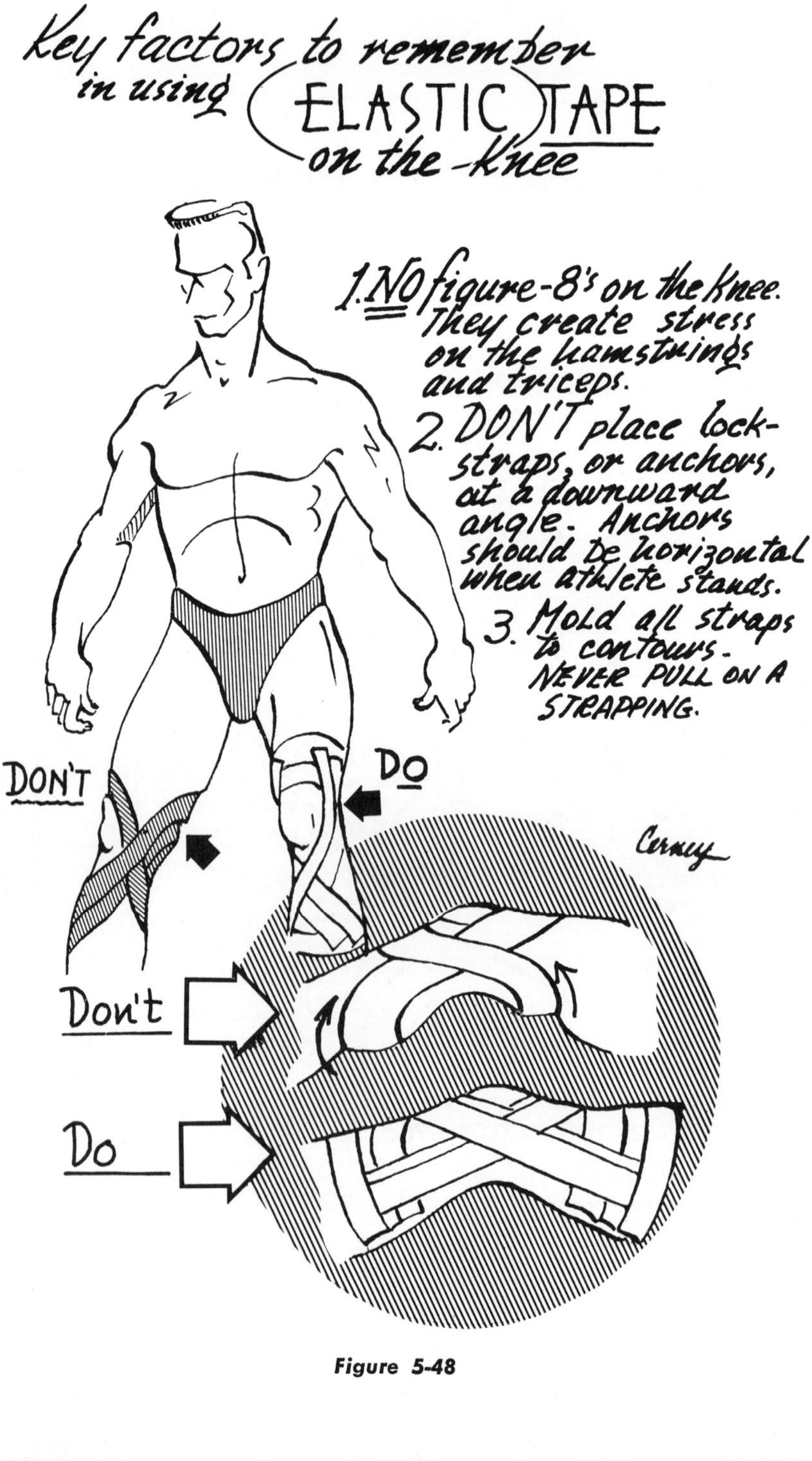
Key factors to remember in using ELASTIC TAPE on the Knee
1. NO figure-8's on the Knee. They create stress on the hamstrings and triceps.
2. DON'T place lock-straps, or anchors, at a downward angle. Anchors should be horizontal when athlete stands.
3. Mold all straps to contours. NEVER PULL ON A STRAPPING.
DON'T
DO
Cerney
Don't
Do

Figure 5-48

SHIN AND LEG INJURIES

Shins are best protected with heavy knee-length wool socks and shin-guards, when necessary. Use hinged guards on the bigger boys for protection. The anterior crest of the tibia is a highly vulnerable area. Its blood supply is inadequate and the periostitis that follows trauma is painful.

Taping Techniques for the Leg

Figure 5-49

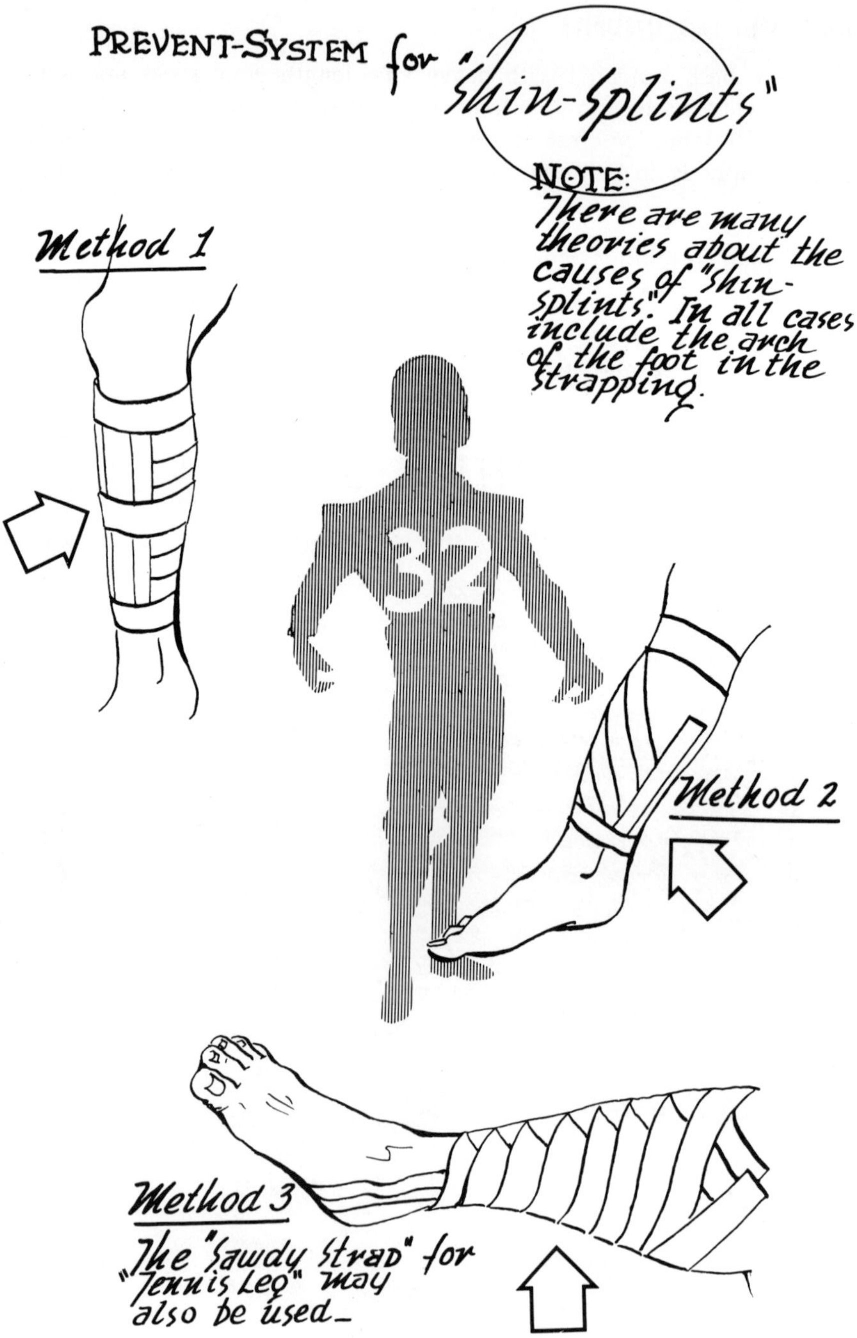
PREVENT-SYSTEM for "Shin-Splints"
NOTE:
There are many theories about the causes of "Shin-Splints". In all cases include the arch of the foot in the strapping.
Method 1
32
Method 2
Method 3
The "Sawdy Strap" for "Tennis Leg" may also be used_

Figure 5-50

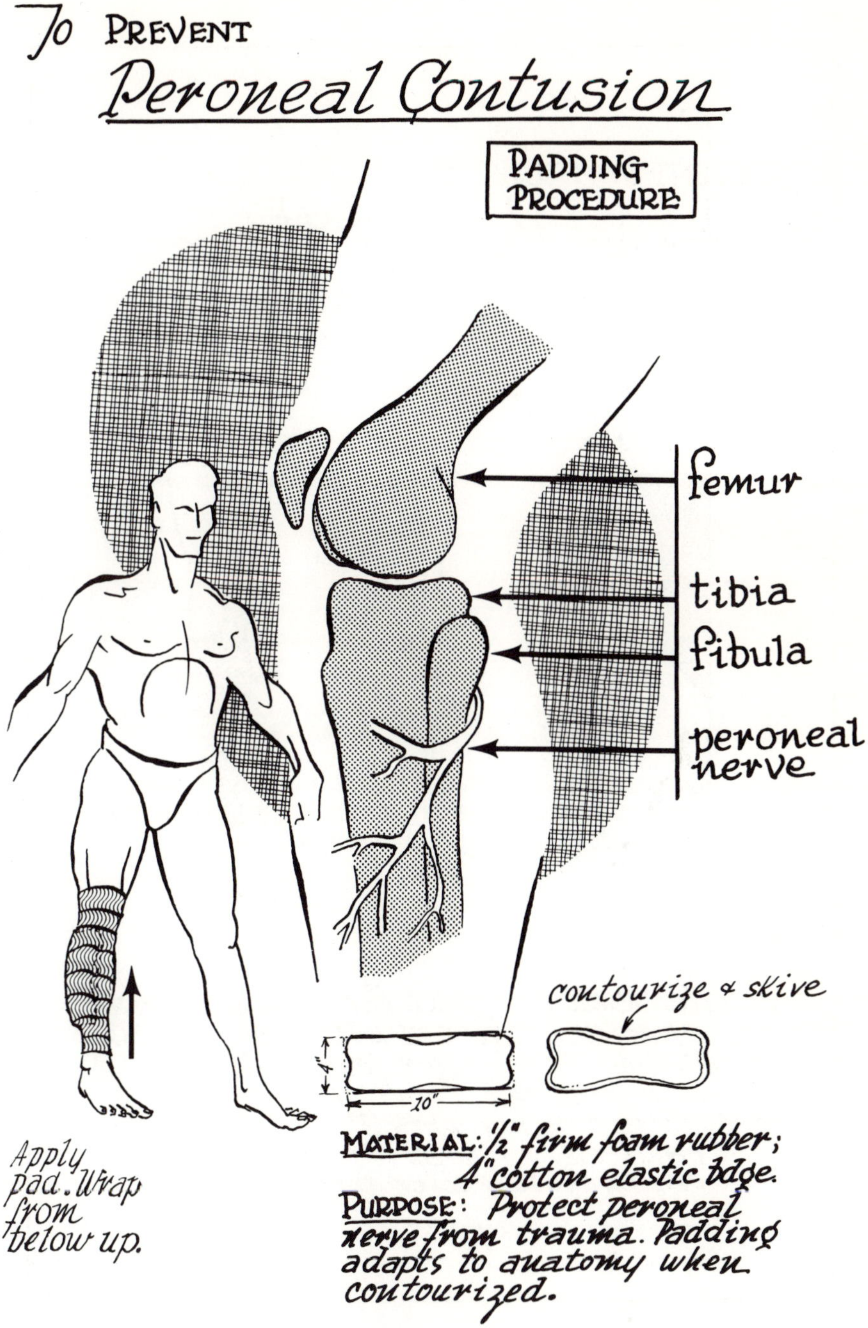
To Prevent
Peroneal Contusion
Padding Procedure:
femur
tibia
fibula
peroneal nerve
contourize & skive
4"
10"
Apply pad. Wrap from below up.
Material: ½" firm foam rubber; 4" cotton elastic bdge.
Purpose: Protect peroneal nerve from trauma. Padding adapts to anatomy when contourized.

Figure 5-51

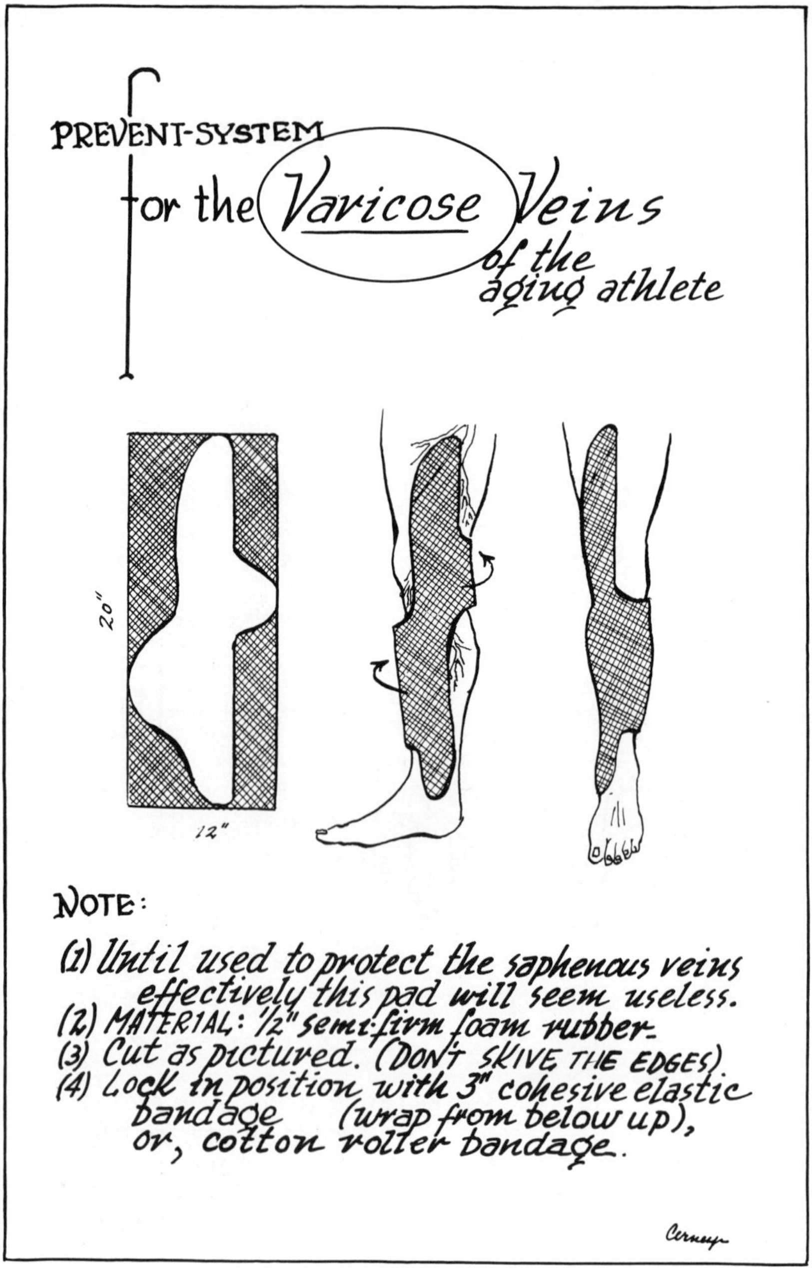
PREVENT-SYSTEM
for the Varicose Veins
of the aging athlete
20"
12"
NOTE:
(1) Until used to protect the saphenous veins effectively this pad will seem useless.
(2) MATERIAL: ½" semi-firm foam rubber.
(3) Cut as pictured. (DON'T SKIVE THE EDGES)
(4) Lock in position with 3" cohesive elastic bandage (wrap from below up), or, cotton roller bandage.
Cerney

Figure 5-52

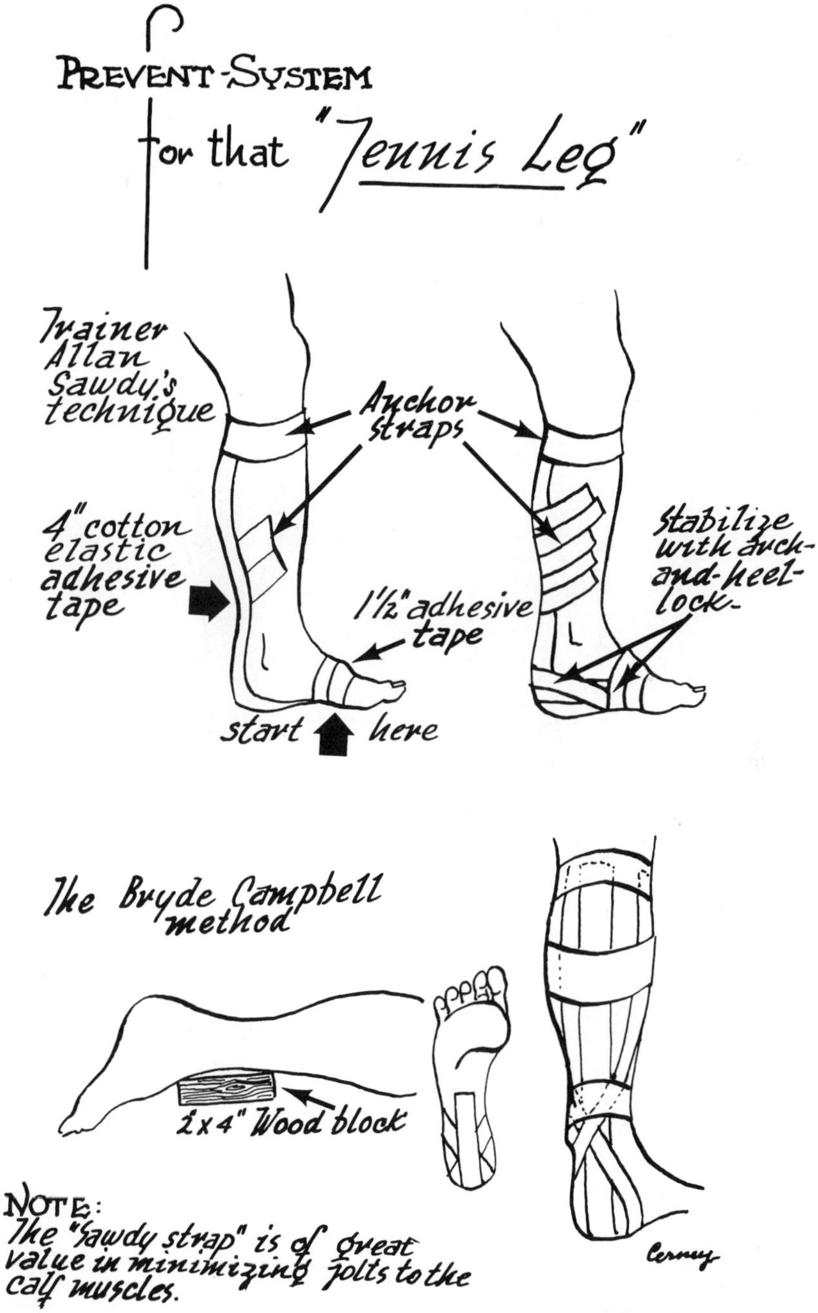
PREVENT-SYSTEM
for that "Tennis Leg"
Trainer Allan Sawdy's technique
Anchor straps
4" cotton elastic adhesive tape
1½" adhesive tape
Stabilize with arch-and-heel-lock
start here
The Brydе Campbell method
2x4" Wood block
NOTE:
The "Sawdy strap" is of great value in minimizing jolts to the calf muscles.
Cerney

Figure 5-53

PREVENT-SYSTEM

for

Herniated Calf Muscle

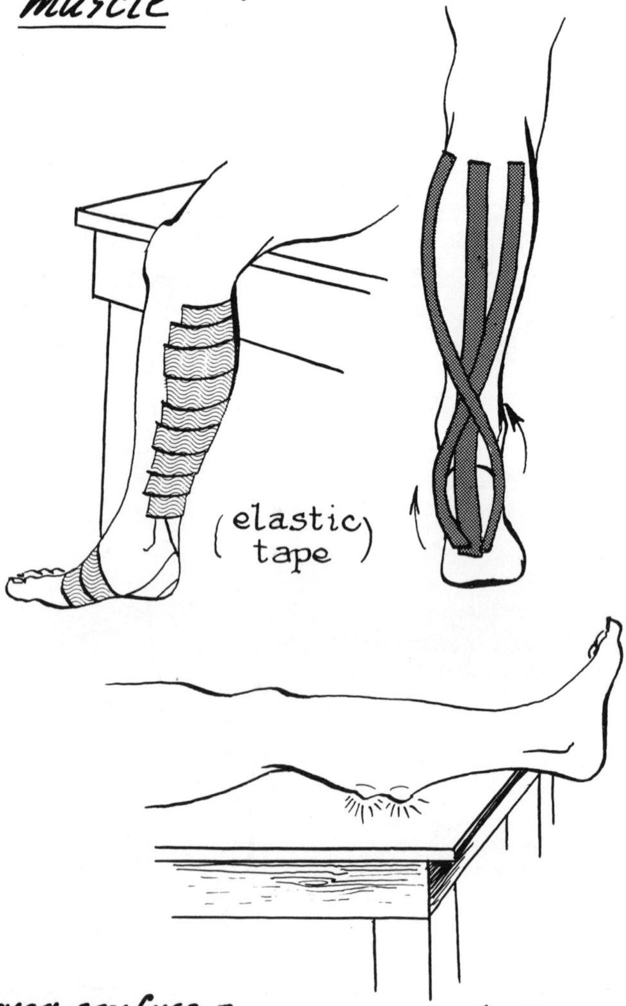

NOTE: Never confuse a muscle herniation with varicose veins.

Figure 5-54

Taping Techniques and Wraps for the Ankle

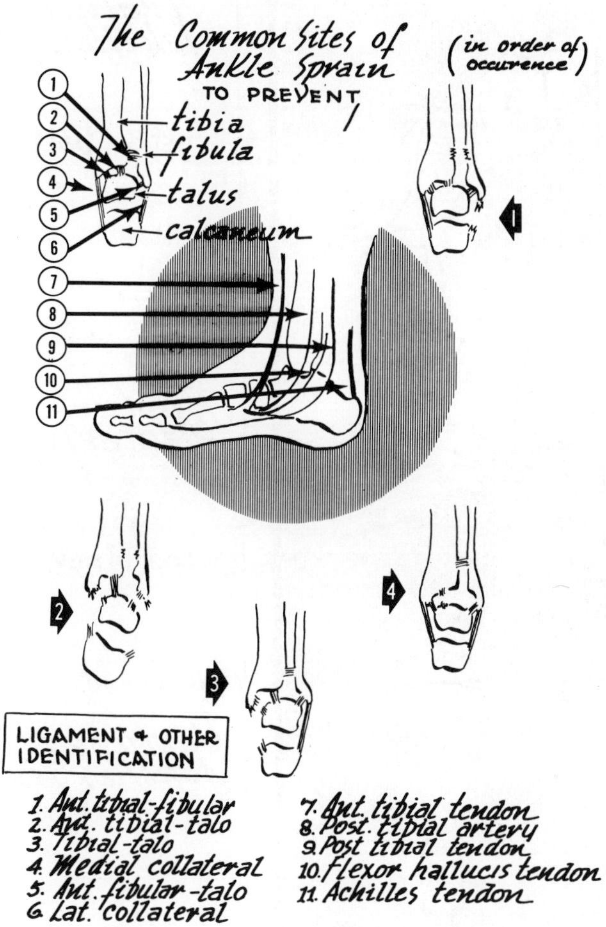

Figure 5-55

ANKLE INJURIES

Because of the incidence of consistent preventive ankle strappings, there are fewer ankle injuries according to some authorities, and more according to others. Sprains, strains, fractures, dislocations, etc., still continue as a result of direct trauma, twisting, or torsion. Violent action may result in fracture, dislocation, or subluxation of any or all bones making up the ankle joint. The foot is immediately affected when the ankle sustains injury.

The fixed-foot syndrome in football creates a lot of problems that

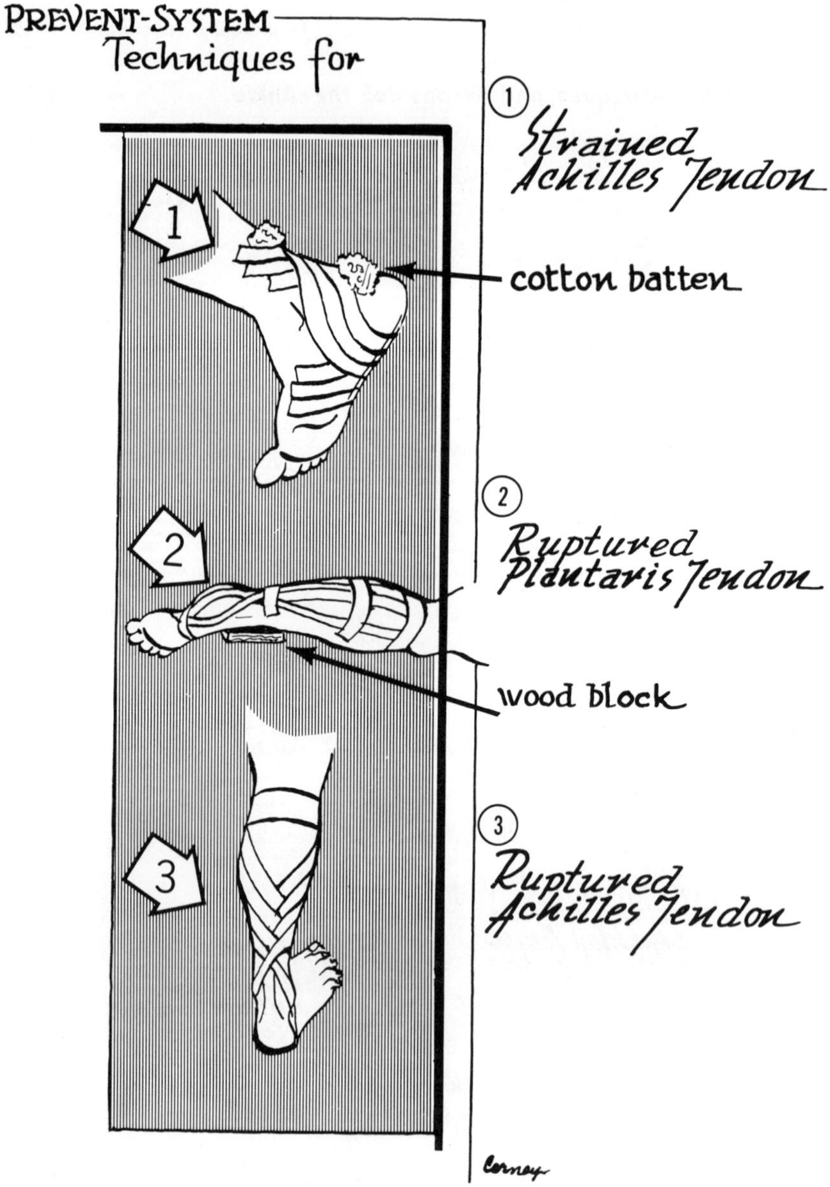

Figure 5-56

arise from a player's being tackled while his foot is anchored to the ground. A 250-pound tackle hits a fast moving 185-pound back who has one foot on *ye auld sod* and something has to give. It may be the ankle, foot, knee, or even the low back where the lumbar vertebrae, the sacroiliac joints, and the low back muscles are located.

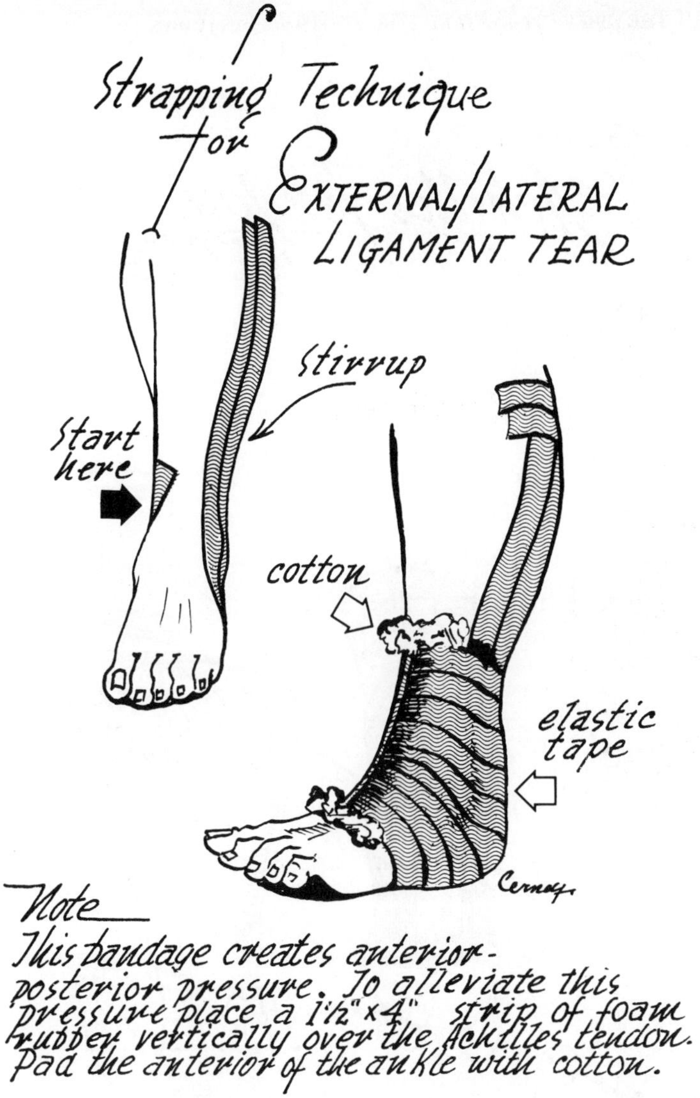

Figure 5-57

Procedures for the Ankle

In football, ankle protection begins: (1) with strappings or wraps; (2) with properly fitted shoes and socks; (3) with changing poor running habits; (4) with checking for foot problems, short leg, tilted pelvis, or a scoliotic spinal column; (5) with checking for poorly rehabilitated old injuries, and (6) with a weight-training program, and isometric or isotonic exercising.

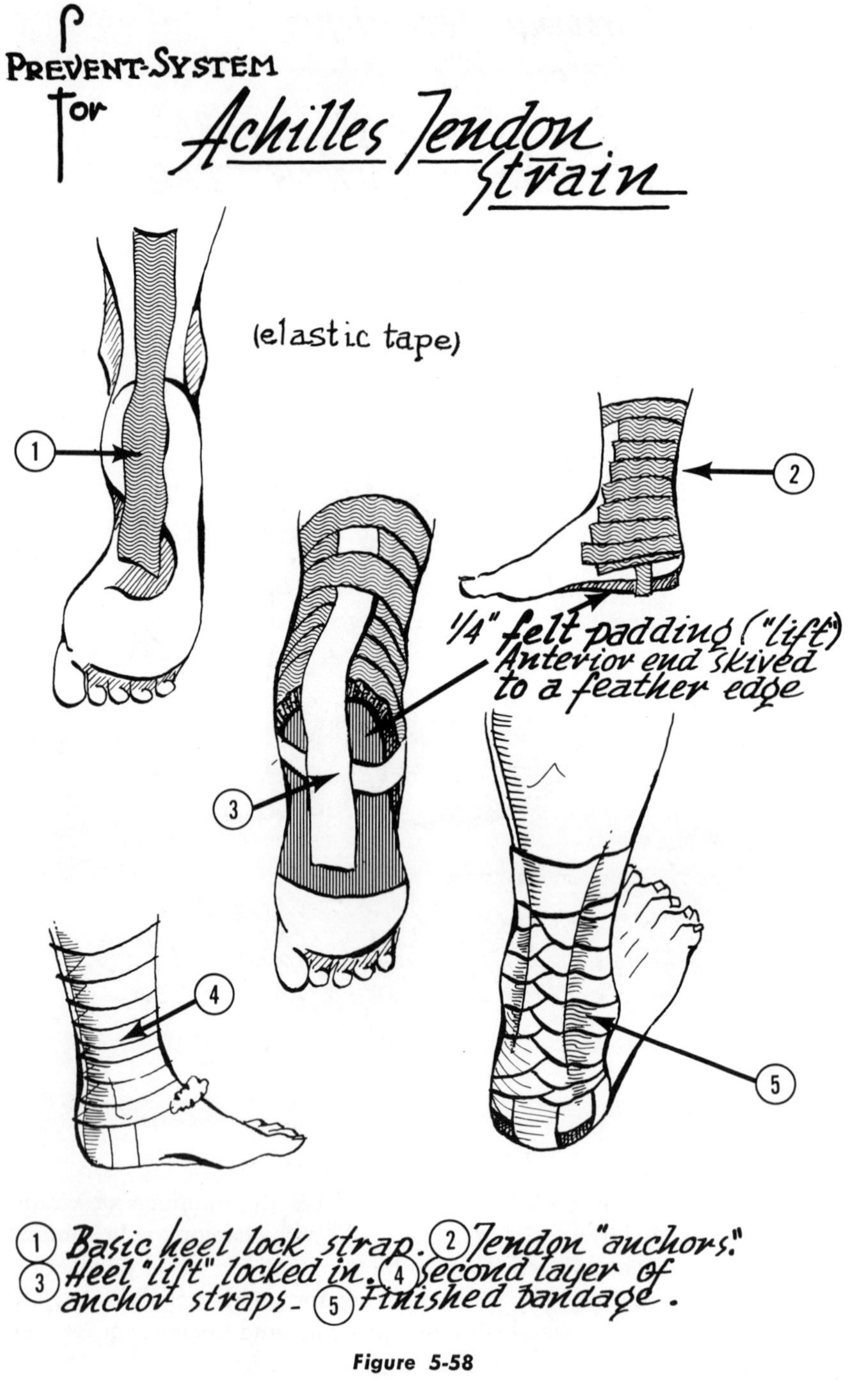
Prevent-System for Achilles Tendon Strain
(elastic tape)
1
2
1/4" felt padding ("lift") Anterior end skived to a feather edge
3
4
5
1 Basic heel lock strap. 2 Tendon "anchors."
3 Heel "lift" locked in. 4 Second layer of anchor straps. 5 Finished bandage.

Figure 5-58

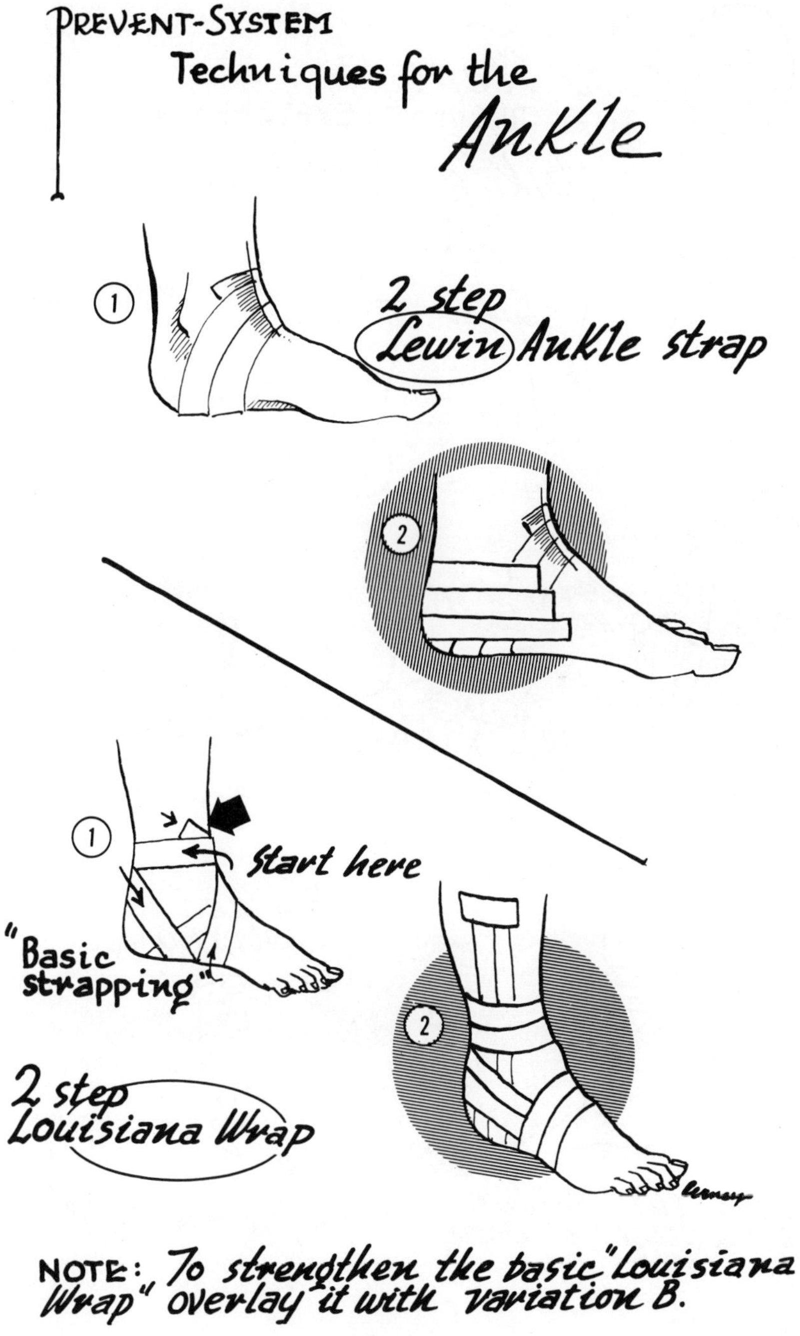
PREVENT-SYSTEM
Techniques for the
Ankle
1
2 step
Lewin Ankle strap
2
1
Start here
"Basic strapping"
2
2 step
Louisiana Wrap
NOTE: To strengthen the basic "Louisiana Wrap" overlay it with variation B.

Figure 5-59

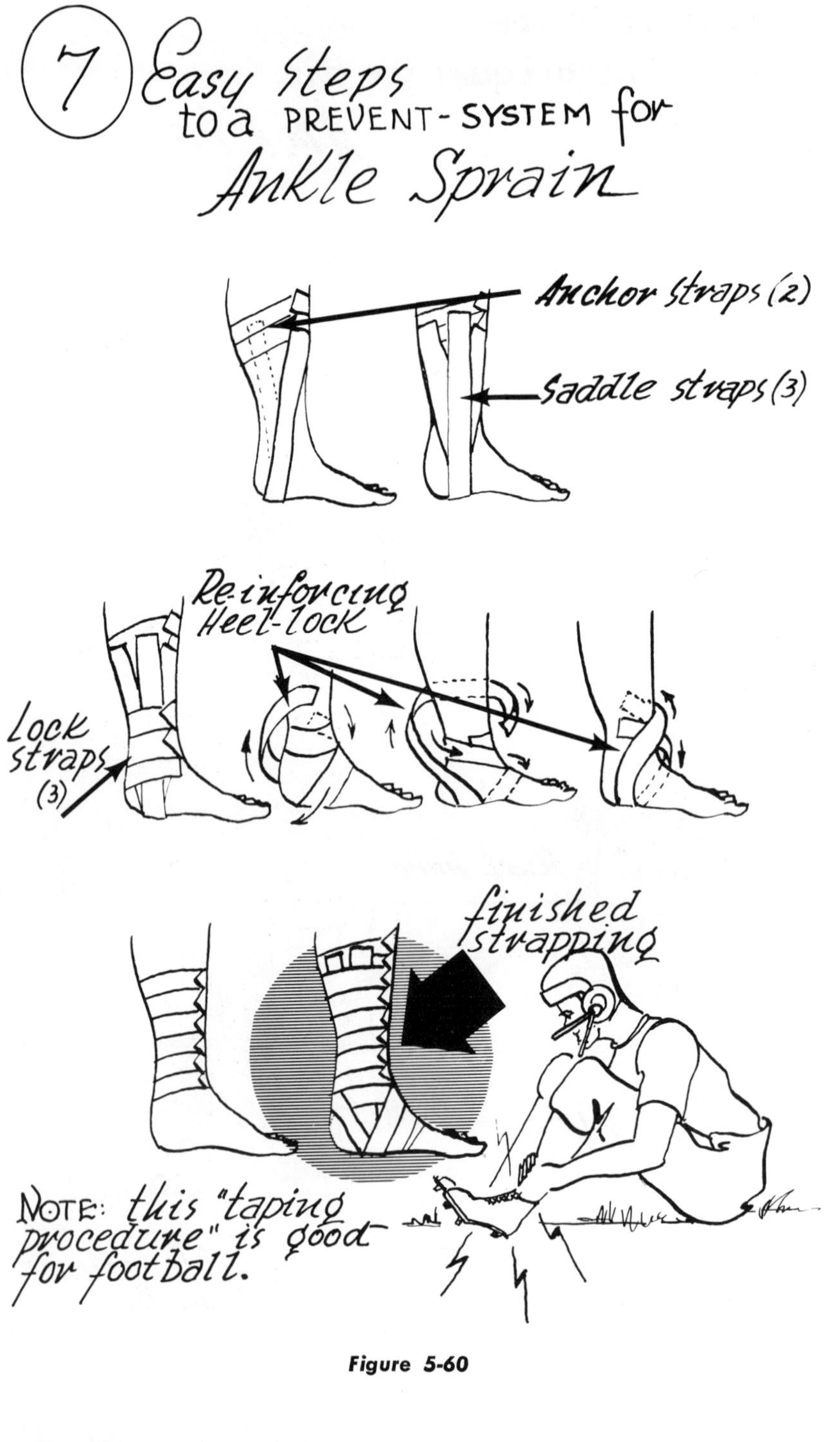
7 Easy Steps to a PREVENT-SYSTEM for Ankle Sprain
Anchor straps (2)
Saddle straps (3)
Re-inforcing Heel-lock
Lock straps (3)
finished strapping
NOTE: this "taping procedure" is good for football.

Figure 5-60

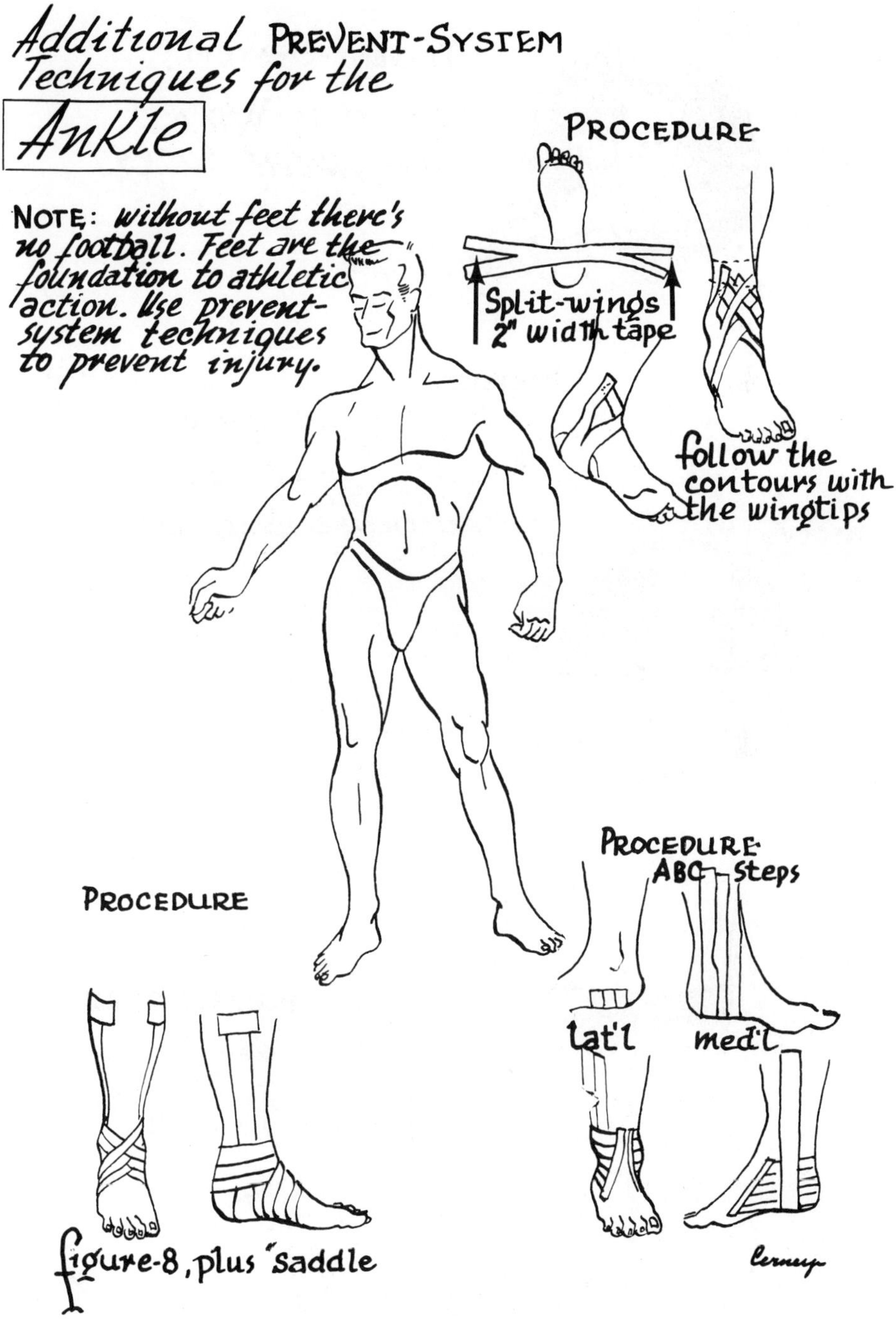
Additional PREVENT-SYSTEM Techniques for the
Ankle
NOTE: without feet there's no football. Feet are the foundation to athletic action. Use prevent-system techniques to prevent injury.
PROCEDURE
Split-wings 2" width tape
follow the contours with the wingtips
PROCEDURE
figure-8, plus "saddle
PROCEDURE ABC Steps
lat'l
med'l

Figure 5-61

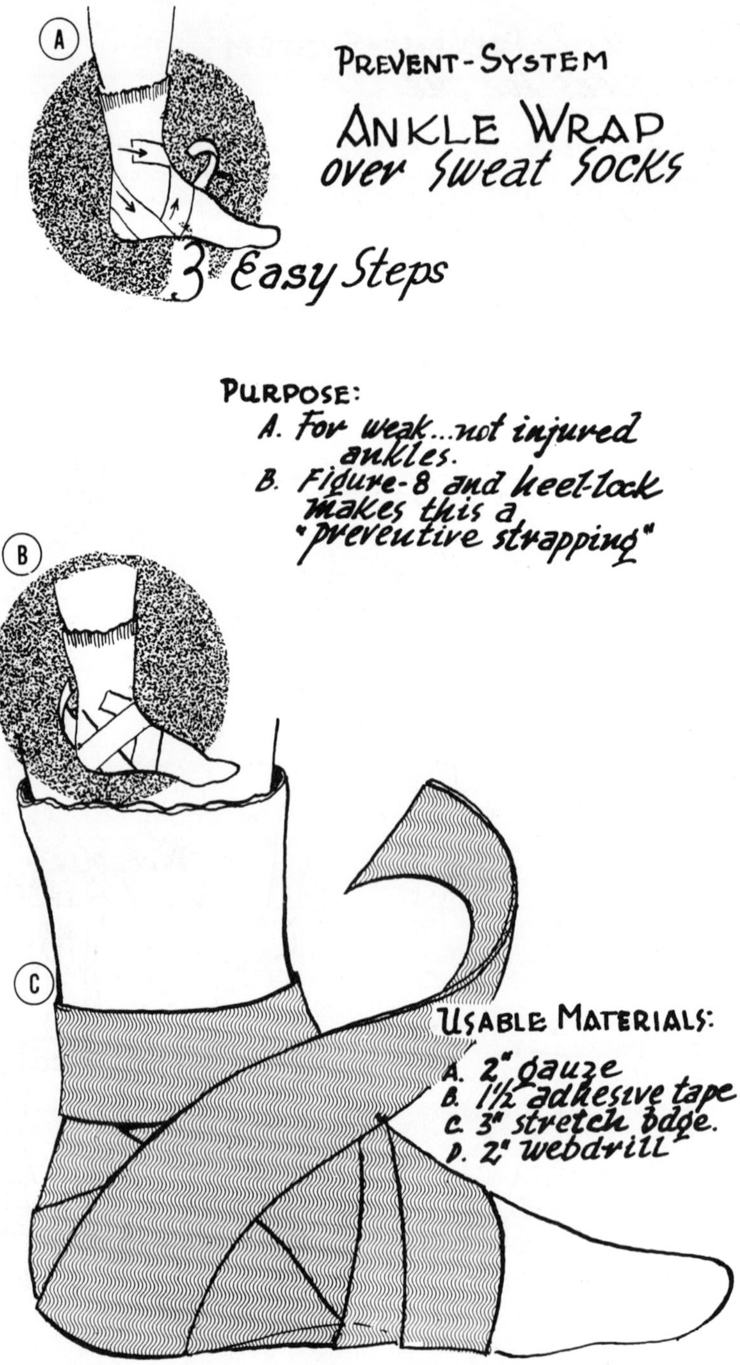
A
PREVENT-SYSTEM
ANKLE WRAP
over Sweat Socks
3 Easy Steps
PURPOSE:
A. For weak...not injured ankles.
B. Figure-8 and heel-lock makes this a "preventive strapping"
B
C
USABLE MATERIALS:
A. 2" gauze
B. 1½ adhesive tape
C. 3" stretch bdge.
D. 2" webdrill

Figure 5-62

FOOT INJURIES

There are many causes for foot problems in sports. Oddly enough, the feet get too little attention in the practice of sports medicine and even less in general practice. Feet are taken for granted. They are something that stick out at right angles to the leg. Too few doctors and too few trainers see the foot as the foundation to the building of athletic performance. Even fewer are conscious of *biomechanics* in the extremity. Without feet in football there is no performance. Without security there is lack of coordination, slowed reflexes, inability to follow through on assignments, lost balance. This is actually the basic cause not only for injuries, but also for inadequacy in playing the game.

"Athlete's foot," misnomer that it is, is only one of many foot problems, and even it is misdiagnosed. Let's take a look at some of these areas where foot problems may begin. A congenitally short first metatarsal segment can lead to postural imbalance as well a caved-in arch. A sagging arch from any cause may be the reason why one or more of your boys is "running on his ankles." Those knock-knees, bowlegs, "weak ankles," "growing pains," leg cramps, ankle and knee injuries, etc., may all have their inception in the human foot. Those varicose veins you see on the heavy boys may have begun in venous circulation being cut off beneath a flattened arch. Muscle pulls in the calf or thigh may have been instigated by foot imbalance. Those so-called "functional neurological disorders of the ankle or knee" may be a poor diagnosis arrived at when someone forgot to check or didn't know specifically how to examine the feet. Many a fracture goes unnoticed and is called a sprain or strain. Achilles tendon and tendon pull or tear begin with foot trouble. The many hallux valgus (bunion joint) and hallux rigiduses, the dorsally contracted toes that are observed in athletes, bursitis, gout, sesamoditis, exostoses, corns, calluses, metatarsalgia, Morton's syndrome, forefoot drop, contracted triceps, extensor tendons pulled up like bowstrings, rotation of the leg and thigh on the foot, peroneal muscle spasm, knotted plantar fascia, excessive sweating, bromodrosis, inability to evert, invert, or adduct the foot on the ankle, and a hundred other problems that lead to athletic inefficiency, may well originate in the foot. The big concern in sports has been in the past with ankles and knees, but as the feet go, so go the ankles and knees. Much to-do has been made over the effects and too little concern has been given the cause. Too little has been done for the Prevent-System in football. It is like taking an aspirin to mask a headache and doing nothing to determine the cause.

Most Foot Problems Begin Early

The majority of foot problems that lead to football injuries began in childhood. They begin long before a youngster goes into a uniform. The biggest preventive you can use is to have athletes get a foot examination by a foot specialist or podiatrist as part of the preseason medical examination. The podiatrist can be a part of the Team-Behind-the-Team. The best athletic shoes, the best quality socks, the best ankle and knee wraps, braces, etc., are to no avail until that foot problem is determined and corrected, or an environment provided that brings foot security as well as foot comfort on the practice and playing fields.

Just as Earl Blaik eliminated the "skinny-necked" applicants for try-outs, so should youngsters with "bad feet" be eliminated automatically to prevent so many of the injuries that are destined to follow. Because the beginning of pain is not always local, because it may be referred, foot problems may have their inception in systemic disease like gout, for example. Foot problems may begin with a febrile disease and a stay in bed. Since foot pains have many origins, it is unwise to think that shoes or adhesive straps are the total answer. This is especially true of systemic diseases and orthopedic inadequacies.

Stop and think about it and remember the number of athletes you know who have had to quit sports because of the feet and legs. How many boxers had to stop fighting? How many track runners quit? How many Babe Ruths, Joe DiMaggios, and Mickey Mantles in baseball had to quit because their extremities couldn't take it any more? How many football players had to give up promising careers? Untold numbers of potential greats have been lost to sports because of their feet, and a thousand alibis were given to hide the real truth that someone had not made a proper diagnosis or used a Prevent-System to ameliorate the problems.

Feet are the foundation of any football team and when it can be demonstrated that 85 percent of all men and women in the United States, given a specialized examination of the feet, have one or more foot problems, it indicates that there is a total inadequacy in American foot health. It points not only to improper foot care, but to a general lack of understanding of the foot in health and disease, and of the role feet play in the body's health and security. Team efficiency loss begins the moment men with bad feet run out on the field.

In my research on thousands and thousands of feet, ankles, knees, pelvises, and spinal columns, and the postural changes from them all I have noted that football players with foot problems not only tire quickly but lose spirit, become uncooperative, and demonstrate emotional problems. They get gloomy about their inability to get going. They get belligerent when they can't "get up and go-go-go" as the coach wants, and they drop out of the game fast. Their reflexes and coordination are faulty, self-control becomes harder, and that essential power-drive so necessary to personal achievement in football dissipates.

As the Muscles Go So Goes the Foot

Remember that there is no such thing as an "arch" in the human foot. At rest, an arch is an arch only in name. In action those twenty-six bones of the foot are no more than the strength of the muscles, tendons, ligaments, and fascia that lock them into a functioning organ.

If for any reason the anterior tibial and the posterior tibial, and the flexor hallucis longus become inadequate, the arch drops. An amazing serial distortion goes through the ankle, the knee, hip, spinal column, shoulders, neck, and head. This change beings with the pronation tilting of the calcaneum (heel bone) followed by tarsal collapse. The foot abducts. The knees roll forward and rotate outwardly. The pelvis tilts

Taping Techniques for the Foot

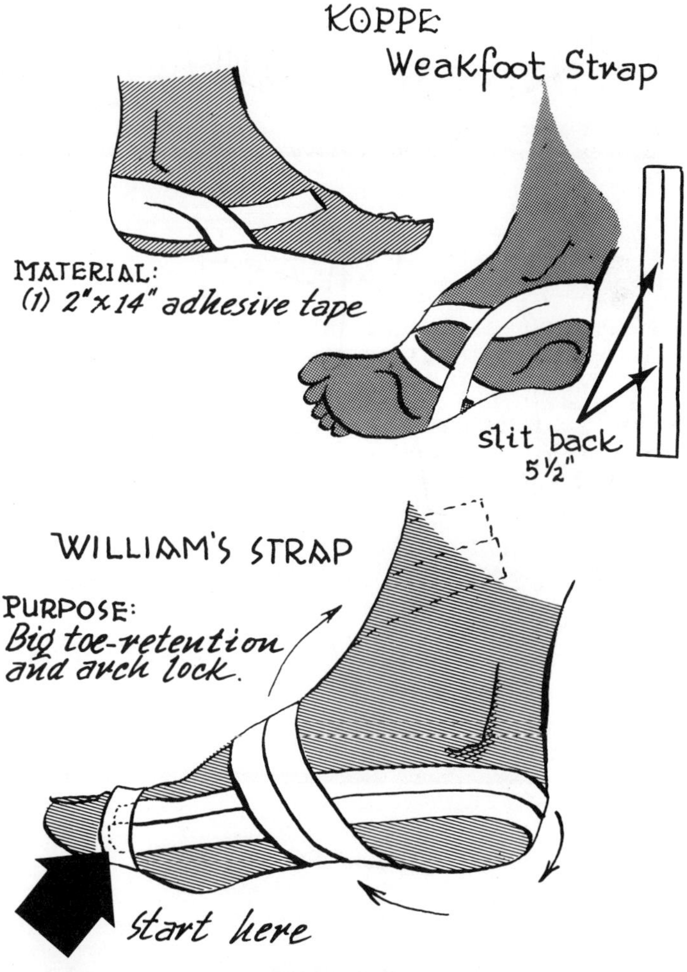

Figure 5-63

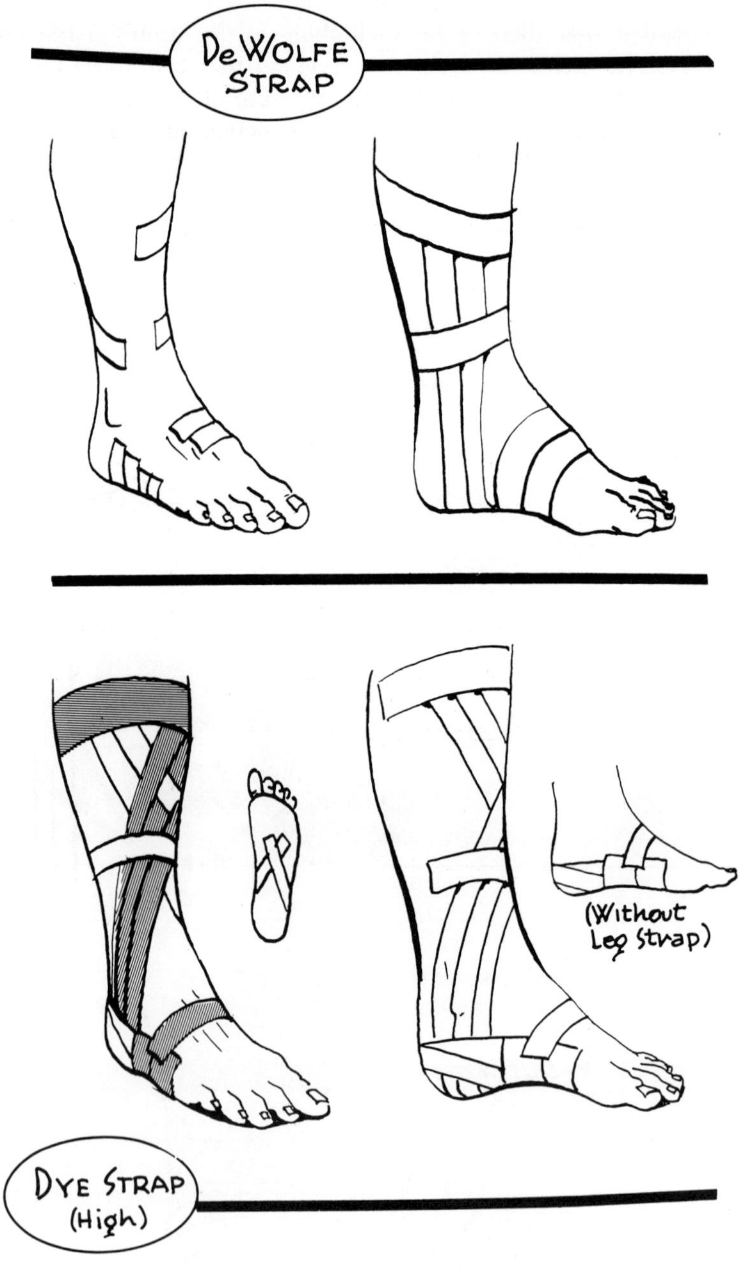

Figure 5-64

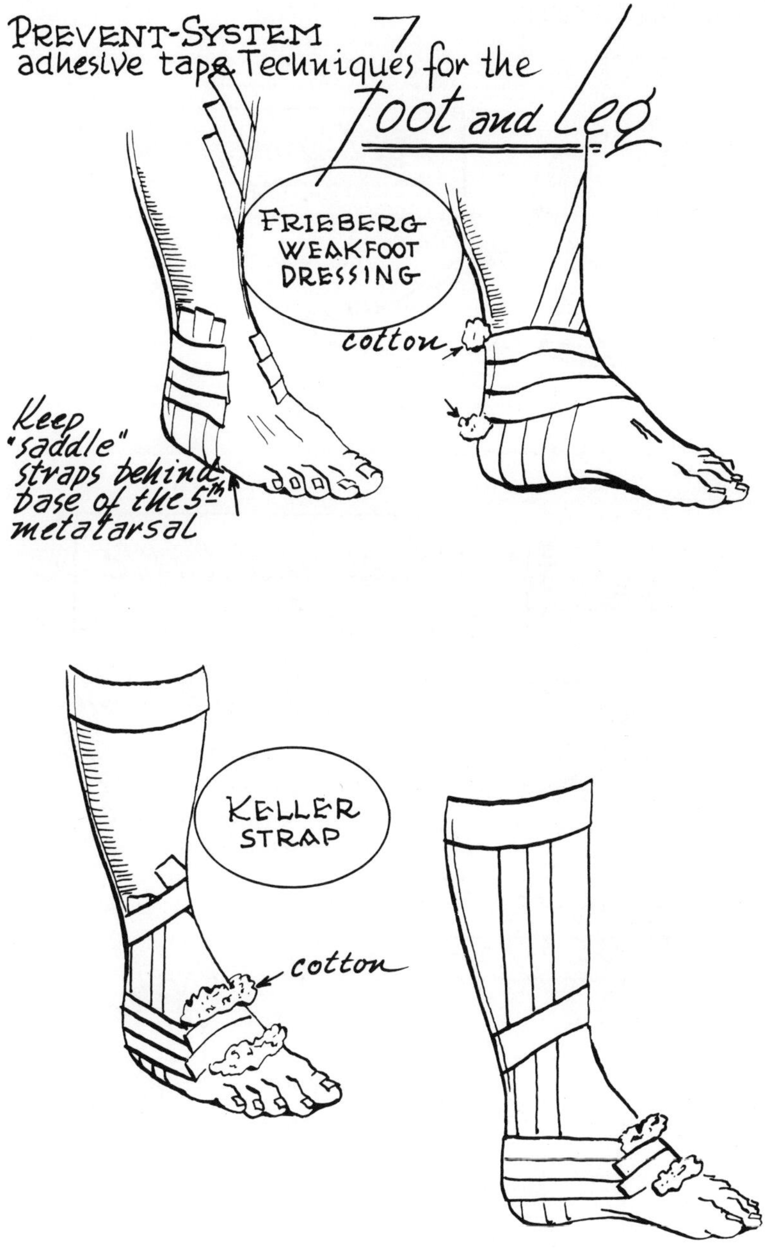
PREVENT-SYSTEM
adhesive tape Techniques for the
Foot and Leg
FRIEBERG
WEAKFOOT
DRESSING
cotton
Keep
"saddle"
straps behind
base of the 5th
metatarsal
KELLER
STRAP
cotton

Figure 5-65

for the Foot.....

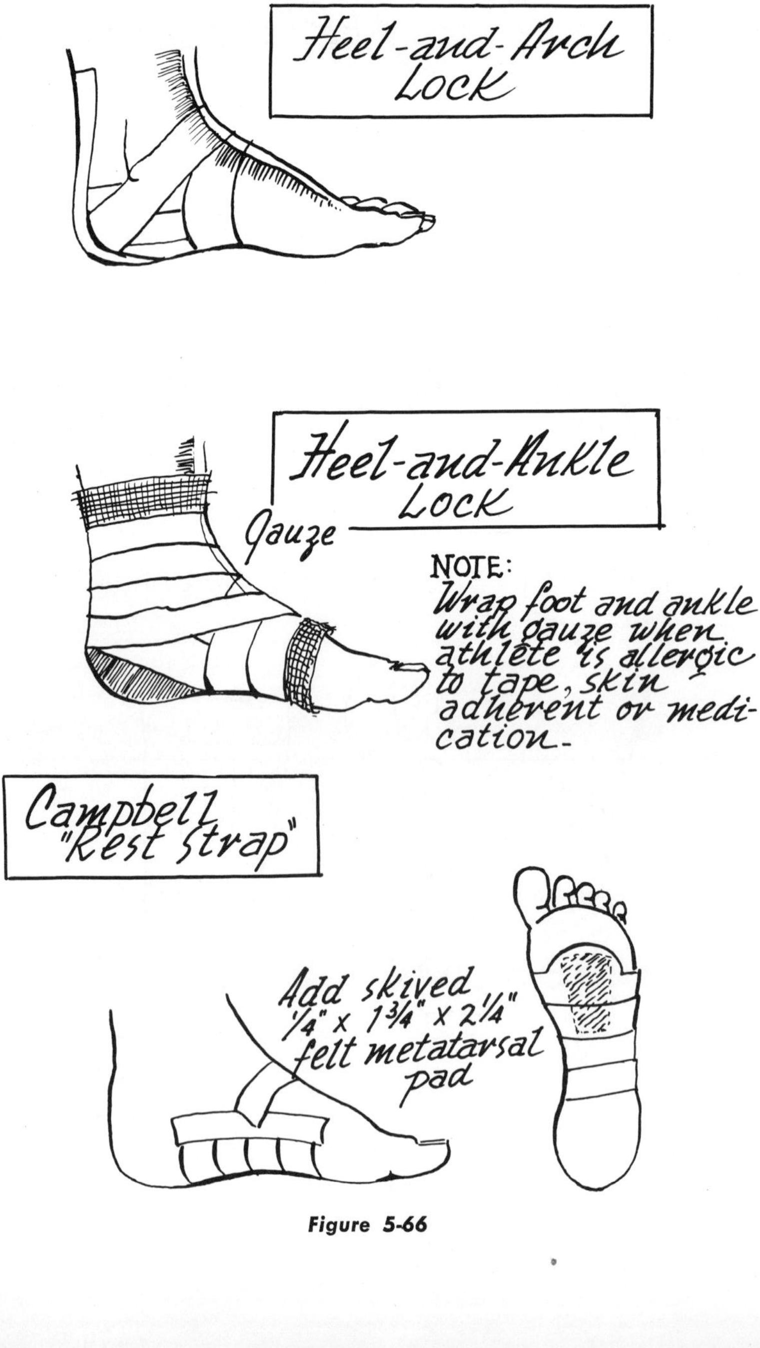

Figure 5-66

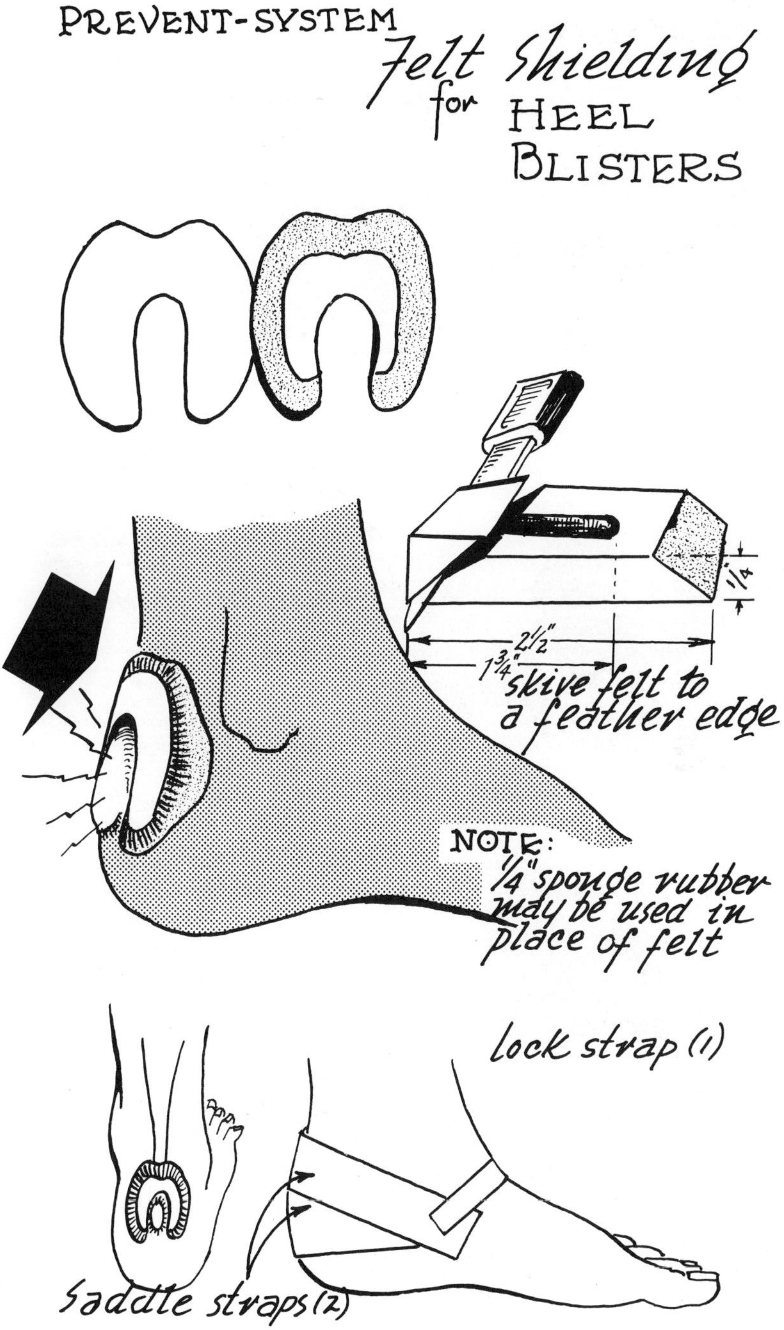
PREVENT-SYSTEM
Felt Shielding for HEEL BLISTERS
1/4
2 1/2"
1 3/4"
skive felt to a feather edge
NOTE:
1/4" sponge rubber may be used in place of felt
lock strap (1)
saddle straps (2)

Figure 5-67

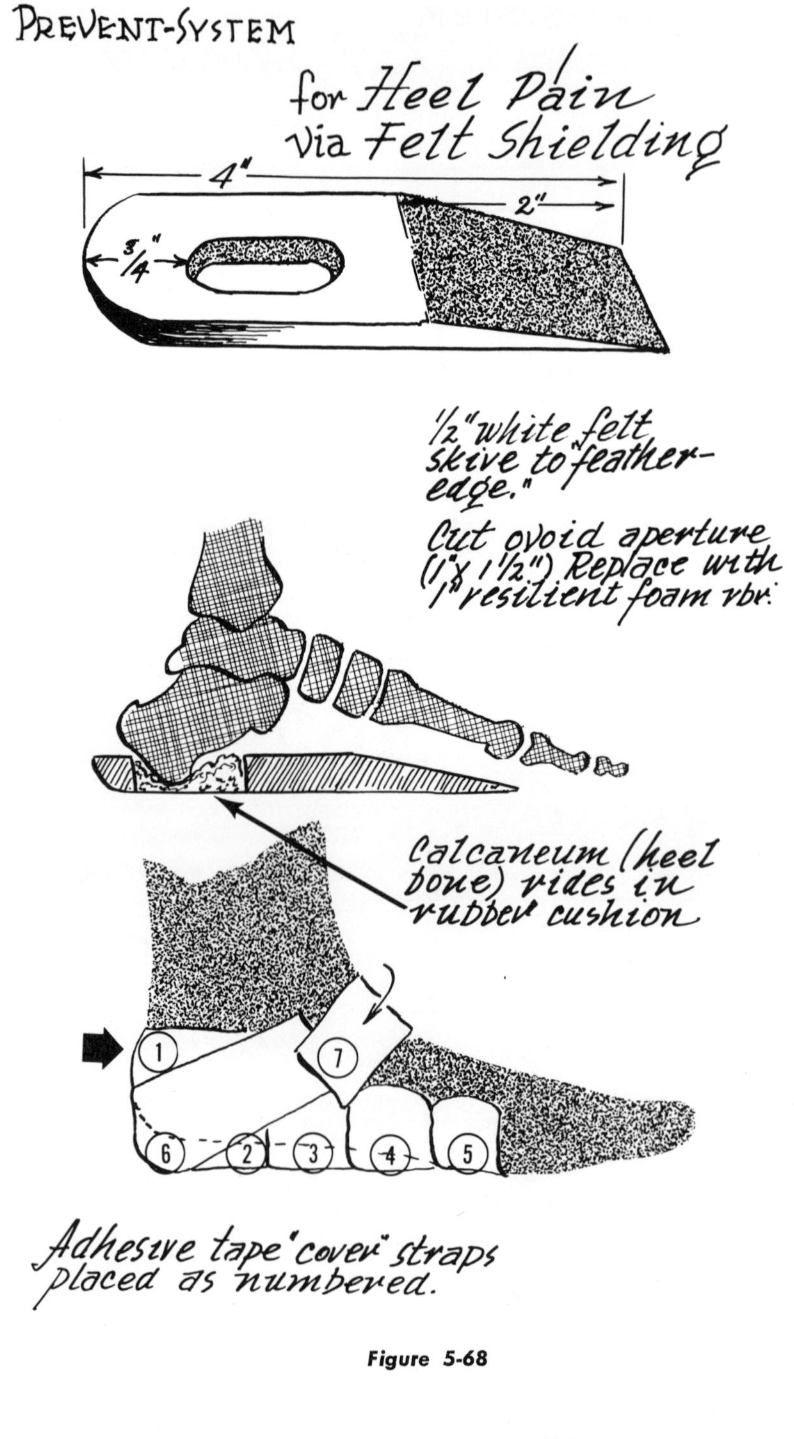
PREVENT-SYSTEM
for Heel Pain
via Felt Shielding
4"
2"
3/4"
1/2" white felt skive to "feather-edge."
Cut ovoid aperture (1" x 1 1/2") Replace with 1" resilient foam rbr.
Calcaneum (heel bone) rides in rubber cushion
1
2
3
4
5
6
7
Adhesive tape "cover" straps placed as numbered.

Figure 5-68

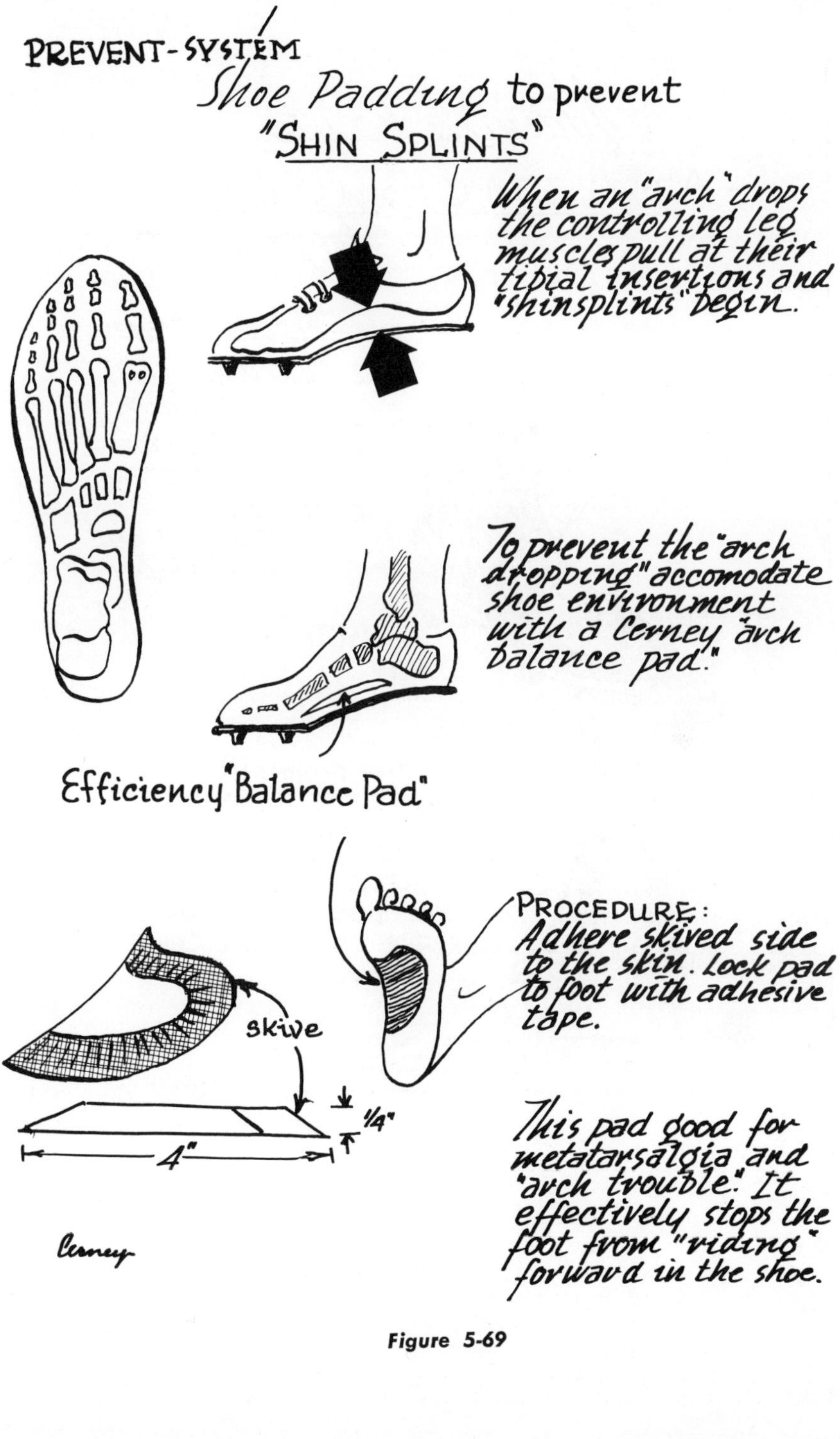
PREVENT-SYSTÉM
Shoe Padding to prevent
"SHIN SPLINTS"
When an "arch" drops the controlling leg muscles pull at their tibial insertions and "shinsplints" begin.
To prevent the "arch dropping" accomodate shoe environment with a Cerney "arch balance pad."
Efficiency "Balance Pad"
PROCEDURE:
Adhere skived side to the skin. Lock pad to foot with adhesive tape.
skive
1/4"
4"
This pad good for metatarsalgia and "arch trouble." It effectively stops the foot from "riding" forward in the shoe.
Cerney

Figure 5-69

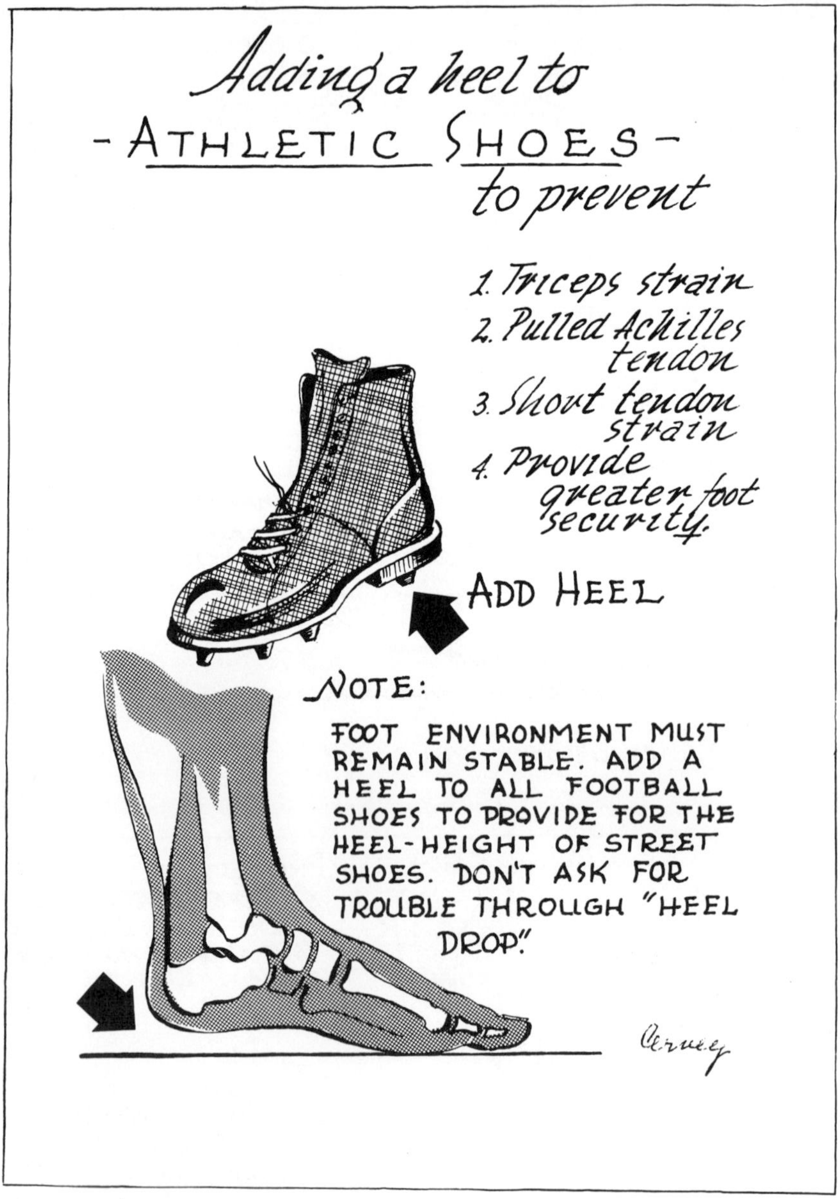
Adding a heel to
- ATHLETIC SHOES -
to prevent
1. Triceps strain
2. Pulled Achilles tendon
3. Short tendon strain
4. Provide greater foot security.
ADD HEEL
NOTE:
FOOT ENVIRONMENT MUST REMAIN STABLE. ADD A HEEL TO ALL FOOTBALL SHOES TO PROVIDE FOR THE HEEL-HEIGHT OF STREET SHOES. DON'T ASK FOR TROUBLE THROUGH "HEEL DROP."

Figure 5-70

anteriorly. That triangular chunk of bone, the sacrum, upon which the spinal column sits rolls forward. This puts strain on the sacroiliac joints and these begin to ache. Spinal curvatures distort or accentuate. The belly pots and the shoulders and head thrust forward.

Now get that picture in mind. Then stop and think about some of those boys you've seen running down the field panting and sweating. The next time you see that serial distortion from foot to head in an athlete, realize that a foot problem may be its primary cause.

The human foot was meant for weight bearing. The human foot was designed for flexibility and action. Normally springy, it was meant to take jarring blows away from the pelvis and spine, from the knees and ankles, from the abdominal organs and even the brain. Run that kid with foot trouble and you can predict where he's going to start hurting. You will even, as you become more adept at your observations, predict his future sites of injury! If the Prevent-System is not used and the foot problem is not corrected, the best player on the squad becomes the world's worst the moment he develops foot trouble!

The Prevent-System, as far as the feet are concerned, begins with that preseason medical examination. *Know that foot!* Everything above the foot depends on it. Beware of bad ankle strappings, fatigue, poorly fitted arch supports, poorly fitted shoes and socks, ineffective shoe padding, inefficient care of the legs and feet after fracturing or febrile illness, nutritional deficiencies, gastrointestinal problems leading to toxic waste in the body, circulatory deficiencies, and distortions of the normal alignment of the pelvis and spinal column.

Appendix I

LEGAL STRATEGIES FOR YOUR PREVENT-SYSTEM

THE LEGAL ASPECTS OF SPORTS

Whether you want to think about it or not, the legal aspects of sports hang like an atomic cloud. They blanket everything over which we once worried not a whit. Today, in an era of fantastic malpractice awards, we have to be totally conscious in our Prevent-System of the legal aspect of sports and how the prevention of athletic injuries is *the* place to begin.

As a member of the Team-Behind-the-Team are you personally covered by insurance? Are you free of the possibility of being accused of negligence, dereliction of moral duty, or tort liability? Is laudable purpose, good faith, and honesty on your part enough to free you from being accused of legal manhandling? Are you likely to avoid a lawsuit even if employed by the state? Can you actually be accused of assault and battery because you well-meaningly manipulated a dislocated thumb and said, "Now, you'll be just as good as new?" Let's look at what the authorities have to say about all this.

Burke Shartel and Marcus L. Plant, professors of Law at the University of Michigan, stress the importance of procuring a patient's consent (in our case from the athlete and/or the athlete's parents or guardian) to any medical treatment, and the dangers of confining a patient against his will. Liability may be imposed for assault and battery or for false imprisonment if patient's or athlete's rights are violated in these respects.

> It is worth emphasizing that the basis of liability in these cases is that the physician's conduct (in this case the coach) is wrongful even though his act was done in medically competent manner, and regardless of his good faith, or his honesty, or the fact he was motivated by a laudable purpose. The theory of the claim here is basically different from one founded on negligence or malpractice.[1]

The difference between *tort liability* and *negligence* was indicated by the Colorado Supreme Court in the case of Cady vs. Fraser (122 Colo., 252 at 255, p. 2, 422, M.L.C. 1947–52, p. 464 (1950)).

> Negligence in treatment . . . and treatment without employment, presents basically different claims . . . the one is basically on the existence of a contract and authority for service, and the other upon the lack of such contract or authority. The one is based on lack of care or skill in the performance of services contracted for, and the other on wrongful trespass on the person regardless of the skill or care employed. The assertion of one is the denial of the other. Both claims cannot exist at the same time.[2]

When an athlete is hurt a coach seldom thinks about his legal liabilities. His concern is for the youngster, his injury, and how to get the boy

[1] B. Shartel and M.L. Plant, *The Law of Medical Practice* (Springfield, Illinois: Charles C. Thomas, Publisher, 1959), p. 151.

[2] Shartel and Plant, ibid.

or girl back into the game if he's in condition to go back. Today it's not a matter of athletic injury. It's a matter of legal liabilities of the coach and other members of the Team-Behind-the-Team as well. Today an overt action, or no action, may lead to an entire chain of legal consequences stemming from two words: *contributory negligence.* Too little care, or too little too late, or any act that aggravates the original injury could leave the coach and the rest of the Team-Behind-the-Team wide open to personal liability for the boy's injury, plus a suit for negligence. To cut down the possibilities of negligence I would like to list twenty key factors that may guide a coach's thinking not only in dealing with injury prevention problems but also in preventing the consequences of legal action that go with them.

Twenty Ways to Throw a Block into "Contributory Negligence"

1. Screen the candidate in your yearly preseason interview. Don't give anyone the chance to go out on the field for tryouts until he has gone through a complete medical and athletic examination.

2. The coach should obtain a complete medical history from the team physician and confer with him on all the participants' operations, illnesses, injuries, etc., where pertinent.

3. The team physician's signed approval of the participant must be in the athletic department file.

4. The trainer's signed athletic examination findings must be on file in the athletic department office.

5. Permission to participate cards, signed by parents or legal guardian, must be on file.

6. A coach should insist that the team have a doctor and a trainer, because he himself is not legally permitted to do either the trainer's or the doctor's job. To do so makes him vulnerable to legal action.

7. A coach should run on field (when the referee beckons) with his trainer, to assess the injury and make decisions. It indicates his personal interest and attention.

8. He should take the trainer or team doctor's decision as gospel and not fight it even though the game and the need for the athlete is crucial. The injured boy's life and physical well-being is more crucial than the score.

9. The coach should demand that all suspected injuries be x-rayed (for example, ankle "sprains," shoulder "strains," etc.). *Know* whether or not a fracture is involved.

10. A coach should never personally touch the athlete. Don't massage his muscles or manipulate his bones or joints.

11. The coach should render accepted or standard first aid procedures *only* when a team doctor or trainer is neither present nor available. Get the injured player to the local hospital immediately. The coach should render no therapy. Prescribe nothing. Say nothing. Most of all offer no consolations such as, "You'll be good as new."

12. Demand that a doctor and trainer be present at all games and that at least a trainer be present at all practice sessions where injuries are at their worst. When a physician cannot be in attendance for any reason see that a standby physician is available. One astute coach has his equipment manager phone the team physician in advance each day to assure his attendance.

13. Carry a heavy liability insurance policy and insurance for the entire staff. Your athletes must be covered. Permit absolutely no athlete to participate unless he is covered by insurance for practices and games traveling on games away (on *any* type of conveyance).

14. The coach must at no time say that the injured athlete does not have to see a physician.

15. He must permit no previously injured athlete to return to practice until the doctor pronounces him 100 percent rehabiliated and this is verified by the trainer's athletic examination and the physician's signed approval is on file. In addition, the parent or guardian's written approval for the boy's return should also be on file. In other words, the coach must cover himself at all times. It's his personal Prevent-System in action.

16. The coach must have a trained "rescue squad" for practices and games. They should know how to carry a litter, use the two-man carry and operate all emergency equipment necessary for first aid procedures. He should make sure that the ambulance crew is completely schooled in the handling of all traumatic cases, particularly injuries of the back, neck, and head.

17. The coach will insist that tumbling techniques be taught to all athletes not only to develop faster reflexes and timing but to prevent injuries.

18. The coach should never send an athlete into a practice or game who is hurt or ill. Remember, you are liable for sending an injured boy into the game even if he has wilfully hidden his injury from you. To say "I didn't even know he was injured" is no alibi in the eyes of the law. Coaches are liable and guilty of negligence due to ignorance. So keep your eyes open.

19. A coach should never rely on low financial status to keep a suit from being brought against him. This kind of thinking cannot only lose him his job, but put him in hock for the rest of his life.

20. Remember that each and every participant is your first and last consideration and the game secondary. To this there is no alternative.

Waivers: Are They of Value?

Are waivers signed by parents or legal guardians of any legal value? The answer is no! Parental or guardians' signatures are strictly a good-will measure. They have little or no legal value and the boy can bring suit against everyone concerned including his parents! With the Prevent-System in mind the coach should clearly abide by the doctor's decision to exclude the boy from athletics. He should not risk his own or the boy's future by permitting any situation which may make him guilty of negligence or of not taking reasonable precautions. To some this will sound like a coldblooded approach but that's exactly how the matter has to be handled where injuries and waivers are concerned. If the coach demonstrates warmth, understanding, concern, and has a working Team-Behind-the-Team that fills the bill on all reasonable precaution and services then he will never be guilty of negligence. He will have served the boy to the best of his ability.

A growing volume of lawsuits claiming negligence on the part of coaches, trainers, team physicians, athletic directors, and other allied athletic department personnel, emphasizes the necessity to set up a program to prevent football injuries. Under the existing umbrella of responsibility the athletic director, as well as the team physician and coach, has to be sharply aware of this negligence factor. "Negligence by the physician," said Dr. A.A. Savastano of the University of Rhode Island at the Seventh Post-Graduate Conference on the Medical Aspects of Sports, "is failure to act as a reasonable prudent physician under the same particular circumstances." Dr. Savastano pointed out that with the increase of negligence suits in sports injuries that team physicians, coaches, and trainers, as well as school administrators, were being involved. He stressed that physicians are not immune from suit even though they are rendering a gratis service or are employed by institutions owned by local government or the state. "In order to reduce the incidence of tort-liability-malpractice claims," he said, "it is well for a team physician to use good medical judgment, follow and control all sports injuries, have a good relationship with trainers, keep parents of an injured athlete well informed, never promise complete cures, and not permit anybody to pressure him to allow an athlete to play if he has not fully recovered from injury. In turn a team physician should always be adequately covered by malpractice insurance, either institutional, individual, or both." [3]

He indicated that efforts are often made to override the doctor; that parents write to the athletic director, coach or other school administrators, and sign release forms permitting youngsters to play football despite warnings against this. It is vital to remember that what holds true of the physician is just as binding on the rest of the Team-Behind-the-Team. Dr. Savastano puts it very succinctly:

> It is to be remembered that the statute of limitations does not begin until the child becomes of age. The same may be said of a release by the minor himself. It is recommended that when a team physician deems an individual unfit to participate in any given sport or sports, he should notify, in writing, the parents, the athlete, and the school or college, as to his findings, that, contrary to his recommendations, the boy is participating in sports. He will do well to write a second time stating his objections to continued participation.[4]

The athletic director should not permit this participation in the first place, but for the sake of the records he should have a copy of all communications (with the doctor or otherwise) on file in the athlete's athletic career file and another copy in the school records. This is not just vital data on the handling of injury, but is also an exemplification of thoroughness of the school's Prevent-System in caring for, and about, the football participant.

Maintain permanent records on all injuries!

For the protection of the school and all athletic department personnel, as well as for the protection of the athlete, maintain consistently clear and complete records. Your records should reveal the state and nature of the injury as well as its cause and what was done for it, by whom it was attended, what fees were charged if any, whether the bill was handled by an insurance company, the school's athletic fund, or by parents, and the exact degree of recuperation as designated by the team doctor and the trainer's athletic examination report. The trainer's report should show the percentage or degree of rehabilitation.

[3] A.A. Savastano, author's lecture notes, Seventh Postgraduate Conference on Medical Aspects of Sports, University of Rhode Island.

[4] A.A. Savastano, ibid.

Negligence: Primary Headache in Athletic Injuries

Because of slipshod procedures and the lack of a Prevent-System in many high schools and small colleges, it is amazing that more irate parents have not initiated more law suits. Any observant person can go through schools not using the Prevent-System and turn up one flagrant violation after another contributing to injury and *negligence*.

Today there has to be complete recognition on the part of the team doctor, trainer, coach, athletic director, and school principal or president of all areas within the athletic department where negligence may be demonstrated in the performance of duty, in the prevention of injuries, and their care, and in the failure to use accepted and standardized methods and facilities. Anyone in the athletic department can be held liable for "accidents" or injuries in the department's program, despite laws indicating that the school district is immune from legal action. This means that no working member of the athletic department is ever immune! To determine where you stand on this matter check with the legal department of your local board of education. Understand all laws on personal liability. Remember that youngsters in the school system are minors, and a parent with a grievance about injury to his or her child can bring suit and attempt to prove negligence. And what will an enterprising attorney look for? He will look for the weak links in your Prevent-System!

According to Dr. Allan J. Ryan, of the University of Wisconsin, the law holds that participation in organized interscholastic and intercollegiate sport is a *privilege and not a right* of the individual. Said Dr. Ryan, "Various hazards of different sports have been acknowledged by the courts as being accepted by the individual participant in advance. They bear down hard on negligence and it is this defect that we must avoid in our efforts to qualify athletes for safe and effective sports competition."[5] To dispel the possibility of *contributory negligence* the athletic department has to set up a program designed to close the loopholes that open it to a liability suit. With this in mind I'm going to cover some of the weak links such as permission-to-participate-cards, injury reports, permits, travel releases etc. with each being exemplified.

Permission to Participate Cards

"Permission to Participate" cards must be signed by the parents or legal guardian. This is a legal ploy, a waiver of liability. Here's the hooker: *A child, when he comes of age,* can *cause suit to be brought against any or all members of the athletic department!* It should be repeated that he may also bring suit against his own parents or guardian!

[5] A.J. Ryan, *Medicine in Sports Newsletter* 10 (July 1970), pp. 4–5.

As long as you are working with minors you have an obligation. Remember that no parent can sign his child's rights away! Responsibility continues to belong to the person or persons working with that minor in football. Athletic department personnel *can* be held liable if negligence can be proved. The point is: close every loophole. Such as it is, a permission to participate card is a place to start. Purchasing the best gear, hiring likable and capable coaches, covering the youngster and all other personnel with insurance, getting the parents involved, etc., are all part and parcel of the Prevent-System.

There are certain advantages to having parents sign a waiver against holding school employees responsible for injuries incurred during intramural or interscholastic sports. The parents, in signing a permission to participate form, tacitly admit: (1) that they are officially aware of the youngster's participation; (2) that they are aware of the school's stand on the matter, and that every effort will be made to protect the participant; (3) that by establishing responsibility for payment of injury care the parent assumes this responsibility; (4) that on this card the parent may indicate sports in which he does not want his son or daughter to participate; and (5) that with the signing of this card the parent is indicating a *partnership agreement* with the athletic department, and in so doing the permission card becomes legal evidence of the parents' awareness of the boy's participation. Now let's take a look at that important Injury Report: (Examples of reports and forms follow later.)

The Injury Report System

In setting up a system of reports, waivers, permits, etc., the athletic director should develop an injury report system which provides detailed information so that at no time can the Team-Behind-the-Team be accused of "contributing to negligence." Yes, it is more paper work, and there are more details to be handled, but oh, how valuable these measures are in the case of litigation! One ounce of prevention saves the entire department. This system should include: eligibility certification, athletic permits, health reports, the trainer's report, the coach's report, and the school injury report.

The coach, in reporting to the athletic director, describes the nature or circumstance of the injury, what care was instituted, his recommendations, and his comment on the attitude of the player. *The trainer* in his report to the coach and athletic director indicates how he handled the player, the treatment or first aid he used, the exact procedure he used in getting the athlete to the doctor or hospital, as well as all the signs and symptoms that he observed. *The doctor* indicates his diagnosis of the problem and his recommendations to correct the problem. When surgery, physical therapy, etc., are to be used he must report this as well in a subsequent followup statement. In the Prevent-System the doctor must issue a signed release *only* when the participant is 100 percent ready for action. If the participant is not released, the doctor must report why and indicate the rehabilitation or other procedures necessary to achieve this 100 percent function. *The school injury report* is a final step. This presents the combined actions of the Team-Behind-the-Team working for the welfare of the given participant. One copy goes to the school's files. Another goes into the athlete's athletic career file. All reports should be in triplicate with the the coach receiving one of them. The doctor and trainer should keep copies of their reports for their own files.

Eligibility Regulations

Eligibility regulations are a method of preventing injuries to the unqualified. A fair-standard program should be maintained to benefit everyone concerned. Issues to be decided upon, and maintained are: age limits, grades, required attendance, and sincerity about playing football; transferring from school to school; health examinations; previous tryouts for a professional team; previous professional experience; gambling or drinking (that has been publicly proved); playing under an assumed name; having practiced with a professional or semiprofessional team; years of previous competition; size; weight; character; behavior; physical condition; signed permission by the parents or legal guardian; and finally, clearance by the team doctor and trainer as well as the coach in his pre-season screening. The following is an example of an eligibility status form that an athletic director may use in his Prevent-System.

Always think twice before putting into print statements on a permit card that may lead to trouble. For example, the statement that *the school is not liable for any injuries* arouses parental ire and can prove to be a bomb waiting to burst. In protecting your Prevent-System also check for the authenticity of signatures. Compare signatures on permits with signatures on file known to be legitimate.

There is no *ideal* permit card. Local conditions, laws, rules and regulations in each school district establish the type, style, and content of the permit card. There are many ways to treat such a permit. It may be in the form of a letter which may establish an excellent homey touch that can be of healthy public relations value. It may be supplemented by a health report on the opposite side of the card. Some permits request vital medical history to which the parents have to affix their signatures. This proves to be very valuable in the prevention of future athletic injuries. This same permit may also include the waiver of liability during travel. In other words, it may be as simple or as complex as the athletic director cares to make it. In any event it demonstrates the school's best inten-

Special Note: *Before putting the following forms into print have them checked by the school attorney. Every region has different laws and requirements and your school's legal advisor is your final authority.*

ELIGIBILITY STATUS FORM

My full name is ____________ birthday __________________.
(print) month/day/year

My address is ____.
(number) (street) (city) (state)

I live at this address with my parents/guardian. Yes___no___.

I understand that after I have signed this form that I may not participate in athletics outside the school during the season without forfeiting eligibility to compete for my school. Yes___no___.

I understand I must accept no awards of any kind other than school presentations for athletic achievement. Yes___no___.

I understand that if I am offered gifts or awards I will first consult with my coach or school principal. Yes___no___.

I, or my family, has health and accident insurance that covers football and travel. Yes___no___.

____
Signature

(over)

Figure A-1a. *Side one*

tions. At no time is it meant to be a whitewash or an absolution of all responsibility. Its purpose is to promote partnership between parents and athlete, and the school and its athletic department. You have communicated and established a common understanding and that's the name of the game.

MAINTAIN YOUR ELIGIBILITY

You are not eligible if:

1. You are over 19 years of age by September 1.
2. You have competed in sports for four seasons.
3. You are a high school graduate.
4. You have played with another team in the same sport during the season.
5. You have accepted awards from anyone other than this school.
6. No physical examination is on file.
7. You are not yet out of grammar school.
8. You have failed to return your eligibility card filled out in full.
9. You have competed as a professional or against professionals.
10. You have been a member of some "All-Star" team.
11. Your grades are not up to par.
12. You did not pass in 15 hours of work in the previous semester.
13. You enrolled later than (date)______________.
14. You transferred from another school without your parents moving into this school district.
15. You transferred from a public to private school.
16. You entered competition under an assumed name.
17. You are not in regular attendance and passing three full-time classes this semester.

Figure A-1b. *Side two*

ATHLETIC ELIGIBILITY HOME SIGNATURE FORM

To be filled out only by parents or guardian:

1. What illnesses has your son/daughter had?

____

____

Polio___ Diabetes___ T.B.___ Heart Disease______
Hernia___ Mononucleosis___ Rheumatic fever______
Epilepsy___ Kidney ailments___ Rupture______

2. What injuries? (broken bones, wounds, etc.)

____

____

When?____

3. What operations has he had?

____

____

When?____

4. Does he have trouble with his eyes?__________
5. Against what diseases is he currently immunized?

____

____

I understand that at the beginning of each inter-school athletic program my son must have a physical examination. His examination may be by the family doctor. I understand the school renders a complete physical examination in the Athletic Department. I understand the necessity, and have purchased insurance that covers football injuries.

____
Signature (parent or legal guardian)

____
Date

(over)

Figure A-2a. *Side one*

I have read the requirements for athletic participation at _______________school as indicated on the reverse side of this card and I hereby request that you permit my son/daughter_________________to participate in_______________(sport) for the season of 19_______. I agree that no school employee, school organization, school district, or aide will be held liable for any accident or injury received by him/her as a result of being engaged in athletic activity. I also agree that those mentioned above will not be held responsible for payment of any bills incurred by my son/daughter due to injury.

________ ____

Date Signature (Parent or legal guardian)

Figure A-2b. *Side two*

TRAVEL RELEASE RESPONSIBILITY WAIVER

School____________________________

Address___________________________

Date______________________________

Student______________________________ has my permission to accompany ___________________ (team, school, or group) on the trip/trips to_________ ____________________________________(place).

I hereby release______________________________ (school or Board of Education), any of its employees, or the driver of the vehicle from any responsibility in case of an accident resulting in the injury or death of my child in the course of this trip/these trips.

Signed_____________________ (parent or legal guardian)

Telephone____________________

Address______________________

____

Figure A-3

Note: Similar travel forms should be made out for band members, cheerleaders, team managers, etc., or other students or parents attending out-of-town games. To this form you may add something on the responsibility for transportation costs; add or delete as is desirable for your purpose and circumstance. Once again check out the legal aspects on travel releases with the school's attorney before putting the form into print.

How to Set Up an Athletic Permit and Health Report

Athletic permits may be combined with the family physician's Health Report if a team doctor is not available. This report should indicate athletic department policy on injury and who is responsible for the payment of bills incurred. Also included in this permit or report should be the signatures of the athlete as well as that of the parents or guardian. All such signatures indicate a partnership agreement between parents, athlete, and school. When the family physician handles the preseason physical examination because the team has no doctor, the athletic director will have him utilize a form such as follows. Parents, as well as a doctor, should fill in the record and sign it. The doctor may desire to make changes of his own.

HEALTH REPORT

Doctor: Do not complete this form until the opposite side of this card has been filled in by the participant's parents.

EXAMINATION:

Head & Neck	Heart	Thorax
Eyes	Valves	Lungs R___ L___
Ears	Rhythm	Xrays necessary?
Nose	B/P	
Throat	P/P	Abdomen
Cervical bones	Exercise tolerance	
Tonsils	Recovery time	Hernia
Teeth		Rupture
Cervical glands		Musculature
	Reflexes	Testes Descended?
	Eyes	
	Elbow	
	Knee	
	Foot	

Laboratory tests

Urine: sugar___ albumin___ S.G.___ protein____

Blood: sugar_____

Statistics:

Height__________ Weight__________ Record of inoculations

Are there any factors prohibiting the boy/girl from participation in the school's athletic program?

Please explain:

Approved__________ Not Approved________

Date________________ Signed____________________
(Physician)

(Address) (Telephone)

Figure A-4a. *Health Report. Side one, to be filled out by family physician.*

PARENTS' REPORT

The welfare of your child is our concern and to maintain complete records to determine whether he/she is eligible for sports we need your cooperation. Fill in the following:

Check the sports you approve for his participation:

Baseball ______ Swimming ______
Basketball ______ Tennis ______
Football ______ Track ______
Gymnastics ______ Wrestling ______

Which of the following has your child had?

Heart ailments ______ Muscle/joint pain ______
Injuries ______ Tuberculosis ______
Rheumatic fever ______ Allergies ______
False teeth ______ Operations ______
Epilepsy ______ "Shots" ______
Other illnesses ______________________

____

Insurance:

Do you have health and accident insurance that covers football and other sports? Yes___No____
(Note: No athlete will be issued gear or be permitted on the playing field unless he has full insurance coverage.)

Has your child ever been told by a physician not to participate in sports at any time? Yes___No_____

Signed______________________
(Parent or legal guardian)

Participant:______________________

Address______________________

Date__________Telephone______

Figure A-4b. Side two, to be filled out by parents or guardians.

DOCTOR'S RELEASE FORM

Student____________________ Date______________

1. Is <u>not</u> to participate in any practice or game for ______ days or until otherwise indicated.

2. May have restricted practice: Yes___No___with the following recommendations:

____

____

3. He may participate fully in any practice or game. Yes___No___

Signature_________________
(Physician)

<u>Note</u>: This form must also be signed by the parent.

Signature_________________
(Parent or legal guardian)

Figure A-5

PHYSICIANS REQUISITION FORM
FOR SUPPLEMENTARY TREATMENT BY THE TRAINER

The following therapy is prescribed for:

Student____________________ Date___________

Parent's Name______________ Address_______________

___Maintain daily sterile dressings
___Cold packs: Ice___No Ice___
___Whirlpool Baths Time___Temp.____
___Analgesic pack Night___Day___
___Contrast baths
___Massage
___Crutches___Canes___
___Adhesive Tape Support
___Stretch Bandage Support
___Exercises
___Rehabilitation
Physical Therapy
___Contractile Current
___Short Wave
___Immobilization

Treatment Schedule:

The athlete is required to return to this office for final check up. He is not to return to active participation until I have signed his release and this release is in the hands of the Athletic Director of ____________________School.

Signature______________________
(Physician)

Address________________________

Figure A-6

INJURY TREATMENT AUTHORIZATION FORM

Name____________________ Date____________________

Address____
(Street) (City) (State)

School____________________ Address____________________

The above student of _____________school, a member of our __________team, is hereby authorized to receive attention from you as is necessary for his injury. If complications are present call this office. Bill this school for services rendered and return this authorization form. Please indicate if therapy is completed.

____
Athletic Director

Figure A-7

INJURY TREATMENT SERVICE REQUEST

School____________________

Address____________________

Date____________________

Sport____________________

Doctor____________________

Please Examine
Treat
X-ray } ______________________________
(student)

for injury received during athletic activity. When rendering your bill please also forward this authorization. This school will not be responsible for unauthorized handling of injuries.

____
Athletic Director

Figure A-8

COACHES' INJURY REPORT FORM*

Sport__________

Student_______________ was injured in game/practice/traveling (date)__________(place)___________ (time)________. The student was injured while playing for or on school facilities: Yes_______ No_____

Nature of Suspected Injury:

Abdominal injury	___	Fracture	___
Abrasion	___	Laceration	___
Concussion	___	Muscle tear	___
Contusion	___	Stab wound	___
Dental damage	___	Strain	___
Dislocation	___	Sprain	___

Description of Injury, Site, and Circumstances of Accident:

Disposition of Case:

1. First aid in the field (describe)__________
   ____
2. First aid in the Training Room ____________
3. Student instructed to go home and see family doctor? Yes___No___
4. Ambulance was called? Yes___No___
5. Referred to: Dr.__________Hospital_________
6. Student was taken home by?_________________
   __________________(Give names)
7. Injured student instructed not to report in until physician signs his Release Form?____

Date_________________

FOLLOW-UP:

1. Student attended by Dr._________Hospital____
2. Student sought professional care. Yes___No___
3. Parent permitted student to see doctor. Yes___No___
4. Release form on file. Yes___No___

Signed_____________________
(coach)

Date______________________

* This form is to be filed in the Athletic Director's office within 24 hours.

Figure A-9a
Figure A-9b

The Whys of Parental Consent

James S. Feurig, M.D. Director, Health Center, and team physician at Michigan State University, says:

> The consent forms obtained from the parents of underage athletes are, in practically all instances, the "general consent" type. In essence they authorize responsible personnel to provide or procure medical care to the underage athlete when something occurs to said athlete when he or she is participating in a sport or functioning as a member of a team in a specific team assignment. It is generally, and also legally, assumed that this consent covers minor medical or surgical situations. The only occasion for which it is regarded as being all-inclusive will be instances of emergency where it is medically nonfeasible to delay the implementation of the indicated treatment procedures, or where it has been impossible to contact the respective parent and continued delay is medically unwarranted. In either

MEDICAL CONSENT FORM*

Patient____________________

Permission is hereby granted to the Director of the Health Center to proceed with any medical or minor surgical treatment, x-ray examinations and immunizations for the above named student. In the event of serious illness, the need for major surgery, or significant accidental injury, I understand that an attempt will be made by the attending physician to contact me in the most expeditious way possible. If said physician is not able to communicate with me, the treatment necessary for the best interest of the above named student may be given.

If student will be under twenty-one at first enrollment at MSU, parent or guardian should sign; if student will be twenty-one or older at first enrollment, the student should sign.

____________	____________	____________
Name	Relationship to student	Date

*By permission of the Michigan State University Health Center.

Figure A-10

of these instances it is wise to have two or more physicians properly concurring that immediate treatment is needed or that continued delay is not proper.[6]

Michigan State University uses the permission form (Figure A-10 on page 241) in its active files for every one of its athletes.

THE ADMINISTRATOR AND THE INSURANCE PROBLEM

Schools in some states are self-insured. Other state school systems depend on private commercial carriers and the cost of the insurance program is maintained by the school athletic fund, the parents, special athletic funds furnished by Booster groups, athletic department funds, or a combination of two or more. Any insurance program you have should encompass the adults as well as athletes, cheerleaders, bandsmen, etc. The Team-Behind-the-Team should be covered by insurance as well as all associated personnel. There should be insurance in your Prevent-System against all contingences that could possibly arise. The trainer, as well as the team physician, should be covered by malpractice insurance. The coaches should all be covered. Leave no loopholes through which the haunting cry of "negligence" can enter.

Who is responsible for insurance payment? An important part of protection in the Prevent-System is insurance. The question of who pays for it at high school level is a big concern and responsibility, for insurance payment varies in each state. The responsible parties may be grouped roughly as: (1) The athletic association of each school, (2) the athletic funds of an entire school system or board of education, (3) each athlete's family, or, (4) specially purchased insurance called family health and accident insurance.

In maintaining the Prevent-System, the athletic director indicates at the beginning of each season, and on all printed literature sent home, that no athlete will be issued gear or even be permitted on the practice field unless he has insurance coverage. The athletic director will check with parents to determine if the family health and accident policy covers contact sports (most of them don't). He will advise all athletes, if the school is not covered by insurance, that their private insurance *must cover football,* or they cannot play. If coverage is complete and an injury occurs, the athletic director should be responsible for filling out all forms and sending them to the insurance carrier. When preliminary forms are required, he should also fill these out. He should maintain in the school files a complete record of all injuries and claims, and of how, when, and

[6] J.S. Feurig, *Medicine in Sports Newsletter,* March, 1969.

where each was paid. He should also know of any bills that were not paid and why.

There are many forms of insurance. Some policies are impractical and a waste of money as far as protection is concerned. Others are excellent. So far there is no uniform coverage for athletes throughout the United States. Each state has its own program, and this is often unfair to the very boys and girls whom they ask to participate. All types of coverage should be given consideration by the athletic director, the school administrator, and the board of education before a choice is made. Politics or friendships should play no role in the choice of carrier. For your Prevent-System I submit the following simplified breakdown to provide a basic understanding of the available coverages:

Types of Insurance Coverage for Athletes

1. *State high school athletic association insurance:* By this method each school pays a given amount into the state association for protection against big medical bills.

2. *State association nonprofit insurance corporation:* This is a financially independent group that is controlled by the state association.

3. *Privately controlled companies.*

4. *Combinations of coverages:*

   a. *Maximum payment plan* with each injury to be paid for up to a specific amount after all bills are submitted. The premium on this coverage is costly.

   b. *Indemnity plan* which is the least costly.

Appendix II

PREVENT-SYSTEM TECHNIQUES FOR FOOTBALL PLAYERS BY POSITION

Author's note: This system was devised and successfully fielded by myself at amateur and professional levels. Mimeograph it, staple it, and distribute it to each candidate. This will save a lot of talking and explanation, and it will lower your yearly injury rate!

TACKLERS

Rules for Preventing Tackling Injuries

Work out all year round! Football is never seasonal. A good football player is *always* in good shape, so keep your endurance, your strength, and your reflexes up to par at all times. See the trainer about your weight-training and isometric program. Play handball, soccer, and swim. Sign in for gymnastic training and tumbling techniques.

No heavy gear is to be worn in initial spring or summer training programs. Helmets, lightweight shirts, and shorts only are to be worn. Train in tennis or gym shoes and run, run, run. *Do not* run on hard surfaces or on the track. Stick to the turf. At no time in the spring and summer should you start running from a crouched position. Stretch *all* your muscles, especially the thighs. Work out until sweating. You will be instructed when you can suit up.

To avoid head injuries set your eye on the target. Keep your eyes open! Keep your chin up and your both feet on the ground as you make contact. Don't dive! Don't make straight on tackles! When suiting up, check the suspension webs in your helmet and then have the equipment manager or trainer do a double check. Check the anchoring of face guards and chin straps. Be comfortable. Feel secure. Wear a mouthguard at all times on practice field or in games. To prevent head and neck injuries develop a "bull neck." See the trainer for your program.

When making a tackle never totally leave the ground. Stabilize and guide your weight and motion by keeping at least one foot on the ground at all times. Never tackle when your body weight is backward. Drive your weight in fast and hard. Maintain control. Maintaining control prevents injury to your back, shoulder, neck, leg, or arm.

Follow through on the approach to contact. Don't pause! Don't stop! HIT! Impetus pays off and prevents injury. Take advantage of your momentum and hit hard. Stay on top as you take your man down. Don't let him fall on you. Stay on top in making a head-and-shoulder tackle. Ride the ball carrier. Save yourself all the way. When your contact is made and your tackle is solid bring your knees up. *Never* permit your legs to drag out behind you!

All early-season tackling is to be done on a dummy. Tackling techniques will be given you on the field. Develop faith and confidence in yourself by hitting the dummies before hitting live targets. This is especially true for first year men.

Where a body-across tackle is used cut the runner's flight with your full weight. Hit him chest on. Grasp him with your arms. Twist! This saves you from being hurt.

If head-on tackles are unavoidable do not tackle low! Do not close your eyes! This may be the blindspot in which you lose your teeth, so keep your vision unrestricted and your head up.

Never relax in making a tackle. Maintain muscle and tendon tension at all times. Don't relax even when the referee blows the play dead. Relax only when the game is over and the last whistle is blown. Never drive in for a tackle with just one arm or leg. Hit with the shoulder or hip padding.

Complete equipment is mandatory! At no time go out on the practice field or participate in a game without full gear.

Don't fight out from under a pileup. Don't knee, gouge, or kick. Lie there and wait. Conserve energy without relaxing. Save your energy for the next play. Never throw your shoulder at the wrong side. If you miss your tackle dive, land on your hands, ease to your shoulder, and roll. Don't hit the turf on your belly, face, or elbows.

If fear of tackling arises report to me. Let's talk it out. Good tacklers are not born. They are made. If you have been benched with an injury, don't expect to go right back to tackling once more. The team doctor will tell you when. One more thing, when you've tackled and ridden your man to the ground, and the play is whistled dead, give him a hand up! That's sportsmanship the way we want to play it!

BLOCKERS

Rules for Preventing Blocking Injuries

Never throw a block when relaxed. Keep tight and tense at all times. When the game is over, *that's* the time to relax. Never stop when you make contact with your target. Keep driving. Wear your target down within legal bounds. When blocking a man larger than yourself, never block with anything less than a leg block. It's less damaging to you and more effective on him. Remember that blocking is the interference that wins games. In every offensive play somebody gets thrown a block, a shoulder or leg block, or even gets clipped.

Don't kid yourself about body blocking. Hit your man just above the knees with your hip and the small of your back. When making a shoulder block, stay on your feet. Deflect your man enough to make a hole. Take him out and keep going. When you use that leg block, drive it in! Ram him back. Never fail to hit *first*! Block hard. The harder you block, the less susceptible you are to injury. Beat him to it every time!

Protect your hands and arms. Keep them close to your body in a pileup. Never try to fight up out of the stack. Wait! Don't relax! Never stop being alert; a tough competitor will soon salt you away. Never leave your hands open on the ground. Never use a fist! With your palms up make a hard driving charge. Keep your butt down as you take hard charging steps. Throwing a fist or forearm may result in a paralyzing judo chop from your opponent when you try it again. Don't try it!

Never stand up to do your blocking. Keep digging. Keep low. Above all don't telegraph your next method of contact. Take your stance, squat, lean forward, and get the knuckles of both hands on the scrimmage line. Keep your head up and your buttocks down. Never deliver a block with your feet close together.

For problems with gear, check with your trainer. If your pads or equipment do not fit, or are causing pressure and irritation, your trainer, or the equipment manager, will issue new equipment or pads as needed.

Keep this in mind. Linemen are often injured because of their failure to remember the rules and fundamentals. The moment they forget the position they are playing, forget how to use their hands, or forget how to charge, that's the moment they are open to injury!

PUNTERS

Rules for Preventing Punting Injuries

The punter is one of the team's greatest defensive weapons, and he is as susceptible to injury as any other man on the team. He is subject to being roughed-up whether or not there are penalties for the act. Because punters and place-kickers can win or lose a game for the team, they, particularly are subject to rough handling and to other types of injury. In brief here's the story:

Punters are injured when kicking for height or distance without proper warm-up or conditioning. At no time are you to go out on the field cold. Warm up until sweating and stay under wraps. Punters are hurt when they fail to practice form, when they fail to use plenty of leg exercises, when they are not getting protection from the half-backs, when taking the ball from center less than twelve yards, or when fear of getting smeared gets stronger than fundamental knowledge of how to take care of themselves. They are injured when they fail to relax when hit, or if they use low cut shoes, when a high cut with padded tongue would save arthritic hurt to the top of the foot and the front of the ankle. Grand-standing with a barefoot kick is out! It inevitably leads to foot trouble.

PASSERS

Rules for Preventing Injuries to Passers

The good passer (quarterback or other backfield man) maintains calmness and accuracy. He spots his receiver, gives him the right kind of lead, and rifles the ball. But passers, like any other backfield man, are subject to injuries. To avoid such injuries here are the points where passers get hurt and what to avoid:

Passers get hurt when the passer is not in good physical or mental condition, when he's not physically tough to take being tackled and panics and when he stands to pass with legs straight. Bend your knees slightly. When hit, relax. Passers are injured when the throwing arm is cocked back and the shoulder muscles are bunched. The arm becomes a lever when hit.

Passers get hurt when jump-passing and getting hit in mid-air. Its a desperation move. Don't try it!

Warm up completely! Under no circumstance go into the game "cold." Learn how to feint. Start and stop fast. When and if you get tackled try to roll with it. Don't resist! Flow with it. Keep your elbows tucked into your sides. To keep from getting decked, move out of the slot as fast as possible.

LINEMEN

Rules for Preventing Injuries to Linemen

Linemen are injured too often because of their failure to stick to the rules. Their position on the line, the use of their hands, charging, etc., all contribute to possible injury if improperly handled. When taking your stance on the line, have one foot forward of the other at a comfortable space apart (usually shoulder width). Squat, lean forward with the knuckles of one or both hands touching the scrimmage line. Keep your head up, buttocks down, and prepare for contact.

In using your hands to prevent injury keep your hands still, use them to maintain balance. When you charge bring those hands up fast, grasp your competitor's shoulders, dig in, keep your body low, flip him on his face. Another technique is to place the palms of your hands under his chin. Forcibly raise your competitor's head and thrust it backward. (Use on tall men.) You may also drive your opponent by thrusting with the palm of your hand (not the heel of your hand) on his head. When your opponent charges in very low, push his face down, place your hands on his head as you force him down and leapfrog over him. The next time around, fake him out. Go down low as if to make a submarine charge. When your man goes down, spring over the top of him again. Land on all fours and go!

Linemen sustain injuries when they fail to keep their elbows and knees in, when they fail to wear their mouthpieces, facemasks or other protective gear, when they fail to report broken gear, when they fail to remain tense throughout the play, when they permit their hands to get stepped on, and when there is two-on-one blocking. Big linemen sustain injuries in the early season when they don't warm up properly and do not stretch thigh muscles; when they do deep knee bends; when they do not practice fast crouch starts all-year-round. *If you have had previous knee injuries or torn thigh muscles you are not permitted to do deep knee bends, the duck walk, etc.*

BACKFIELD MEN

Rules for Preventing Injuries to Backfield Men

Backfield men owe their position on the squad to their ability to run and skirt the ends, or kick or pass the ball, and otherwise alertly move that ball forward when on an offensive. Good backfield men remain calm. They are fast, shifty, and usually have a second sense about knowing how to diagnose a play if they are on defense. Backfield men are key men who can't afford to be injured, so they have to use every method of injury prevention possible. Let's take a look at some pointers.

Backfield men are subject to injury when they use an improper stance. For example, when you're on offensive keep your feet in line and your hands on your knees or on the ground. Backfield men get hurt when they run *without* high knee action, and when they run with knees or elbows sticking out so that these body parts become handles to grasp. They get hurt when they run high through the line (remain low), when they telegraph the play by "pointing" with feet, body or eyes and get nailed, and when bucking a hard massed line. If yardage is that important hurtle over the top. Otherwise skirt the end, pass, or boot the ball. Backfield men get hurt when tackling with an arm, when they are improperly conditioned, when they have old injuries that have been given improper care, when they have both feet planted and get clipped from behind or on the "blind" side, when they get a hard shoulder block to the thigh, or when a two-on-one tackle is made with the legs apart.

Always use the proper stance. Lean slightly forward. Bend your knees slightly. On offense keep your feet in line. Your hands may be on your knees or knuckled down to the ground. Run with high knee action. Never run high through the line. Stop "birddog pointing" and telegraphing with your eyes, knees, feet, or the lean of your body. If you're a quarterback, move out of the slot immediately with each play. Don't wait! If you get hit, relax and roll with the fall. Don't panic under pressure because it leads to injury. If you are apprehensive, check yourself out of the game for a few plays. Never go into a game cold. Warm up until sweating. Stay in your warm-up clothes until ready to go out on the field. Keep your cool at all times. Run with your elbows glued to your sides even as your knees come up driving high and hard. Learn to feint your man out of position. It saves getting decked. It saves getting hurt, and that too, is the name of the game. That's prevention!

SIMPLIFIED DIRECTIONS FOR TUMBLING

From a squat position. Squat, palms down on the turf with knees between your elbows. Place chin on chest. Lean forward. Shove off with the feet. Roll forward on the back of the neck and shoulders with knees tucked in tight to the chest. Clasp your shins as you go over and snap to an upright position.

From an upright position. Stand on your feet and lean forward. Go through the same movements as from the squat position. Chin-to-chest, lean forward, shove off with the feet, tuck head in, hit back of neck and shoulders as the knees come in tight to the chest. Clasp legs and snap upright as you make a smooth flowing tumble. Hit your feet and run!

From a running position. Take off running and dive. Take your weight on your hands in a smooth rolling ball, tuck your head in. Quickly transfer your weight from the hands to the back of your neck and shoulders and roll. Come to your feet and keep running.

HOW TO DO SHOULDER ROLLS

From standing position. Start with feet apart and lean forward. Throw your left arm up. Now snap it toward the ground. Bend at the elbow. Take your body weight on the elbow as you hit the turf. Transfer the flow of weight immediately to the left shoulder as you roll forward and over. Tuck your head in. As your right hand touches the ground push off and roll to your feet all in one freeflowing complete motion.

From a running position. Relax and fall easily. Now go through the same movement as above from a run. Snap the arm forward and down. Roll on the left shoulder. Push up and off with the right hand. Roll easily to your feet and keep running.

Do the reverse of this for a backward roll.

SWIMMING

Swimming was once condemned as a body conditioner for football men. So was weight training. It was forbidden to athletes whose prime interest was football. Today however football coaches realize the value of swimming as a supplemental exercise in the conditioning of football players. What is remarkable is that those who specialize in swimming seldom excel in other sports because a good swimmer must be loose and completely relaxed. His muscles and joints have to be trained for swimming and for very little else to get the best performance. The opposite is true of football! For conditioning the football player, for injury rehabilitation, for assisting recovery from new injuries, and in the prevention of new injuries, swimming is an asset for football players. If you are recovering from an operation, a fracture, dislocation, muscle damage, or ligamentous strain *use a heated swimming pool* for faster recovery. In reestablishing the function of a body part or in general rehabilitation, *do not swim in a cold pool!*

FOOD CONTROL

A team is no better than its ability to learn fundamentals and get into shape for competition. Most injuries are due to failure to be in condition. Therefore, to win like a champion you have to condition like one. Proper diet is one such procedure. Here's a suggested program to follow:

1. No candy or pastries.
2. No greasy or fried foods (french fries, hamburgers, etc.).
3. No cola drinks.
4. No alcoholic beverages.
5. Eat a *big breakfast*. The breakfast you eat determines your afternoon energy for workouts or games. Cold cereals are of little value. Eat meals regularly! Eat slowly. Chew your food. Relax no matter what goes on around you.
6. Do not eat immediately before, during or immediately after a game. *Eat* at least four hours before a game.
7. You *can* drink water before, during, and after games (unless otherwise instructed). Just be moderate about it.

Elimination. Have a regular bowel movement. Keep your bowels open. When finished get up and leave. Don't sit. If you are having trouble with your elimination consult the trainer or team physician. *DO NOT use harsh laxatives!*

Get into shape gradually!

Most injuries occur in the early season. They result from not being in good condition. They also come at the end of the season if you are tired. Many injuries result from being inadequately warmed up. Remember this: *No player is to go directly into any practice or game without a warm-up!* If you have sustained an injury signal and check yourself out for examination by the trainer or team doctor. When you are recovering from an injury check in with the trainer for special physical therapy or exercises. No player will be returned to the field until the injury is 100 percent rehabilitated.

Sleep is a must!

Sleep is necessary for everyone. Good football performance is difficult without it. If an outside job cuts into your practice or sleep time, drop either the sport or the job. Or arrange it so that there is no interference with or from either. Sleep in a cool room on a firm mattress. Take a warm shower before bedtime. Have a glass of warm milk before bedding down.

Stimulants. No matter what you hear or what you see advertised DON'T use cola drinks, coffee, tobacco, alcohol, aspirin or other drugs as stimulants! The use of "hard" drugs ("uppers" and "downers") will automatically dismiss you from the team.

Mental conditioning. Remember you are out there to win! Have pride in your football form and physique. Polish your technique. Learn all football fundamentals perfectly, so that you have complete confidence in yourself. Stick to the training rules and you will not only think like a champion but be one too!

SOME SPECIFIC DO'S IN INJURY PREVENTION

DO be covered completely by insurance. No gear will be issued nor will you be permitted on the practice field until you have said insurance coverage.

DO play when you're in good condition. Do not play when ill or injured. Never hide your injuries. Report them immediately. Save yourself and be twice as good when you're needed most.

DO report all broken gear. Wear all protective devices (mouthguard, faceguard, jock cup, etc.).

DO report old injuries for the sake of the record.

DO keep tense throughout the game (except quarterbacks) and don't let yourself relax during halftime.

DO take supplementary vitamins and minerals if the trainer or team doctor suggests them.

DO get physical therapy treatment for muscles inside plaster casts to keep them from shrinking. Electrotherapy and massage by the trainer are effective in getting you back on the squad sooner if you have been injured.

DO forget the I-Am-A-Hero stuff. Be out there to play football NOT play to the grandstand! If you have been decked do not run off the field! Stay down until instructed what to do by the trainer or team doctor. Accept their help.

DO get your old injury areas taped. Old injuries are the doorways to new injuries so prevent this possibility. At no time are you to apply adhesive tape (for any reason) on yourself!

DO dress at least forty-five minutes before game time.

DO warm up until sweating freely. Then go under wraps. Don't sit on a bench with your legs tucked under. Sit with your legs stretched out front.

DO prevent blisters on your feet by rubbing them with petroleum jelly. Put on a lightweight pair of socks and dust them with talcum powder. Put on regulation sweat socks over them. This reduces friction problems.

DO know the plays!

DO know the rules.

DO learn to tumble and roll with a fall. Stick to the rules of health and you'll be a champion all the way!

INDEX